C000181486

Yorkshire
WOMEN AT WAR

WOMEN'S LAND ARMY   and   WOMEN'S TIMBER CORPS
1917 - 1919 and 1939 - 1950   1942 - 1946

DURING THE FIRST AND SECOND WORLD WARS, OVER 240,000 LAND GIRLS AND LUMBER JILLS
PROVIDED FOOD AND TIMBER FOR THE WAR EFFORTS. ON BEHALF OF OUR NATION, WE
EXTEND OUR THANKS AND APPRECIATION FOR THE COMMITMENT AND ENDEAVOUR
SHOWN BY THESE YOUNG WOMEN.

This tribute was unveiled by
HRH The Countess of Wessex GCVO
21st October 2014

'A great response by the women of our country to the call of duty in the nation's hour
of danger and need ... and for this, the nation owes them an everlasting debt'

Her late Majesty Queen Elizabeth The Queen Mother
Patron of the Women's Land Army and Women's Timber Corps

This book is dedicated to the memory of Miss Jacob-Smith MBE, who organised the Women's Land Army in North Yorkshire (1939–1945) and later the whole of Yorkshire (1945–1950); to Lady Margery Lawson Tancred, founder of the first Land Girl hostel in 1917; and to all members of the Women's Land Army.

WLA Veterans at an Enactment.

WLA

Yorkshire
WOMEN AT WAR

STORY OF THE WOMEN'S LAND ARMY HOSTELS

MARION JEFFERIES

Pen & Sword
MILITARY

Published in 2015 by
PEN & SWORD MILITARY
An imprint of
Pen & Sword Books Ltd
47 Church Street, Barnsley
South Yorkshire
S70 2AS

ISBN 978 1 47384 909 9

A CIP catalogue record for this book is
available from the British Library

Printed and bound in England
By CPI Group (UK) Ltd, Croydon, CR0 4YY

Pen & Sword Books Ltd incorporates the Imprints of Pen & Sword Aviation,
Pen & Sword Family History, Pen & Sword Maritime, Pen & Sword Military,
Pen & Sword Discovery, Pen & Sword Politics, Pen & Sword Atlas,
Pen & Sword Archaeology, Wharncliffe Local History, Leo Cooper,
Wharncliffe True Crime, Wharncliffe Transport, Pen & Sword Select,
Pen & Sword Military Classics, The Praetorian Press, Claymore Press,
Remember When, Seaforth Publishing and Frontline Publishing

For a complete list of Pen & Sword titles please contact
PEN & SWORD BOOKS LIMITED
47 Church Street, Barnsley, South Yorkshire, S70 2AS, England
E-mail: enquiries@pen-and-sword.co.uk
Website: www.pen-and-sword.co.uk

Contents

Acknowledgements

A SPECIAL MENTION MUST BE MADE to the Yorkshire Museum of Farming at Murton Park, York, and Eden Camp, Malton, for making their archives available. Also to the members of Pollington History Group who showed the author round the vast site over two farms. Buildings were explored and a valuable insight was given to the lives of the WLA girls at this hostel.

The author acknowledges the tremendous help received in the form of information and photographs from a great many WLA veterans and from their relatives.

Every effort has been made to contact the copyright owners of photos. Should any owners of photos desire their names included please supply details to the publisher, who will endeavour to correct the information in subsequent editions.

WLA girls working together in 1947 in the North Riding. (*Murton Farming Museum*)

Introduction

BRITAIN OWES A HUGE DEBT OF GRATITUDE to the members of the Women's Land Army who played a crucial role in farming, ensuring that the people of this country did not starve during the First and Second World Wars.

During the First World War, there were tremendous barriers against the idea of women working on the land. Farmers were antagonistic towards the employment of women and their male workers were fearful that their own jobs would be threatened by a less well-paid labour force. In 1915, well meaning titled ladies, known as the 'Lilac Bonnet Brigade' tried to entice the middle classes to get involved in farming work. These ladies had no understanding of the real hardships involved. Their greatest problem in getting large numbers of women to take over the jobs of men sent to fight, was the question of how to accommodate them. For various reasons, many farmers could not be persuaded to have Land Girls billeted on their farms.

In response to the lack of accommodation on farms, special hostels were created for the Land Girls. The first hostel opened in 1915 at Aldborough, Boroughbridge in North Yorkshire. It was established due to the pioneering work of Lady Margery Lawson Tancred. This lady was concerned about the working lives of the women in the local area and formed groups to tackle their problems. She was later involved as a welfare officer in the Second World War.

Other trial hostels appeared in 1916, and were run by genteel ladies of the county. In 1917, the Women's Land Army (WLA) was officially founded as a civilian force. It was not until 1918, however, that the accommodation problem was really seriously tackled and by that time it was too late.

By 1938, preparations for the ensuing war were being made and in 1939 the Women's Land Army was revived. It faced most of the same problems encountered during the First World War, such as the hostility of farmers and the lack of accommodation for the women workers. The 'home lives' of the Land Girls, in billets or hostels, were of major importance. The accommodation problem had to be resolved quickly, so that the women could concentrate on their job of growing food for the nation. However, it is sometimes forgotten that this task continued for five years after the war, when the nation continued to suffer tremendous hardships and long-term rationing. The WLA was finally disbanded in 1950.

Medal awarded to veteran WLA members in 2008.

Many books have been published about the working adventures of Land Girls and the often wonderful social life enjoyed by members. Yet little has been reported about the day-to-day running of the WLA hostels and even their locations. Tales of life in the Land Army, remembered fondly by the authors, have usually been written in the first person and reflect a very personal aspect of WLA life, focusing on their working day or leisure activities.

The majority of existing WLA memoirs or studies also generally refer to the southern counties of Britain. In contrast, the present book reveals the history of the organisation and identifies the location, management and daily life within the WLA hostel residences in Yorkshire. The county had the largest WLA recruitment numbers in the country and Yorkshire members not only worked on farms but, throughout the period, Yorkshire girls were in great demand all over Britain. Over 25,000 were recruited in the county from 1939 to 1950.

In 1939, Lady Denman, the Head of the WLA, made use of her Women's Institute contacts to organise the Land Army. As in the First World War, these women were chiefly from the upper middle classes and some were titled ladies. One such was Lady Celia Coates, who recruited Miss Winifred Jacob-Smith for the task of mobilising the women's workforce in Yorkshire. At a Knaresborough Women's Institute meeting in 1938, Lady Coates, who stuttered very badly, spoke

Women's Land Army

Women's Timber Corps

The Government wishes to express to you its profound gratitude for your unsparing efforts as a loyal and devoted member of the Women's Land Army/Women's Timber Corps at a time when our country depended upon you for its survival.

Gordon Brown

July 2008

Rt Hon Gordon Brown MP
Prime Minister

Certificate, without a name, awarded to Second World War Veterans, 2008.

privately to Winifred Jacob-Smith about the WLA. 'If war broke out, would you be responsible for organising, and running the WLA in Yorkshire?' She asked. Lady Coates explained that this would involve the setting up of hostels.

Not all ladies of her background had experience in agriculture, but Miss Jacob-Smith had trained both in administration and agriculture. Ordinary Land Girls had very little contact with Lady Denman, the WLA Head Office or even the County Office. The local representatives (reps) were their main link with the Land Army administration. In some hostels the girls had little contact even with the reps, as some tended just to meet with the hostel warden to discuss problems. Reps were supposed to go once a month to visit girls billeted on farms, to check that they were happy, well fed and had suitable washing facilities. They also visited the hostels, where problems usually centred round the choice of warden and how to improve the services the hostel provided to the girls. The choice of warden could turn out to be unfortunate and the selection of forewomen was often made at random. Conflict was inevitable!

Few official records on the WLA remain, however some of the original recording cards are held at the Imperial War Museum (with microfiche copies at The National Archives in Kew). Each record card contained the girl's name, address, age, occupation, date of enrolment and date of the termination of the contract. In some cases work was also mentioned.

These, unfortunately, are incomplete. There is also a lack of evidence about local hostels in public libraries or the County Record Office. Today, most local parishioners often know little about the location or history of the former WLA hostel in their town or village. Perhaps the indifference to the essential work of the WLA among the authorities caused records to be lost or destroyed? It is only in relatively recent years that interest in the WLA has been revived.

After the Second World War had ended, letters of thanks were sent to Land Girls from the then Queen. Unfortunately, some of the women's names were not spelt correctly and their full service history was not recognised. When, in 2008, the British Government tried to make amends for their oversight in neglecting the work of the WLA, they showed further indifference. Medals were sent to surviving members, along with a certificate signed by the Prime Minister Gordon Brown. The name of the recipient was left blank, however, and they were expected to have their own names inscribed. This upset many WLA veterans.

Recently there has been a resurgence of interest and some further recognition of the crucial work of the Women's Land Army. Unveiled in 2005, at Whitehall in London the Memorial to the Women of World War Two sculpted by John W Mills, illustrates the outfits worn by the various Women's Services, including the uniform of the Women's Land Army.

Peter Naylor from Yorkshire created another memorial to the WLA at Fochabers in Scotland, on donated Crown Land. The metal piece features a group of enthusiastic Land Girls sitting on a farm gate, leaning into each other as they look out over the Moray Estate. Prince Charles, as the Duke of Rothesay,

Veterans at the WLA Memorial at Fochabers, Scotland. (*Muriel Berzin Collection*)

unveiled the memorial in October 2012 and he stressed that this was the first permanent memorial to the WLA. A similar monument to the Lumber Jills of the Women's Timber Corps, who were also part of the WLA, can be seen at Aberfoyle in Scotland.

On 21 October 2014, there was an official dedication of the WLA Tribute Memorial to the Land Girls and the Lumber Jills at the National Memorial Arboretum, in Airewas, near Lichfield in Staffordshire. Sculptor Denise Dutton depicted a Land Girl and a member of the Women's Timber Corps standing side by side. It was erected after a three-year campaign by the Staffordshire Food and Farming Union raised a total of £85,000.

Present at that ceremony was a former Land Girl from Ripon, North Yorkshire. At 101 years old, Kay Fawell is a wonderful example of the enthusiastic dedication of these great women. She is discussed in the final chapter of this book, within the section on Easingwold Hostel. Muriel Berzins (née French), aged ninety-one, (whose story is recounted in the section on Howden Hostel), Dorothy Taylor, who has done so much towards keeping information flowing between the WLA girls, and Iris Newbold, all represented Yorkshire at the ceremony.

As already discussed, most books about the WLA have predominantly reported on life in the South of England. This book attempts to redress the balance, since today in Yorkshire and across the North of England there is a thirst for knowledge from the children and grandchildren of the WLA girls. A real excitement has developed, as seen in the activities of re-enactment groups, especially in Yorkshire, and new exhibitions and displays in museums all over the country.

In Britain there is a lack of information about the life in the WLA hostels, despite the existence of 696 hostels by 1944. This book concentrates on the hostels in Yorkshire and identifies around fifty, detailing their location and,

Countess of Wessex talking to Muriel at Official Dedication of WLA Memorial. (*Muriel Berzin Collection*)

where possible, the management style within each hostel. The list of hostel locations in the final chapter of the book is as comprehensive as possible, in light of the poor state of WLA records held by all the major sources.

Time has taken its toll, too, on the recollections of the WLA veterans. However, many stories of life in the hostels are included here. Material for the book has been gleaned from newspapers, websites, memoirs, and from many letters, emails and telephone conversations. The duplicate record books kept by Miss Winifred Jacob-Smith were a key source of information on the WLA in Yorkshire during World War Two. These books, about eighty in number, record her visits to the farms where Land Girls were billeted and her inspections of the hostels. Four hostels are covered in detail within this book and these accounts draw on the records that Miss Jacob-Smith made. The author has edited these records and pruned some of the more trivial details for easier reading.

Miss Jacob-Smith had very strong views about the welfare of the WLA girls and she kept a record of each member, detailing her personality, appearance and other facts which would perhaps not be recognised as proper in the modern age. To protect the identities of some of these women, the author has not mentioned their names. The names of veterans interviewed by the author are included, however, as well as some members of the hostel staff.

Life in the WLA hostels was often insular, as they were sometimes very remote from towns. The girls worked fourteen hours a day; they came back from work tired and dirty and the hostel was their home. Food, comfort, and suitable clothing were their main priorities. Events outside the hostel were often secondary to everyday life in the hostel, as there was little media bombardment, apart from the wireless broadcasts. Even these were limited by the availability and life of the wireless batteries and warden interference. The girls rarely saw newspapers. Miss Jacob-Smith made little reference in her books to the war or politics in general.

Land Girls whose families or boyfriends were fighting would wait anxiously when the telegraph boy arrived at the hostel. Those residing in hostels near to airfields would watch the bombers going out and count them in on their return. One girl from Jersey had escaped the Nazis on the last boat leaving the island. She moved with her mother and father to Barnsley, where she joined the WLA and was sent to Moat Hall Hostel in Ouseburn and later to Arkendale Hall. She was so worried about the plight of the people in Jersey that she wrote a letter to her Member of Parliament.

There is little reference in the records of WLA hostels to celebrations on Victory in Europe Day (VE Day) in 1945. Working all day in the fields without access to the wireless or newspapers, many Land Girls did not know straight away that it was a special day. Yet, some took part in Land Army 'Thanksgiving Parades'. One group of girls from the Keyingham Hostel, working at Spurn Point in East Yorkshire, were so excited by the news that they threw their hats into the River Humber. Other girls had relatives or friends who were still fighting in the Far East, so VE Day meant little to them.

The work of the WLA continued long after the official end of the war and until 1950 Land Girls were helping to boost food production during post-war austerity.

During the following chapters, readers will discover the foundations of the WLA hostel policy during the First World War and how hostels were implemented throughout Yorkshire from 1939 to 1950. The book has a serious intent and yet, thanks to the joviality of the dozens of veterans interviewed by the author, it is also illumined by many light-hearted stories.

.

CHAPTER ONE

The Origins of Hostel Accommodation for Women Working in Agriculture

In the nineteenth century, Britain's prosperity was measured by the export of manufacturing goods, in return for raw materials and food from the colonies and North America. Farming was in a recession during part of the nineteenth century. When the First World War broke out in 1914, the country was ill prepared for the shortages about to occur. By 1916, after a poor harvest, there was a national food crisis, as British merchant ships were targeted by German U-Boats.

In response, the new coalition government under Lloyd George intervened in agricultural policy. Run down farms and grasslands were brought back to cultivation under the direction of County Agricultural Executive Committees; by 1918, 1.75 million acres of grassland had been ploughed up to grow wheat. Men were desperately needed for the Front Line and so female labour became a priority.

By 1900, female agricultural labour was deemed a threat to femininity. This view was jealously guarded by many working men who feared that their own conditions would be threatened by lower paid women workers. Farmers in the Craven area of North Yorkshire commented that much of the work done on their farms would be degrading to women, and that female land workers were considered socially inferior to domestic servants. (Bullock, 2002.)

The Women's Farm and Garden Union (later Association) was founded in 1899, by a group of women who were concerned about the lack of education and employment opportunities for female labourers working on the land. When war broke out in 1914, the Women's National Land Service Corps was formed as an off-shoot of the main organisation. Its purpose was to replace the labour lost to male enlistment and to avoid disruption to food production. An appeal was made 'for all young, strong, educated women... to come and take a short training course for work on the land'. This group was later developed into the Women's Land Army, which was founded in 1917.

The 'Lilac Bonnet Brigade' and other recruiting agencies

In 1915, the Board of Agriculture tried to induce farmers to employ female labour by enlisting the help of titled ladies in recruiting women workers. These ladies were called the 'Lilac Bonnet Brigade' by farmers and the general public. Their efforts met with little success, however.

In 1915, the Women's Farm and Garden Union attempted to look after the interests of those women committed to farm work. With three million men away fighting, there was a real need for more women to become involved in the production of food. Traditionally, on small, family-run farms tasks like milking, butter-making, poultry keeping and hay-making had been done by the female members of the family. This practice was extended by the Board of Agriculture, and by 1917 there were over 250,000 female labourers working on farms. (Lloyd George, 1938).

At first, the prejudice of Yorkshire farmers towards taking on female workers seemed almost insurmountable. Some of their views were summed up at a meeting of Ryedale farmers in 1916. Mr A Peters, the Agent for the Earl of Feversham's estate, told the meeting that he had a letter from the University of Leeds, requesting farmers in the district to take on women trainees at their farms for a fortnight. Mr Hebron told the meeting that he would put his name down to get a woman trainee who could help his wife, but he could not get one for love nor money. As to the women coming to work on farms, he thought it was a farce and that they were simply out on a 'spooning' expedition, trying to catch husbands. A woman's proper place was in the home, he insisted.

However, another farmer at the meeting, a Mr Stockill, said that he found women workers satisfactory and several members of the club also signified their willingness to train women on the farm. (*Yorkshire Post and Leeds Intelligencer*, 27 May 1916.)

The Women's National Land Service Corps, led by Mrs Roland Wilkins, was formed in 1916. The organisation, which moved around the country, consisted of middle class educated ladies who tried to recruit local female labour. Enthusiasm for labouring was largely confined to the ladies of the Corps, who had little idea of what really rough work entailed. Working class women knew only too well and avoided it at all costs.

There was opposition from working class women against these recruitment drives made by stylish titled ladies. During a meeting at Darlington in 1916, one woman with six children who was canvassed told the recruiter to go home and liberate her own servants! Another woman who was asked to work on a farm replied, "When you have something better to do for the country than ride about in a motor car dressed in furs and set me an example, I'll come out and do my bit!" As we will see, Lady Mabel Smith would do exactly that!

Part of the new wartime workforce included women who had been active in the Suffragette Movement. Six days after the declaration of war, all suffragette prisoners were released and the Government Boards of Agriculture and Trade jointly issued an appeal to women, to 'Come forward and do your bit' for the war effort. Women everywhere swiftly answered the patriotic appeal. In the words of Emmeline Pankhurst: 'What is the use of fighting for the vote if we have not got a country to vote in?'

By March 1915, one million women had joined the paid labour force. Not only working class women, but those who were educated and more accustomed to being waited on by servants. Women of all social classes would also manage to get involved in farm labouring.

Lady Margery Lawson Tancred, a later photo taken just before the Second World War. (*Courtesy of her family*)

Early hostel accommodation

In 1916, the Conference of North Riding Farmers agreed in principle to employ female workers, but concerns were also expressed about the provision of lodging for these women. The farmers' concerns were justified by the experiences of early Land Girls, who were frequently housed in makeshift accommodation in any available church or village hall.

They had tin basins on trestle tables and jugs of hot water with which to wash. They slept on ticking mattresses filled with straw and often spent the night accompanied by the various additional inhabitants of the building, like beetles. As the Women's National Land Service Corps had no uniform, instead the women wore gym slips or overalls. They ate a basic diet of soup, rice and potatoes and had to buy whatever cooking equipment and pans they could afford. The low wages paid to Land Girls meant that it was difficult for women to be self-supporting, let alone find their own accommodation. Cottages could be rented singly or jointly, but a certain amount of variation existed, depending on whether or not a woman had another source of income.

Even the government recognised that there was a problem with the living standards of Land Girls, mainly because of their lack funds and low wages. The

Journal of the Board of Agriculture, published in October 1918, recommended that the only way their living expenses could be reduced further was by building up a community of female farm workers. This would provide lower rents, and a communal kitchen and messing arrangements would also reduce the cost of their food. In the first instance, the *Journal* explained, they would need to have a community house, containing a kitchen and dining room, common rooms for society and also bedrooms. It should be let at rates within the means of women engaged upon a farm. The purpose of the community house would not be to secure a uniform institutional mode of existence, but to leave as much freedom and diversity as possible on a fundamentally economical basis. The community should be managed by a paid person acting under the committee of the residents.

Before this report, various experiments in hostel accommodation had been tested in Yorkshire, beginning in 1915. Lady Margery Lawson Tancred founded the first hostel for 'Land Women' in the Boroughbridge area. (The Lawson Tancred family believe that this was located at Heaton House, Aldborough, near Boroughbridge.) At the time, Lady Margery was a local woman of twenty-five and she would continue to do a tremendous amount of work with the Land Girls during the war.

Agricultural training for women

So that Land Girls should be of value to the farmer it was thought desirable that they should have some kind of grounding in the industry. Throughout the country, women were soon undertaking training in agriculture. In 1915, the *Journal of the Board of Agriculture* reported on the 'Agricultural Education of Women', detailing a scheme in West Yorkshire. On the 312 acres comprising Manor Farm in Garforth, near Leeds (later associated with University of Leeds), women students attended the dairy school run by the Yorkshire Council for Education.

The students resided in a house in Garforth, under the supervision of the dairy instructress. During milking, individual farmers did not have the time to supervise the work of trainees, but the training school could give students the close supervision lacking in on the job training. Over terms of six weeks, successive classes in skills like butter-making were held at the farm, running from April to October. Eight pupils were enrolled at any one time and they were nearly all women.

The Yorkshire Council for Education also conducted five short courses for women at Garforth, consisting of two weeks with thirty women present. The training involved practical milking, separation, cleaning the dairy and utensils, feeding calves, pigs, and poultry, loading hay, cleaning turnips and mangels and any other potential seasonal tasks on the farm.

Early dairy school c.1892.
(*Murton Farming Museum*)

Women who undertook practical training on farms were also accommodated in nearby lodgings or hostels, but those attending registered training centres had a more regimented life.

The Elkington Estate, Lincolnshire

On 15 May 1916, Captain Smythe, the owner of the Elkington Estate and Lady Wilton, the tenant of Elkington Hall, made arrangements to start a training station at Elkington. Elkington, near Louth, is in the East Lindsey district of Lincolnshire, just over the border of the East Riding of Yorkshire, separated by the River Humber. Free instruction lasting two weeks was given at the new training station, with board and lodging supplied at five shillings a week. Wages were paid to the trainees by the estate, at the rate of three pence an hour, to cover the cost of their board and lodgings.

The training station catered for twelve women at a time. Under the guidance of a forewoman they were expected to carry out any work on the estate allocated to them, such as weeding corn, hoeing roots, hay-making and milking. Those on milking duty were to be at the dairy by 6.00 am. Others would rise at that time, tidy their bedrooms and make the bed, performing all domestic duties before breakfast at 7.00 am. After breakfast, they would assemble at 7.45 am.

The students would be placed under the direction of an appointed forewoman, or instructress, and would carry out her orders and instructions when at work. Beginning work at 8.00 am, they had an hour for lunch at midday.

Work was finished at 5.00 pm, with a meat tea at 5.45 pm. Bed was at 9.00 pm and lights were put out by 9.30 pm.

Every student was expected to take her turn assisting the cook matron in preparing the meals and taking the midday meal to other students. This would mean that one day out of the fortnight's training, would be given over to domestic work. (Twinch, 1990.)

Women who undertook the course at Elkington did so on the undertaking that they would work on the land in the Lindsey area afterwards, provided they were offered suitable wages and conditions. It was decided that the minimum wage paid to students by farmers should be board and lodging, plus six shillings a week. Women of all backgrounds and levels of education passed through the training. It was found that the farmers preferred the more educated women, although all those placed were satisfactory. (Dowling, 1916.) Most farmers required women to do weeding or similar work, but those, perhaps from a wealthier background, who had experience of riding were put to work with horses.

Free accommodation for six women was provided by Lady Wilton and the parish also handed over the local institute to act as a canteen and recreation room. Cooking appliances and all the necessary crockery and cutlery were supplied by Captain Smythe. Mr Benjamin Stone, the Elkington Estate Manager, acted as the local secretary and was responsible for planning the work completed by the Land Girls each day. He also arranged for the women to be conveyed to and from the training station.

A cook-matron was engaged from the local village and she was paid fifteen shillings a week. The instructress was also a Lincolnshire woman used to working on the land, and she was paid sixpence more than the training women. The scheme was a success. In an area where there was formerly great prejudice against women workers, as a result of the training scheme farmers began to employ women with enthusiasm. (Dowling, 1916.)

The Bawtry Training Centre, South Yorkshire

In 1916, Mrs de Wilton, a Canadian woman farmer, came to Britain to help the war effort. She had successfully run a Canadian farm of 328 acres for nearly ten years, using an almost entirely female labour force. At Bawtry in South Yorkshire, she took over the empty Butler's House next to the local hall, which was large enough to house a dozen women. There she gave two weeks' hospitality and training to women who wished to learn agricultural skills, ensuring that each recruit was passed on to an employer already able to do many basic farm duties.

Mrs de Wilton's social connections brought her into contact with Mrs Herbert Peake, the Secretary of the Women's War Agricultural Committee (WWAC) in South Yorkshire, who was particularly interested in getting educated women on to the land. The Committee subsequently employed Mrs De Wilton as instructress and principal of the Bawtry Training Centre.

Mrs Peake also undertook to consult with Major Peake, to establish a larger training centre, which would later become the Bawtry Training Centre, at Plum Tree Farm near Doncaster. A house on Major Peake's estate then stood empty. It was located in the centre of some hundreds of acres of glorious farmland and it was a roomy hospitable house, with fine farm buildings occupied by horses, cows, calves, pigs, sheep and poultry. There was also farming equipment and tools, guarded by a bailiff.

Within a week of acquiring the house, Mrs Peake had furnished it to accommodate twenty recruits. A cook and housemaid were hired to ensure the comfort of the recruits. (*Country Life*, 1916.) By the end of their two weeks' training, the recruits at Bawtry were able to carry out farm yard duties of stock feeding and grooming, stable and byre cleaning, spreading manure and planting seed potatoes. They had also practised harnessing horses to carts; and used a range of implements; and assisted in sheep dipping, weeding, ditching, harrowing and rolling the seed bed.

Four Bawtry trainees went to work at a farm near South Cave in Yorkshire, where they were employed in weeding, shifting, dumping and spreading twenty tons of manure. They were soon trusted with the mower, the bind reaper and the plough. As one of these girls stated, 'Where a Bawtry girl goes I now feel confident that we can gain the confidence of the farmers who dwell in the neighbourhood of her work.' (*Country Life*, 24 June 1916.)

Unfortunately, the training centre closed during its first winter because of the shortage of applicants. In a report of work carried out in the West Riding under Lord Selborne's scheme for women workers, it was stated that over 1,000 women had volunteered for work in the West Riding, yet only thirty-two farmers had applied for women workers.

Lord Selbourne had been appointed President of the Board of Agriculture in 1915. As a former First Lord of the Admiralty he therefore understood more than anyone how serious the interruption of foodstuffs might be in the event of hostilities and loss of shipping. He realised that women would be the only new source of labour and committees were needed to deal with women's labour. Training was essential. (Twinch, 1990.)

However, the Bawtry Training Centre brought other similar centres into being. Another pioneer in the recruitment of women to agriculture, Christopher Turner started one in Lincolnshire. In 1916, Major Dent placed a cottage to accommodate four experienced female workers, on the condition that farmers who were willing to employ female labour could be found in the Ribston district, near Wetherby. Lady Ancaster started with six recruits under an instructress at Grimthorpe in East Yorkshire.

Lady Sykes added accommodation to the existing training provision at Eddlethorpe near Malton. Eddlethorpe was a house and estate owned by her husband, Sir Mark Sykes 6th Baronet of Sledmere. Sir Mark had already proposed to the War Office that agricultural workers of East Yorkshire should be signed up as reservist drivers. In 1913, his efforts led to the formation of the Wagoners' Special Reserve, which became part of the Army Service Corps in 1914, driving wagons with supplies of food, fodder and ammunition for the Front Line. Men were enrolled in the Wagoners' Special Reserve from Pickering, Sherburn and Aldborough. In light of her husband's interests, it is hardly surprising that Lady Sykes became so involved with the Land Girls.

Other Yorkshire gentlewomen followed Lady Sykes' lead. The ladies of the County mixed socially and exchanged ideas and no doubt it became fashionable to get involved in women's agricultural training. Lady Dorothy Wood (later the Countess of Halifax) started a similar programme by training three girls at her farm in Garrowby, East Yorkshire. Lady Chetwynde was also ready to start a similar enterprise. As already mentioned, in 1915 Lady Lawson Tancred started the first Land Girls' hostel in the Boroughbridge area.

Lady Lawson Tancred must have been aware of the work of the Wagoners' Special Reserve, since some men from her own village enrolled, and she was probably inspired by their efforts to help Land Girls take over some of their work. Lady Lawson Tancred later moved to Aldborough Hall, and so could not take on more recruits, but she had already done pioneering work with women in the Ripon district and helped with recruits in North Yorkshire.

On 17 May 1916, the *Yorkshire Post and Leeds Intelligencer* reported on a meeting to promote women's agricultural work in the West Riding. At the meeting, Mrs R F Merrick had explained that a group of ladies had been doing farm work in the Wetherby district and were handing over their wages to a British Farmers Red Cross Sale held at Wetherby. Mrs Foster of Stockeld Park, Yorkshire, volunteered to train three women under her farm bailiff.

At the meeting, it was also revealed that Lady Mabel Smith, the sister of Earl Fitzwilliam, had written a letter to the Rotherham Board of Guardians telling them that she was going to work on a farm for six months. She said it was her way of serving her country at present. She apologised for not attending the meeting, but said that if anything really important required her presence then she could no doubt get a day off.

Speaking before the meeting, Lady Harewood urged the ladies in the district to find out how many local farmers were willing to take in women and train them. Any farmers doing so would receive a grant of ten shillings per week for a fortnight, from the West Riding County Council. She urged the need for a training centre to be established in the West Riding and pointed out the success of Mrs Peake's centre at Bawtry, and the value of combining a trained instructress with accommodation. She also praised the example set by Lady Mabel Smith.

In February 1916, the East Riding Council considered exempting older girls from school attendance in the Howden area, to relieve their mothers from domestic duties and free them for farm work. This was intended to help solve the shortage of labour. Farmers were asked to utilise women from the towns, and in order for them to do so a properly organised centre would be established at Howden, where the women could be housed and to which a farmer in need of hands could apply. (*Yorkshire Post and Intelligencer*, 7 February 1916.)

Over in the East Riding, Mrs Philip Reckitt had made an urgent appeal for garments for women agricultural workers in 1915 (*Hull Daily Mail*, 26 January 1915). This came to the attention of Lady Sykes of Eddlethorpe, who became the Chairman of the local Women's Workers Agricultural Committee. In May 1917, Lady Sykes, together with Mrs Philip Reckitt and Mrs Edwin Robinson became involved in establishing training centres at Eddlethorpe and at Sutton (*Hull Daily Mail*, 5 May 1917).

These training centres taught recruits farming skills for three weeks, during which time they would learn about horses and cows, how to spread manure, hoe, cut up turnips and do other manual work. They were provided with suitable accommodation and their railway fares. As housing the trainees was difficult, a plea was made for the offer of a cottage to serve as a hostel, located within the reach of two or three farms. The government would be prepared to furnish the cottages for seven or eight women.

In 1917, 130 women potato pickers were housed at Ousefleet Hall, near Goole (*Hull Daily Mail*, 21 November 1917). In the *Yorkshire Evening Post* (6 November 1917), Lady Mabel Smith reported on the useful work done by these women in lifting potatoes on the larger farms. In the past this had been done by Irish casual workers and their assistance had helped the farmers to get in their crops, which otherwise they would have had difficulty in doing. She added that the girls were billeted at Ousefleet. One hundred and eighty-seven girls had passed through Ousefleet, ninety-four of which were National Service volunteers from as far away as Cumberland.

At first, the better educated agricultural volunteers were catered for in a different way from the less educated women. When interviewing for Women's Land Corps forewomen's jobs in 1916, it was stated that among the 'towns bred' women of the educated class, a large number were willing and eager to qualify for forewomen's posts. At least 5,000 were required to command squads of workers prepared to go on tour among different farms, wherever their services were demanded.

'The Government wanted women who were intelligent yet stupid enough to do farm work!' In 'The Notes on War Service', the Board of Trade stated that

What to wear if you have the money!   National Service Poster (First World War)

women and girls of high social standing 'will at once learn to milk and will let the other inhabitants see them going, in suitable working dress, to and from work day after day. Smart fashionable attire was marketed by the exclusive shops in London for the high standing recruits. Then, their social inferiors will not be slow to follow their example.' (Twinch, 1990.)

In 1918, Harrods issued an advertisement for suitable Women's Land Army clothing. Boots specially made for farm work cost thirty-seven shillings and sixpence. The jackets recommended were made of beautifully cut best corduroy, with button pockets and converted storm collars. This attire was far beyond the average wage of female farm workers.

During the early months of the war, many a capable woman was denied training and opportunities because she was deemed uneducated. (Twinch, 1990.) By the 1918 harvest, however, every volunteer, trained or untrained, was welcome. Following the German offensive in the spring of 1918, a further 22,654 Grade One (the most physically able) men were called up, leaving a vast gap in the farming workforce. Women became even more important in saving the harvest that year, together with prisoners of war, low category soldiers, volunteers, policemen and public school boys.

The formation of the Women's Land Army

Despite initial resistance in the farming communities, in February 1917 the Women's Land Army was formed. It was much less well-known than its World War Two successor, but it also attempted to provide a full-time, well regulated female work force. (Bullock, 2002.) It was administered by the War Office and funded by the Board of Agriculture and Fisheries.

There were three sections within the Women's Land Army: Agriculture, Forage, and Timber Cutting. The first inspectors were appointed in 1917, and paid women officials were used in each county.

In April 1917, Vinidcome Hostel in New Church on the Isle of Wight, was the first WLA hostel to be opened under the National Service and Board of Agricultural Scheme. The training of women on farms proceeded all over the country. It was stated that the housing and welfare of the worker in every instance was to be considered, in order that the women could start well on the land, under comfortable home conditions. Forty thousand more women were needed in that year alone and many more in 1918. The women were to be supplied with free board and lodging during their training. They would be clothed at no personal expense, and their uniform would include one free outfit, as well as thigh boots, breeches, two overalls and a hat.

WLA recruits would be sent to specially selected farms, under the care and protection of supervisors appointed by the Women's War Agricultural Committees. The assurance was given that no parent need be afraid for the future of their daughter. Skilled women would always demand good wages for farm, garden and dairy work. One thousand new training centres were to be established by the WLA all over the country.

As soon as the trained recruit started her independent career, she would receive not less than eighteen shillings a week, with bonuses for special work and harvesting. Some women questioned whether they could live on eighteen shillings a week, but the hostel and billeting scheme answered that their experience in the munition centres had proved that female workers could be housed and fed for fifteen shillings a week.

In some cases, the farm workers' hostels were within country mansions or cottages. Additional arrangements made by the WWAC and such bodies as the Girls' Friendly Society, offered free or low cost accommodation to ensure that the land workers had a surplus of cash for their own needs. (*Nottingham Evening Post*, 26 March 1917).

The Young Women's Christian Association (YWCA) also played a key role in housing Land Girls, encouraging independence whilst keeping an eye on morality. The YWCA opened its doors to women agricultural workers and even organised a convalescent home in Margate for Land Girls. The involvement of the YWCA in Women's Land Army accommodation became essential by the Second World War and especially in Yorkshire.

In 1916, it had already been suggested that women's agricultural training would take place at organised centres, where the recruits would reside together in one central hostel, under the supervision of an instructress and a housekeeper. By 1917, the Women's Land Army badly needed this type of accommodation. The hostels were usually established in the centre of a district where there were several farms suitable for training.

The instructress played a vital role in training new recruits at these centres. She needed to give all her attention to the work of training and she also had to be experienced in farm work, so that she could gauge the suitability of the recruit for the various kinds of labour. Gradually, the amount of work given to each trainee would be increased. She would make sure no girl, in her enthusiasm, exceeded her powers.

It was hoped that at these centres recruits who mostly came from the towns would appreciate the companionship of girls of their own age and an esprit de corps would be established. (*Country Life*, 1916.)

In the South of Yorkshire, there was a major WLA recruiting drive in 1917. In March 1917, WLA girls marched through Sheffield in the charge of Miss H Andrew. Several newspapers at the time commented that the girls looked full of health and vigour! In the *Yorkshire Herald* (7 May 1917), an article entitled 'What is being done in the North Riding', discussed the sceptical attitude of the local farmers towards the women land workers and how at first they had tailored the work to fit the capabilities of the women workers. Throughout the county, women were to be trained in winnowing, turnip cutting, threshing, preparing food for cattle, planting potatoes and cabbages and clearing the land.

Women were also recruited to the WLA for timber cutting. Britain was now dependent on home-grown timber because of the enemy blockades. Timber was needed for pit-props, for the railway, army huts and many other essential services. The terms of service were similar to those in the agricultural scheme. All necessary travel expenses in connection with employment were to be defrayed, and during periods of unemployment, the women's board and lodging was guaranteed for four weeks.

In some areas, problems of accommodation were to be overcome by housing women in specially fitted-out railway carriages, as in Northallerton. In December 1916, the *Yorkshire Post* reported that the Agricultural Committee had opened three training centres, with one specialising in milking. In order to fill them, advertisements had been placed in Yorkshire newspapers, which resulted in eighty replies. It was apparent that the great industrial towns, of the West Riding would provide a splendid supply of women land workers. The great difficulty was in providing housing for them. To help start this, three disused railway carriages were acquired and converted into cubicles.

Through the kindness of a farmer in Northallerton, a carriage was put on show as an object lesson. It was decided to ask for the loan of caravans, for the transport and the use of gangs of female workers. (*Yorkshire Post and Intelligencer*, 7 December 1916.) The Matron appointed to oversee the coaches was Miss Carter Squire. She cared for twenty women and soon ten had acquired work. The coaches could only accommodate twelve pupils at a time. The guard's van was transformed into a kitchen and living room, and the compartments were turned into bedrooms. The coaches were heated with hot water pipes.

On Thursday, 20 February 1919, sixty-five women assembled at the coaches and marched in procession with the banner of the Land Workers and the Union Jack flag at the head. The Land Army Song opened the proceedings. Colonel L'Anson and the Revd J Kyle, both local farmers who employed some of these women, spoke encouragingly and gratefully of the work they had done. Lady Bell presented the Good Service Ribbons and two Distinguished Service Bars to Land Girls. She then entertained them, offering a tea followed by games, dancing and songs. Lady Bell played the piano throughout and the evening ended with 'Auld Lang Syne', three cheers for Lady Bell, three cheers for Miss Davies (possibly the Matron) and three cheers for themselves. (*The Landswoman*, April 1919.)

The WLA by 1918

At the inter-county conference of the Women's War Agricultural Executive Committee in York on 4 February 1918, members from the three Ridings of Yorkshire, Durham, Derbyshire Kestevan and Lindsey (Lincolnshire) all attended. Lady Dorothy Wood, Chairman of the West Riding Committee presided. Mrs Edward Lane Fox, representing the West Riding and Mrs W G Eyre the East Riding, acted as Conference Secretaries. The Countess of Harewood, as the wife of the Lord Lieutenant of the West Riding, welcomed the delegates.

During the conference, Lady Bell of the North Riding put forward the motion, 'That in view of the importance of food production, the farmers of the counties here be urged to make fuller use of the services of the women land workers.' Lady Bell went on to elaborate on the excellent training camp in Northallerton, where they had good farmers and the women were largely employed. The first step, she felt, was to overcome the inertia of the farmers in this matter!

Mrs Eyre of the East Riding said that the farmers were pleased to have the girls, but in East Yorkshire there was plenty of labour as 1,030 soldiers had been released to work on the farms. Lady Edith Sykes (née Gorst) reported that trained women land workers were in demand in East Yorkshire. However, there had been great difficulty in placing several women who had been trained at Sledmere. It was most difficult, she claimed, to drag one pound a week for them from the East Riding farmer!

Mrs Greenall of Kestevan, said that in her area of Lincolnshire women workers were plentiful but the main problem was in finding suitable lodging for them. The local cottages were very small and it was almost impossible to get cottagers to take the girls in, as they could not get enough food to feed their own families. Lady Bell said this difficulty might be overcome by having hostels. The problem of billeting women on the farms was that the farmers' wives often expected the girls to do the housework as well as working all day on the farm. (*Yorkshire Post and Intelligencer*, 5 February 1918.)

In 1918 Lady Mabel Smith of Rotherham, who had worked on farms herself, continued to tour Yorkshire preaching about the advantages of agriculture as a career for women. She highlighted the success of the ploughing demonstrations by Land Girls at Aldborough, Knaresborough and Wetherby.

On 1 March 1918, an account was given in the *Yorkshire Evening Post* of a farm managed and run entirely by women. Moor House Farm, in the parish of Scruton, Bedale, was owned by Sir Henry Pease. The North Riding Agricultural Committee had commandeered the derelict farm and staffed it entirely with female agriculturalists in their early twenties and teens, who had been trained at Northallerton, Bawtry and Bedale. The team soon managed to make progress on the 128 acres. They were billeted in cottages in a village a mile away, while the farm house was being converted for them.

Life had been hard for them, as each day involved getting up at 5.00 am and walking to feed the horses by 6.00 am, before heading back to the village for breakfast. They then worked from 8.00 am to 12.00 pm, pulling whins (gorse) without implements, ploughing or harrowing, often doing the same thing in the afternoon, at times crying with the cold. Some found it lonely work and they missed the companionship of other girls. However, they were surprisingly strong and found little difficulty in slinging a 16st bag on their shoulders! There were only two such farms run by women in the whole country, the other being in Devon.

In May 1918 The Hon. Mrs Lane Fox, of the West Riding branch of the WLA, made an appeal for donations of furniture for the hostels at the new training centres for women land workers. Temporary loans were needed of single beds, bedside chests of drawers, blankets, sheets and rugs. Also required were items of furniture for the recreation rooms. In a letter from a reader to the editor of the *Birmingham Mail* (28 August 1918) it was mentioned that 'a piano would be a great boon now that autumn draws near. It is so necessary to have plenty of amusements and entertainment for the girls in the evenings to keep them from the excitement and possible dangers of the streets!'

There was a need to bring all the ideas together under a suitable leader, so the government selected an experienced candidate to head the Women's Land Army.

Meriel Talbot had been appointed the first woman Inspector of the Board of Agriculture and Fisheries. In 1917, she became the Director of the Women's Branch of the Board, in charge of recruitment and co-ordination of the Women's Land Army. She admitted that there was a need for hostel accommodation in addition to billeting on the farms, and also stressed the need for training and education for all the women in the WLA.

The government had demonstrated support for women's agricultural training. In March 1917, a Government Training Sub-Committee, including Mrs Peake, Miss Dent and Professor Seton of Leeds University, agreed to make enquiries about equipping one or more empty country houses as training centres. The Board of Agriculture made a grant of £300 towards the cost.

In 1918, there were 7,000 WLA members and Meriel Talbot envisaged an increase to 12,000. In light of this she identified an urgent need for more adequate supervision of the women workers. Many farmers felt neither they nor the government could control the women's behaviour. There had been examples of 'bad morals' and it was felt that the WLA might be blamed for inadequate supervision. The women themselves had also complained about lack of care and assistance.

By 1919, the Land Army girls in Kesteven, Lincolnshire, on the border with East Yorkshire, were written to personally by the WLA. They were reminded that they were entitled to extra rations and to fill in the relative form to claim the additional food. Yet, the letter also stated that some girls were inclined to stay out rather late in the evenings, which inconvenienced the people with whom they wee billeted. It was stressed that no Land Girl should be out after 9.00 pm, except in exceptional circumstances and then only by arrangement with their landlady.

'It is not just a question of discipline but of health also', the letter explained. They would all be at work early in the morning and have a hard day to get through and could not possibly remain fit and be at their best, unless they kept early hours. If they were wise, the advice read, they would be in bed by 9.30 pm. This letter illustrates some of the fears that the WLA organisers had surrounding discipline on the farms and why the organisation might have reasoned that hostels would help to control the health and work of the girls.

Meriel Talbot suggested that hostels would boost WLA membership as well as bringing additional discipline and routine for the women workers. The hostels would supply workers to several farms and provide transport for them, as already existed for prisoners of war working on farms. A Land Controller, paid by the government, could work from designated hostels, setting work tasks on the local farms. In July 1918, it was envisaged that paid women officers, charged with the welfare of recruits, should be appointed to the hostels. (Bullock, 2002.) All of these plans arose too late, however, as the WLA was disbanded in 1919.

However, another branch of the Women's Services had already been provided with far better hostel accommodation, and this may have been used as a guide for Land Army hostels in the Second World War. The Women's Auxiliary Army Corps (WAAC), which was established in July 1917, had even set up hostels in France. The *Aberdeen Journal* (24 November 1917) gave a detailed account of the WAAC camps and hostels. The comfort of the women was of the first priority. When the draft landed in France, new WAAC recruits would spend their first few days in a Draft Receiving Hostel, before being allocated to a hostel or camp. They would be taken to the recreation room, which could also act as a dining room, where there were bright posters adorning the walls. Perhaps a string of bunting would also be left over from the whist drive for the sergeants working at the base camp.

The WAACs were allowed to decorate their rooms as they liked, so long as they were neat. A show bedroom in the hostel had rose pink casement curtains, a lamp and cushions to match, and photographs and flowers to make the picture complete. There were three or four beds to a room. The beds were sprung, but instead of mattresses they occasionally had old fashioned paillasses, known as 'biscuits'. They had four blankets each.

On the walls a copy of the daily routine would be fixed, for instance: 7.45 am roll call, 8.00 am breakfast and room tidied and swept, 1.00 pm dinner, 6.15 pm supper, 8.45 pm roll call, 9.00 pm bed, and 10.00 pm lights out.

The *Aberdeen Journal* also printed a sample menu from the WAAC canteen:

'Breakfast – Tea, bread and butter, boiled ham, jam.

Dinner – Thick brown stew, potatoes and cabbage, bread pudding.

Tea – Bread and butter jam and cheese.

Supper – Toad in the hole, bread and jam.'

Each WAAC member received twenty-four shillings a week (skilled shorthand typists were paid forty-five shillings) and only twelve shillings and sixpence was deducted for their food. Uniform and accommodation was provided free of charge. In contrast, a WLA girl received eighteen shillings a week, with fifteen shillings deducted for food.

The *Aberdeen Journal* went on to comment that it would have been difficult to find life dull in the WAAC hostel, as the women attended concerts, whist drives, or dances held in various recreation huts. They also sometimes cheered up the wounded soldiers with musical evenings. Women going out to entertainments had to get passes but these were given freely. If they invited men friends to their quarters, passes were also required.

There were also educational opportunities, with French classes and lectures at the YMCA. An early morning bathing parade was a regular feature in camps and hostels near the sea, and sometimes Swedish drill or a walk took place. Hockey practice was also common. Life in the camp varied little from hostel life, except that wooden huts took the place of ordinary dwelling houses. The average camp had a number of sleeping huts, each holding about ten women. There was a separate room for the forewoman in each hut, a dining room, a cookhouse and an ablution hut. There was a separate sleeping hut for the administrator.

This account of life in the WAAC, although somewhat glamorised for publicity purposes, makes the WLA girl's life in 1917 seem poor and inadequate. Most WLA hostels never reached these WAAC standards even during 1941 to 1950.

In 1919, the Association of Landswomen declared that after the demobilisation of the Women's Land Army, it would safeguard the interests of women land workers in every way. The Association was set up to support any women who worked on farms, not just WLA members, and it continued after the disbanding of the WLA. It would institute hostels for those who had no homes to go to and make provision for women in times of sickness and disability or unemployment.

An agricultural subscription would be raised for this.

The lessons learnt from the First World War about hostel accommodation for the WLA were not enforced in Yorkshire until the advent of the Second World War. It was then realised that not only were purpose-built hutments required, but large houses would also have to be requisitioned.

Every woman who helps in agriculture during the war is as truly serving her country as the man who is fighting in the trenches, on the sea, or in the air.

First World War Certificate issued to WLA members in 1919.

...thur Lee
General of Food Production

R. E. Prothero
President of the Board of Agriculture.

by Dann.

The Landswoman magazine, issued in 1919.

CHAPTER TWO

Women's Land Army Hostels from the Second World War to 1950

D URING THE 1930S THERE WAS A DEPRESSION IN BRITISH FARMING and much of the land was fallow. Britain depended on overseas trade for large quantities of raw materials, and around 50 per cent of the nation's food was imported during this time. As imports from the British Empire and Europe had largely supplied Britain's needs, on the outbreak of World War Two in 1939 Britain's access to imported goods was restricted and there were acute shortages of food.

Germany's policies and its advancing army threatened these essential supplies and rationing was inevitable. By 1940, German U-boats were attacking British merchant shipping in an attempt to starve Britain into submission. Consequently, British farming had to make the nation as self-sufficient as possible. Grain was treated as a priority for animal feed. Wheat and potatoes were another necessity and the growing of carrots, tomatoes and vegetables were encouraged. An increase in milk and dairy products was also demanded.

Flax-growing in particular needed to be intensified, as flax was an essential raw material for linen, tent canvas, and webbing for parachute harnesses, fire hoses, ropes, thread and even the fabric for aircraft wings. (Ward, 1988.) Many Land Girls in Easingwold Hostel worked with the growing and the harvesting of this crop. Increasingly the yield of flax was a considerable challenge for British farmers at a time when there were insufficient skilled agricultural workers.

The intensive recruitment drive for the armed forces in 1939 left a labouring gap of 50,000 farm workers. Although the shortage of labour was never fully overcome, it was eased by the introduction of auxiliary farm workers, by local townspeople and most importantly by the Women's Land Army. The Government realised that the WLA, which had been revived in 1939, had inherited many of the same problems that had occurred during World War One. Farmers had conveniently forgotten the splendid dedication of the Land Girls in the past. Hostility was shown once more against employing town girls on farms, especially at the regulation wage of twenty-eight shillings a week!

The WLA was now under the control of the Ministry of Agriculture and Fisheries. Lady Denman was appointed the Honorary Head of the Service, and the WLA Headquarters was based at her home at Balcombe Place, Sussex. Lady Gertrude Mary Denman (née Pearson) was a strong minded woman brought up in great wealth and influence. She challenged the restrictions on opportunities for women and is now remembered for her work with the Women's Institute, the Family Planning Association and the Women's Land Army. She never took her fortunate upbringing for granted and her commitment, in the community, was to women. She experimented with poultry breeding at her home Balcombe Place.

During the First World War, Lady Denman worked with the Ministry of Food and the WLA, assisting Dame Meriel Talbot as an able and loyal administrator. She was a first class organiser and became Chairman of the Ministry, so she was the obvious choice to re-form the Land Army in 1938. Lady Denman was committed to the well-being of many young women who enlisted in the WLA and only resigned in protest against the refusal of the Government to refuse post-war benefits for the Land Girls. (Kramer, 2009.)

Although the WLA had in its title the word 'army', it was a purely civilian force, without many of the advantages that were given to other Women's Services. For the purposes of organising the WLA workforce, England and Wales were divided into seven administrative regions, served by fifty-two county offices. In Yorkshire, within each of the three Ridings the WLA was administered separately, until they united in 1945 for economy and efficiency. The North Riding had been organised by the Secretary, Miss Winifred Jacob-Smith, the daughter of an influential farmer and a very efficient, although somewhat formidable lady. She went on to take over the WLA organisation for the whole of the county of Yorkshire.

The WLA had learnt some lessons from the previous war, especially with regard to hostels. In 1941, Mr Sutherland Harris took over the whole accommodation affair. It was decided that the Ministry of Works would organise the building and maintenance of the WLA hutments. The War Agricultural Executive Committee (WAEC) and the WLA meanwhile, would take responsibility for the requisition of houses. The WEAC and the WLA would work in cooperation to deal with the work, living conditions and welfare of the Land Girls. The Young Women's Christian Association (YWCA) and the WLA would manage the hostels.

Unlike the First World War, the history of the Women's Land Army during 1939-1950 has become public property, widely written about and acknowledged. Former Land Girls have elaborated on their personal experiences of living in varied accommodation within autobiographical reminiscences. Despite the interest in the history of the WLA in the Second World War, very little has been written about the organisation and internal management of the different hostels.

The Craven area of Yorkshire was discussed by Margaret Bullock in her Leeds University PhD thesis in 2002. She writes about the hostels mainly from the point of view of the Land Girls. Some of the information gleaned from her research has been included throughout this book.

The Training Centre at Askham Bryan

In 1939, the three Ridings opened a training centre at the Yorkshire Institute of Agriculture in Askham Bryan, near York (now Askham Bryan Agricultural College). This was financed by the three Ridings and it had been completed in 1936, yet the Institute remained unused until 1939 when the WLA decided to run courses there.

Training started with twenty WLA recruits being trained in tractor driving and dairy farming for two weeks. The first batch of students – twenty from the West Riding and ten each from the East and North Ridings – arrived at the end of October 1939. The WLA proposed to increase the number of trainees to fifty, rising to one hundred by spring 1940. It was expected that the first fifty recruits would help with the training of the second batch and so on. They would each be trained for a fortnight to a month. Several courses were run, but with decreasing numbers.

By March 1940 the Emergency Committee was persuaded that it was not economical or sensible to continue running the courses, for which there was insufficient demand. The Ministry was consulted for the future use of the premises, since such a large institutional building could not be unoccupied during the war. It was requisitioned by the government and disappeared from the local records. (Tallon, Unpublished, undated manuscript held by Askham Bryan Resource Centre.) The present building at Askham Bryan, which now holds the Learning Resources Centre, was originally built in 1936-1939 as a dairy but it was never used for that purpose. Instead it became a science/laboratory building on the ground floor.

Accommodation had been provided at the Institute for fifty trainees. Students slept in the bays upstairs between the beams behind curtains. The farm, market garden, glasshouses and orchard continued in production throughout the war, partly staffed by Land Girls. (Information supplied by Julie Gardner, Learning Resources Manager, Askham Bryan College.)

Draining the land in the East Riding

During the First World War, some areas of Yorkshire with heavy or flooded soils were deemed too difficult for work by women, particularly in the East Riding. Yet, throughout the period of 1939 to 1950 there were many WLA hostels throughout the area. What had changed? Bill Bromwich worked for Priestman brothers and understood the immediate problems:

'that there were about five million acres of fields that could not grow anything because it was sour, acid, boggy and subject to frequent flooding or simply lacking in nutritional value. Drainage and fertilisers together were the answer. For the first time, the government took a proactive position to organise this through the War Agricultural Executive Committees (WarAg), training and employing Land Girls. Every piece of land in Britain was identified and numbered and the farmers were consulted about their drainage problems.' (Bromwich, 2014.)

Priestman Brothers Ltd of Hull had been approached by the government to build tanks for the war effort. As they were a pacifist firm, instead they offered to build equally useful drainage excavators. They were asked by the Ministry of Food to show groups of Land Girls how to drive their excavators and teach them how to cut field drains and improve land fertility. Priestman Brothers introduced a small excavator called the 'Otter' in 1940, which was much smaller than the other excavators. It was designed particularly for use by the Land Girls, as it would be easier to manoeuvre at only four and half tons. The girls also drove the bigger machine, the Priestman 'Cub' with equal skill.

'The training was over two weeks. It involved not only driving the excavators but also handling wire ropes to fit them on to the machines. This was a fearsome job in winter with cold hands. The difficulty of avoiding "kinking" the ropes was crucial. Starting the diesel engine in winter was also a nightmare as it needed a pull-handle to start it and the girls had to hold the cab and swing the handle to turn the engine just like an old car.'

Priestman's drainage equipment operated by the girls.
(*Bill Bromwich, Priestman Collection*)

At first the Land Girls training with Priestman Brothers were billeted at a guest house owned by a Mrs Piercy, and later they were sent to stay on individual farms. Some of the girls were accommodated in a Mrs Smith's supervised house, possibly in one room, in the first instance. They were charged thirty-five shillings a week.

Later by 1943, the training school was moved to another site at Garth Farm, High Fosham. There the girls were accommodated in the farmhouse and in a hut. Even a caravan was utilised for possible housing. Cutlery, plates and heating were provided for the caravan. All additional accommodation was hired locally.

Around 450 to 500 Land Girls trained at the Priestman School. Their draining of poor soils so that the land could be worked easier made many more acres fit for productive farming. Numerous Land Girls from the East Riding were trained in this excavating work, which explains why there was a growth in hostels in the area, as they would have benefited from working in gangs.

In the West Riding, particularly in the Craven area, the Land Girls were all trained as mechanised operatives and most of their time was spent working the fields with tractors. Only those trained in mechanisation were accommodated in hostels in the area. The tractors helped to increase the productivity of the former sheep farming areas with additional ploughing and fertilizing.

* * *

Members of the WLA could not be employed as casual labour, unless they were working from a hostel. In July 1942, 480 women were employed as casual labour from the hostels in Yorkshire. They were paid by the West Riding Agricultural Executive Committee and the Committee also stood the loss when there was less demand for workers at the end of the season. The total number of WLA members working in Yorkshire during July 1942 was 2,494.

In 1941, at a meeting of the East Riding Executive Committee of the National Farmers Union, the lack of accommodation for the WLA was discussed. One of the members, from Cherry Burton, East Riding, said he employed twelve Land Girls but had to fetch them and take them back each day, and so he would welcome a hostel. He was told that a hostel was not viable unless the farms in the area agreed to employ twenty or more girls. However, by 1944 a camp hostel was in existence at Cherry Burton to accommodate volunteers working in the fields during their summer holidays.

WLA numbers of recruits were initially minimal in 1939. In Yorkshire by December 1939, there were only 112, with slightly larger numbers recruited in Lincolnshire, Sussex, Suffolk and Kent. By the following year, 219 were recruited in Yorkshire.

In December 1940, the East, West and North Riding Committees of the WLA had amalgamated. The chairman of the new Yorkshire Committee was Katherine

Lady Graham, with two vice-chairmen, Lady Bingley and Mrs Dunnington-Jefferson. The organising secretary was Miss Jacob-Smith. By 1941, the numbers of Land Girls working in Yorkshire had increased to 1,075. There was by now an urgent need in the county for hostel accommodation.

The WLA turned to the Young Women's Christian Association (YWCA) to help in the daily management of the hostels. In 1939, the YWCA had wholeheartedly responded to the necessity for the provision of hostels for female war and munition workers, in collaboration with the Ministry of Labour and the Ministry of Supply. The organisation believed in training with Christian values. Throughout the period in Britain, it was involved in running 294 Women's Land Army hostels, mobile units and railway rest rooms.

In 1941, the YWCA opened the Ripon and Knaresborough Hostels in the West Riding. Early in 1942, another YWCA hostel was set up at Easingwold in the North Riding. These three hostels were newly built hutments, intended to accommodate the Land Army workers. Hostels for male agricultural workers were already up and running at Brompton, Easingwold, Guisborough, Leeming Bar, Scorton, Sinnington, Whitby, Stokesley, Thirsk, Terrington and Strensall.

In a publicity leaflet published around in 1941, three types of WLA accommodation are outlined: farms, billets and hostels. In addition, accommodation was provided on or near airfields, where the girls lived in houses. They ate in the airfield canteens and were supervised and inspected by the RAF officers. There were also camps near the forests for the Timber Corps, the branch of the WLA devoted to forestry work.

After the war had ended, the Women's Land Army continued to function until 1950, and the hostels became more important than ever. In 1946, there were over a thousand new recruits in the West Riding alone. Many more recruits and hostels were required when the German prisoners of war began to be repatriated. Farmers were unable to employ Germans or Poles unless there were Land Girls present. One farmer from Brandsby Hall, York criticised these arrangements. He had wanted to use Polish workers from the prisoner of war camp at Hovingham, but was told he must ask for Land Girls from the Crayke, Easingwold or Alne Hostels. Only if there were none available could he use the Polish workers.

Farms were regarded as superior to hostels in giving something of a family life to the Land Girls. In 1939, accommodation on farms and in local houses appeared to be the only immediate option. Billets were to be carefully chosen, often being a spare room in a village house. These arrangements gave a certain freedom, enabling a girl to come and go as she liked, yet they could also be solitary. The hostels, however, offered friendly community life.

All types of accommodation in Yorkshire were inspected on a very regular basis by WLA officials, including Miss Jacob-Smith who later organised the WLA in Yorkshire. Hostels also became the distribution centres for the WLA

Girls arriving at Hostel (Stokesley). (*Eden Camp Collection*)

workers. The hostel forewoman would allocate the girls singly or in gangs at the farmer's request.

The hostel organisers would endeavour to see that the Land Girls had an attractive, sociable and relaxing home to return to after a hard, tiring day at work, and this also acted as an effective recruitment campaign. Throughout Yorkshire, Miss Jacob-Smith was instrumental in helping to promote care in the hostels and she provided support for the welfare of the girls.

Billets on farms

As during the First World War, in addition to living in hostels Land Girls were often billeted with a farmer and his family. Some had a wonderful time and were treated as another daughter in the family, and many speak affectionately about their experiences. They enjoyed the kindness they were offered by their hosts and kept in touch long after leaving the Land Army.

Other Land Girls suffered the most terrible conditions, however, and were often extremely lonely because of the isolated locations of some farms. Often a girl from a town would be sent to a farm with no running water or electricity. A candle to aid her to bed was often her only comfort after a gruelling day at work. Sometimes she was the only Land Girl on a remote farm with no bus service or access to people of her own age. It was extremely hard work, especially in the snow, rain and bad weather. Former hairdressers and shop girls could find that they disliked working by themselves in the fields, picking up stones or doing other types of boring and dirty work.

The fact that they were working for the war effort might now seem remote, despite the enticing advertisements that had attracted them to the WLA; the job no longer appeared glamorous compared to some of the other services. Social life was impossible or frowned upon by the farmer and his wife, and girls from the towns missed the communal and social life of the towns or the company of siblings. They also faced the prejudices of the farmer and, in some cases, the uncalled for jealousy and imaginary suspicions of his wife. Occasionally, farmers would try to take liberties with their female workers and the local forewoman or Miss Jacob-Smith would have to intervene and withdraw the girl from the farm, as she states in her diaries.

Some Land Girls were not given their full rations of food in farm billets and were instead served badly cooked, unappetising meals. Two girls at a farm near Whitby were so regularly given rabbit for their evening meal that they came to hate the taste. Their farming hosts were a miserable couple but they did have a pet parrot. He was the only entertainment on the isolated farm and the girls enjoyed the parrot's company. They spent their spare time teaching it to say swear words and in particular, "Not bloody rabbit again!" Their efforts were not appreciated by the farmer and his wife and the girls were told to leave. On another farm, the Land Girls had been working in the fields on a very hot day, and they had taken off their shirts and were working in their bras. The farmer told them to leave so that his sons would not see them! (Both stories recalled by Edna Braithwaite, née Partington).

Many billeting disasters were remembered by Land Girls. One girl had to sleep in the same bed as the farmer's mother and also had a small boy sleeping in the same room, his bed divided from them by a curtain. In another, the Land Girl was petrified when her landlady's husband came to find his wife, wielding an axe, as he had heard that his wife had been 'carrying on' with other men! When shown around a remote farm by a leering old man, a hapless young Land Girl was terrified when he indicated the 'friendly' double-seated toilet and she had visions of being given the daily orders in a very personal manner and place!

There is also the story of four WLA girls working with pest control. As in many farmhouses of the time, there was no electricity at their billet and the only sitting room was also where the farmer and his wife slept. The only wash basin in the house was the same place where the washing up was done, near the kitchen door leading to the yard outside. To reach their beds the Land Girls had to go through a male lodger's room, which led on to the farmer's son's bed. The girls' sleeping quarters were finally reached through a hole in the wall with a makeshift curtain placed over it. So, every day, the girls had to negotiate the two men's bedrooms and go downstairs to wash in public by the back door.

Perhaps their only consolation was that they had each other for company and suffering could be laughed off! This adventure was reported to Miss Jacob-Smith by a rep, who reacted with horror after having inspected the girls' hole-in-the-wall bedroom door. They were removed to hostel premises as soon as possible.

Some Yorkshire Land Girls wanted to fend for themselves, so they asked a farmer if they could sleep in his redundant chicken shed. They cleaned it, put wallpaper on the walls and begged some old furniture from their families. The farmer also gave them a stove and the local villagers helped supply them with crockery etc. and welcomed them into their homes for a weekly bath.

Billets at RAF airfields

Many Land Girls worked near RAF camps. Mary Tetlow was posted to Catterick, where she was billeted in a semi-detached house, one of several in a row of homes originally built as married quarters, situated four miles from RAF Catterick. Mary and her colleagues were led by an RAF sergeant and corporal, and their job was to grow food for the RAF station. An order might come for 300lbs of lettuce or 3cwt of peas for the meals at the station.

Unlike Land Girls in farm billets and hostels, they wore dungarees during the day and put on frocks every evening, when they went for their meals at the NAAFI. They were fortunate as WLA girls usually could not use the NAAFI. They also had a wonderful social life, with considerable freedom, and participated in whatever events were going on at the camp.

Another such arrangement was in place at Linton on Ouse aerodrome, where Elizabeth Gross (née Dickinson), known as Tina, stayed in a house with six other Land Girls. They grew vegetables for the Canadian Air Force and they had a wonderful time. As Tina said: 'We were all young and daft!' They were supposed to cater for themselves but they could always get a meal at the camp. Tina remembered that they did not care about doing any housework and so the house was always dusty. They were visited by someone from the Land Army (probably Lady Celia Coates) and she always arrived on horseback.

At Topcliffe RAF Aerodrome, near Thirsk, in 1942 there was only a small number of Land Army staff. Their work was also supervised by RAF staff and Lady Celia Coates was their Welfare Officer. One former Topcliffe Land Girl, Diana Hester, said that, at first, they lived in luxury in a gracious house originally designed for officers. Each girl had her own room, which was furnished with iron bedsteads, biscuits (three square cushions filled with flock or straw to make a mattress), pillows, linen and blankets. They had built-in cupboards and a coke boiler supplying constant hot water. The girls ate in the

Women's Auxiliary Air Force (WAAF) mess, where Diana recalls the food being wonderful.

However, the WAAFs kept away from the Land Girls, as they said they smelled of the farmyard (which was true to some extent)! There was some resentment felt by the WAAFs, who were well disciplined, neat and spotless, whereas, according to Diana Hester, the Land Girls were 'a carefree, rumbustious lot with hair flying over the shoulders — swaggering along in grubby baggy slacks, merry and uninhibited'. They were allowed to go to the camp entertainments, where they dressed in pretty frocks, silk stockings, dainty shoes and with waved hair and make-up, looking very dainty and feminine. The girls stood out against the soberly clad business-like WAAFs and the men flocked round the Land Girls.

Later, as the camp was taken over by a large influx of Canadians, the Land Girls had to go into WAAF quarters, in a small house in a row of four. A Nissen hut nearby was used for bathing, but it was smelly and ill-ventilated. Certainly, life for Land Girls based at the RAF camps was far preferable when compared with farm billets. (Lynn et al, 1990.)

Women's Timber Corps camps

Timber played an important role in wartime. During the First World War, German submarines targeted ships carrying imports of timber for pit props in the British coal mines. When the next war came, the Forestry Commission realised there would be an acute shortage of workers. By 1942 endless measuring and stocktaking of the woods were required, new trees needed to be planted, together with the felling and transporting of mature trees.

The Women's Timber Corps was an off-shoot of the Land Army, in which volunteers worked at timber camps in the woods, such as Dalby and Cropton Forests, near Pickering and Boltby and Kilburn, between Thirsk and Helmsley. To qualify for the Forestry section of the WLA members had to be over twenty-one years old. The members wore the same uniform as the WLA but not the same hat. A beret completed the uniform instead.

Some lived in private accommodation, but many lived at training centres, such as at Wetherby Camp and Boulby Camp, where girls were shown how to cut trees, saw pit props, load wood, sharpen saws, identify trees, measure and cost wood. After training, the work was allocated depending on ability; the highest level job was becoming a measurer.

The work of a measurer demanded intensive training. She measured the timber and counted the pit props to gauge the earnings of the workers by piece rates. Hard woods – oak, ash, elm, beech, sycamore, were paid at 2d per square foot whereas soft woods were paid at 1½d. The number of each tree was scored on the base and a note taken. She measured the girth and volume was calculated by length times girth. She worked out all the measurements, calculated the wages of and handled the pay packets to the men and women working in several forests. This involved carrying hundreds of pounds in her haversack. (Twinch, 1990.)

Lumber Jills starting on simpler work, like loading lorries, could work their way up. Women from all over the country came to the timber camps at Wetherby and Boulby for training. (Boulby Camp is discussed in more detail later in the book.)

The demand for hostels

In 1941, hostels began to be used more widely, when it became apparent that farms and billets did not live up to expectations. There was also a genuine fear that the behaviour of some girls might tarnish the WLA reputation, should they be allowed too much freedom. Hostels could provide the support and discipline necessary to limit any potential misbehaviour.

The Ministry of Works took over the building and maintenance of the WLA hostels, while the War Agricultural Executive Committee (WAEC) and the WLA managed the women's work, and the Young Women's Christian Association (YWCA) and the WLA organised the the hostels. One of the major problems in running the hostels was the appointment of suitable staff. Numerous advertisements appeared in the Yorkshire newspapers for wardens and assistant wardens for WLA hostels all over the country. Courses were provided by the YWCA wardens at Oxley Hall, now part of the University of Leeds. It proved difficult to find ideal wardens, considered to be kind motherly women, who could earn the respect and confidence of young girls away from home for the first time in their lives.

Many of the wardens appointed proved most unsuitable, as at Dishforth Hostel, for a short time at Arkendale and at the hostel at Stockton on Forest. Another problem was conflict or jealousy between the hostel warden and the forewoman. This was certainly evident at both Blois Hall, near Ripon, and Terrington Hostel. Arguments also occurred between the warden and the assistant warden at Moat Hall, Ouseburn, and Arkendale Hall, and in the case of the latter were disastrous. (All of these hostels are discussed in more detail within later chapters.)

One difficulty of writing about the WLA hostels involved identifying their locations. The management, the Land Girls, and the local newspapers all used different names for each hostel. For example, Stockton Hostel was at Stockton on Forest, near York, and not to be confused with Stockton-on-Tees. Thorpe Audlin was also known as Hillthorpe or East Hardwick. The Goole Hostel mentioned in newspapers could have been either the Pollington or Howden hostel. There were two Sherburn hostels, one at Sherburn in Elmet and the other near Malton. Selby Hostel was also known as Brooklands and the girls called it 'Jumbo Castle'.

In Yorkshire, by June 1943 there were WLA hostels at Ripon, Sherburn in Elmet, Doncaster, Wetherby, Knaresborough, Beckwithshaw, Thorpe Audlin and Little Ouseburn. Hostels for Land Army machinery girls were opened at Settle, Skipton, Bolton by Bowland and Silsden. Shortly afterwards, other hostels were opened at Weeton, Staveley and Gisburn.

The hostels can be divided into three types: purpose-built brick blocks; requisitioned houses; and airfield buildings. Like the farm billets, they varied widely. There were at least fifty hostels in the Yorkshire area by the end of the war, with 696 across the whole country recorded in 1944. By December 1943, there were 5,279 Land Girls in Yorkshire – more than in any other county – and they all had to be accommodated. Many girls from the county were also posted elsewhere with the WLA, to supply demand in other areas. From 1939 to 1950, the 80,000 Land Girls employed by the WLA included 25,000 Yorkshire women who were employed by the WLA either within their home county or across the country.

The ablution block of Knaresborough Hostel still remaining as a Community Centre.

The dining room at Knaresborough Hostel. (*Eden Camp Collection*)

WLA hutments

Many of the hostels were purpose-built to a government plan and opened from late 1941 onwards. These 'hutments' were of different sizes but usually of the same style and plan, able to accommodate from ten to sixty girls. There were two main buildings connected by a passageway. In one section there would be the sleeping quarters and in the other the day quarters, which would consist of combined recreation and dining area also the kitchen etc. A small water tower was common in most of these hostels.

The sick bay and the warden's quarters were beyond the kitchen. The dining and reception rooms were designed to be light, cheerful and attractive. The dining

The dormitory block of Knaresborough Hostel building as it is today.

tables would be placed at one end and at the other, easy chairs, a piano, radio, bookcase, table, tennis table and a sewing machine. Rooms would be provided for drying clothes and boots and also a linen cupboard was desirable. The hutment gardens would be a vital part of the daily life for vegetables, fruit and flowers.

Ten very similar hutment hostels designed to house forty to fifty Land Girls were erected by the Ministry of Agriculture in districts which would provide suitable work for women: at Settle, Skipton, Ripon, Wetherby, Tadcaster, Sherburn, Knaresborough, Goole and Doncaster. It was envisaged that the Land Girls would begin with potato picking, and beet and carrot lifting.

Over 300 hutments were built to the standard plan. The first hostels of this kind to open in the West Riding were at Knaresborough and Ripon. They were originally planned to accommodate male farm workers, but it was decided to use them for the Women's Land Army instead.

Knaresborough Hostel in Chain Lane, Knaresborough, consisted of three blocks, a dormitory, an ablution block and a welfare block. The ablution block contained, in addition to sanitary facilities, baths, shower baths and washing basins, a linen room, a drying room and a foot bath for washing rubber boots. In the welfare block there was a good sized dining room, a recreation room, a kitchen, accommodation for the hostel manager and a sick bay.

In 1941, there were forty Land Girls in Knaresborough Hostel. The hostel is still visible today but the building has been adapted as a community centre. The sleeping block was still much as it was when the Land Girls occupied it. Originally there were sleeping cubicles of about 6ft by 11ft, with curtains hanging across them for privacy. Two to four girls would sleep in the cubicles in tiered bunks. One or two stoves might be placed at either end of the sleeping annexe.

The asbestos roof of the hutment remains, as does the original brick work. No doubt the rain pounding on it would have woken the sleeping girls. The only major change to the outside was made a few years ago when the window glass was replaced with double glazing. The ablution block was located at the one end, as was the boiler room. (Watterson, 2013.)

In the North Riding of Yorkshire another purpose built hostel was opened at Easingwold in December 1941, and additional hostels opened in the North and West Ridings in 1942.

The *Yorkshire Post and Leeds Intelligencer* correspondent wrote about the opening of the very first WLA hostel in Yorkshire in October 1941. This was the Ripon Hostel in Bondgate, Ripon. The journalist noted that the hostel would hold about forty Land Girls, but at present it was only half-full. It was being run by the West Riding Agricultural Executive Committee, in conjunction with the YWCA. Land Girls would leave the hostel to work at nearby farms in the district, commuting by bicycles, which were provided for them and by bus or they were called for by the farmers and returned at the end of the day.

The Ripon hostel consisted of two long huts, one for sleeping and one for recreation and dining. Each girl, on leaving in the morning, would take three large sandwiches, two of meat and one of cheese and a tea cake. The recreation room was decorated in cream and green. A wireless set was provided along with books, magazines and flowers which the girls bought themselves. Outside the hostel was a special bath with running water for the girls to wash the mud off their boots, and they could then go straight to a hot bath or shower before having their evening meal. At first, many queued patiently for the baths, as they had never used showers before and they were a little afraid of the alien water contraptions. There was also a sick bay.

Eileen Jones (née Waddington) recounted her time at the hostel, when there were forty-two girls in the Nissen hut. They slept in two-tier bunks, four girls to a cubicle with a dressing table between them. They each had a drawer and a locker. Eileen shared a 6ft square cubicle with fellow Land Girls named Anna, Renee and Agnes. At 6.30 am, they were woken by a bell, then beds were made and they went to eat breakfast, which usually consisted of porridge and a fried egg or sausage, in spite of food rationing!

Every morning the hostel forewoman made a roll call and they were given different jobs. There was more fun to be had when working in a gang, Eileen remembered. The work was varied and might be helping the Forestry Commission to cut and clear trees or picking sprouts in a snow-covered field. As they filled the sacks with sprouts, all they could see when they raised their heads were further acres of sprouts ready to be picked. They were glad of the chance to warm up in the cowshed, in order to eat their dripping sandwiches. (Jones, E.)

Many of these buildings were used after the WLA was disbanded in 1950, to house people with mental health problems, and this was also the fate of Ripon, Bubwith and Tadcaster (Whixley). Some buildings were also used to house prisoners of war before repatriation, as well as Poles and displaced persons.

Requisitioned houses

The government requisitioned houses for the use of the WLA throughout the war. These were often in the centre of village life but could also be miles from the nearest habitation. They sometimes appeared quite magnificent from the outside and the Land Girls genuinely appreciated the chance to live in these lovely old places. Houses requisitioned in Yorkshire included Alne House (now a Cheshire Home), Beacon Garth, Blois Hall, Muston Lodge (now a hotel). Stockton House accommodated forty-five Land Girls, with a hutment extension to the rear which housed a further eight girls, as well as the warden, assistant cook and a room for Miss Jacob-Smith when needed.

All the requisitioned houses were carefully inspected by a Ministry of Works official and a WLA representative. The houses chosen were usually situated on or near the old boundaries of the three Yorkshire Ridings. (Since that time, the areas of the three Ridings have changed and the county boundary has diminished.) Mary Sutherland, a WLA Pioneer Warden who visited hostels all over England and Wales, wrote an article for the WLA newsletter, *Land Army News*. She explained that the requisitioned hostels:

> 'might be in the depths of the country with a long winding avenue, a mansion, an old hall, or even a very modern house equipped with an Aga Cooker. In one...there were marvellous bathrooms in different colours with sunken in baths complete with various gadgets for hot and cold sprays...or it might be a house in street in a small country town or village.'

However, some houses considered for requisition did have drawbacks, examples of which will be recounted below.

In the Yorkshire Farming Museum archives there are the original records of preliminary visits made by the WLA to houses they were considering for requisition. Many of these were inspected in 1942 and in 1943, when further billets were urgently required. Miss Jowett, the WLA Hostels Officer, kept records of her visits to each hostel in a duplicate book. She was eventually married in December 1943, to Lt. Commander (E) H Barrett RN, and resigned her Land Army job. Miss Jowett's records of the following requisitioned country houses, which were retained by Miss Jacob-Smith, include the following:

Rolston Hall, near Hornsey in the East Riding, was inspected in March 1943. It was an old house in excellent condition, with central heating, and needed very little doing to it, although it had been empty for three years. Forty to fifty Land

Rolston Hall Hostel, East Riding, as it is today.

Girls could be easily accommodated, Miss Jowett concluded, together with a staff sufficient to look after them. The reception room was exceptionally good, with parquet flooring. The maid's sitting room and cloakroom was suggested as a good warden's room and office and it was near a room with a basin and lavatory.

There were three sinks on the ground floor, one sink on the first floor, three baths and ten basins and three lavatories. The old nursery would make a good sick bay, the record notes. The Ministry of Works inspector suggested that there might be a drainage problem, so to start with the hostel should only accommodate twelve to twenty girls. The double Aga in the kitchen, which the Ministry of Works regarded as a nuisance, would be replaced by the usual coal burning range and would take up less room. This hostel was occupied by the WLA from autumn 1943 to March 1946. It is now a fine country residence.

Aldborough Hall, at Piecebridge near Darlington (then in North Yorkshire), was inspected by the Ministry of Works, Newcastle and the WLA in April 1943. Whilst there was no other suitable house in an area where accommodation was urgently needed, there were several drawbacks to Aldborough Hall. It was isolated with no bus service running nearby. The room space was limited but rooms were lofty, with large windows, so ventilation would be no problem, and there was no heating other than fireplaces. The only cooking facility was a single electric ring in the kitchen. Four lavatories, three baths and five washbasins would be required. It was decided that placing forty girls there would strain the accommodation to its limit. Despite considerable investigation, it has not been possible to ascertain whether or not this house was used by the WLA.

The Bothy, The Gardens, at Warter Priory Pocklington in the East Riding was visited in March 1943. Miss Jowett concluded that the Bothy was most suitable as a hostel, as it was modern, centrally heated and in a very good condition. There was sufficient room to house twenty girls in twelve cubicles, six of which were 12ft by 6ft, with one spare cubicle for a sick bay. There was a dining room and a kitchen, six lavatories and two bathrooms. Some alteration would be needed with new passageways and a new kitchen range would be required. Miss Jowett's final comments noted that the premises were excellent but only twenty girls should use the Bothy, as there was not much space for recreation and the kitchen was not large. The Bothy was never in fact used by the WLA; it is believed that the owners were unwilling to have a large number of girls working with male farm labourers.

Rosedale House, Hunmanby, East Riding, was visited by the representatives from the Ministry of Works and the WLA on 3 March 1943. This was a small, modern detached house standing on the road between Bridlington and Filey. It was on the train line to Bridlington and so it was most accessible, and also near to the village of Hunmanby. Rosedale House had been knocked about by the army. Some of the grates needed repairing, a lot of plaster had come down, and the house generally needed decorating. It was possible to house twenty girls there, leaving two rooms for staff and a small sick bay.

The YWCA then stated that they would require three rooms for staff, so there could only be sixteen girls on the premises. There were additional drawbacks too. For instance, there was no heating, save for the fireplaces and the range needed replacing. The drainage would have to be repaired by the Ministry of Works, as it was not adequate. It was also suggested that the scullery should be divided to make a drying room with a boiler of sufficient size for the girls to do their washing.

The WLA came to the conclusion that Rosebank was very accessible and, with the alterations, would make a good small hostel. The present owners, who now run a bed and breakfast business at the house, do not know if the house was ever used by the WLA.

Muston Lodge, Filey, East Riding was visited by Miss Jowett in March 1943. There would be room for twenty-two girls and four staff, Miss Jowett decided. It was a pleasant old house, equipped with fireplaces in all the rooms. The dining room and the recreation room were both new rooms. An excellent drying room could be made from the pantry, which had a side door to a lobby where the girls could leave their wellingtons. The front bathroom could be altered to contain two baths, two basins and two lavatories. The drainage would have to be improved, as a cesspit was used, but the electricity supply was on the mains, as was the water supply. A new range would have to be installed in the kitchen, together with a sink. There were plenty of outbuildings, providing accommodation for a WLA transport vehicle and bicycles.

Muston was used by the WLA from spring 1944 to spring 1946. It is now a hotel, trading under another name.

Grange Garth, near Malton, North Yorkshire was visited by a representative of the Ministry of Works and the WLA on 30 March 1943. It was a small house standing by the local church and a short distance from the village of Wintringham. It was a one and a half mile walk to the main Scarborough to Malton Road, however, so it was rather inaccessible. The Ministry of Health had formerly requisitioned Grange Garth and so it was in good condition. About eighteen girls, three staff and a sick bay could be accommodated there.

Further changes still needed to be made, though. The drainage was into a cesspool, which was thought to be inadequate. There was mains water and lighting was by calor gas. There were no fireplaces in the rooms and the kitchen range was inadequate. It was suggested that the bath downstairs should be taken out and a lavatory and two wash basins be put in the bathroom upstairs, with the whole room rearranged to take two baths.

Records show that a Miss Cholmley had owned the house at the beginning of the war. She had invited evacuees to live in the house, yet unfortunately she suffered a fall, broke her hip and died suddenly. The house was then requisitioned by the Ministry of Health and preparations for the WLA occupation were made. The present farmer of the land, a relative of Miss Cholmley, said that it was very possible that the house was used by the WLA but he has no proof of it. The land around the house was heavily used by the military, and today he frequently finds unexploded bombs and hand grenades in the area.

Aireville, Gargrave Road, Skipton, West Riding: Miss Jowett visited this house with Mr White Smith from the Ministry of Works. It was a large Victorian mansion, about half a mile from Skipton, and had already been used by the ATS. The grounds were large and the house would accommodate fifty girls with sufficient staff. The drainage, which was by septic tank, was thought to be sufficient, and the house had a mains water supply. The lighting was by gas and there was central heating, but only a small boiler, which just heated a few radiators in the passages and in a few rooms. The cooking facilities were good, with two large ranges and another old-fashioned gas range in the courtyard. There was good light and ventilation from the numerous windows.

There were two good rooms for recreation and a good dining room. A small room, with cupboards, could be used as a sitting room for the warden. Four rooms upstairs were required for staff sleeping quarters, and the remainder were needed by the West Riding WAEC for offices. The outbuildings were sufficient for bicycles and a van. In the grounds were a block of additional Nissen huts, with an excellent ablution section containing two baths, eight wash basins and six lavatories and an ironing room. These huts would sleep forty-eight girls and a member of staff. If only thirty to forty girls were housed here, then no further sanitary fittings would be needed in the house, the inspectors decided. The girls could sleep in the huts and the house could be used for recreational purposes.

Miss Jowett, after visiting Aireville again in July 1943 and meeting with Mr White Smith from the Ministry of Works, decided that Aireville would not be occupied by the WLA. A purpose-built hutment already had been created locally, in Shortbank Rd, Skipton.

The Greens, Station Road, Masham, West Riding (now North Yorkshire), was visited by Miss Jowett and a representative of the Ministry of Works on 23 June 1943. It was found to be an attractive small house on the outskirts of Masham, with a good garden and lovely views. It had an inadequate kitchen, however, in which the large range would have to be replaced. There was a nice dining room and a very good recreation room with a conservatory.

Bathing facilities were adequate, with two baths, two basins and two lavatories upstairs, as well as a basin and lavatory downstairs. The drainage was by septic tank, which would need to be improved. Water, electricity and gas supplies were all drawn from the mains. Radiators were run from the gas mains. The general condition of the hostel was good, with no sign of the roof or gutters needing attention, nor any sign of dry rot. The Greens would make a nice small hostel, accommodating sixteen girls and two staff, Miss Jowett judged.

The hostel opened soon after the inspection in 1943 and closed in spring 1946. The National Farmers' Union (NFU) gave a gratuity to Land Girls who had been in the hostel for nine months of sixpence a week, and five girls received a cheque for the maximum amount cheque at the 1945 Christmas party (*The Land Girl*, Feb 1946).

Bryon, Sedburgh, West Riding (now Cumbria): In June 1943, Miss Jowett visited this property with Mr Chippendale from the Ministry of Works. It was described as a nice house, with an attractive garden. In the area between thirty-two to forty hostel places were required, but this house would only accommodate eighteen girls. To house more would require building a hut on the north side, on the only spare ground. There were three reception rooms, a kitchen, small larder and cloakroom with a wash basin and lavatory. On the first floor there were six rooms, one very small, and a bathroom containing a bath and basin. One room would make an excellent drying room. Water, drainage and gas were on the mains and electricity was generated from the owner's own plant. There were gas fireplaces in the bedrooms and a stove in the hall. The cooking facilities were deemed inadequate but the general comment was good. Nevertheless, by the end of 1943, it was decided that this house was not to be used by the WLA.

Staveley Hall, near Knaresborough, West Riding (now North Yorkshire): The Hall was visited by Miss Jowett on 20 July 1943. At the time it was occupied by fifteen Land Girls who had arrived only the day before, even though the Ministry of Works had not finished the building alterations and there were workmen everywhere. The basins, two lavatories and a bath were in working order, and most of the work had been completed.

The Warden, Mrs Whittingham, who had previously been the Assistant Warden at Blois Hall, and the Assistant Warden Mrs Horner had carried on nobly in the dormitories, dining room and recreation room, making it all look attractive, although the linoleum was not down. Lady Lawson Tancred, the Welfare Officer and Miss Jacob-Smith came to meet the new inhabitants. Lady Lawson Tancred had been involved with the training of Land Girls in World War One and she spoke to the girls, telling them that she had started the very first hostel for Land Girls in 1915, before the WLA had officially been formed.

Miss Jowett made a further visit to the hostel a month later, when she collected the new Cook from the station and took her to the hostel. The Cook, she wrote, was 'a nice girl of nineteen' and Miss Jowett hoped she would fit in well. The hostel was looking good, but the drainage system was not yet completed, nor was the drying room, but it was just a matter of fitting the racks and whitewashing the walls. In February there was a problem with overflowing toilets at the hostel, and there was a leak over the stairs.

When the hostel closed in 1944, the girls were moved to Arkendale Hall, a few miles away.

Cappelside, Cravenside, West Riding: In June 1943, Miss Jowett, along with Mr Chippendale, went to see how much of the Cappelside garden might be requisitioned. It was suggested that a piece of the hay field could also make a lawn to face the terrace and at the back of a house half an acre could be used as vegetable plot. Cappleside had two dormitories, each sleeping eight to ten girls. There were three baths; ten to twelve wash basins and six toilets. There was a large kitchen and recreation room.

In July 1943, Miss Rushworth drove WLA officials Miss Jowett and Miss Crook to this hostel from the Huddersfield Rally on the Sunday evening. They were greeted by Mrs Gorden, the Assistant Warden from Sherburn in Elmet Hostel, who was in charge of Cappelside. The hostel looked most attractive, the three inspectors reported. Miss Jowett also commented on their splendid supper of cold ham and salad with boiled eggs, followed by apple tart and custard. Coffee and peaches finished off the meal. Whether the hostel girls were treated to such luxury is debatable!

Miss Crook and Miss Jowett went over the hostel and talked to some of the various girls who had been working that day. They left the next day at 9.30 am, to visit the girls working in the fields at Gargrave and those learning to drive at Skipton. Later that day, the group visited the Skipton Market and the Skipton Hostel, which was a hutment type. Here, they had lunch with Mrs Gorden, who was the Assistant Warden of Sherburn-in-Elmet who was presently in charge of Cappleside. The Ministry of Works driver joined them for the meal.

Holden Clough, Craven, West Riding (now North Yorkshire): In June 1943, when visiting the hostel Miss Jowett proposed to requisition the land from the front of the house to the stream and to the road. Land would also be taken from the house to the swimming pool. The rest of the park could then be ploughed for a vegetable garden.

In July, Miss Jowett revisited Holden Clough and watched the girls making their sandwiches in the morning. The hostel was clean and a cook was arriving during that week, which would help to relive the staff shortage. The two Wardens, the Misses Dick, were said to natter and fuss rather a lot. The girls seemed 'rather a nice lot', Miss Jowett felt, although she only saw a few, as eighteen were on holiday and four were at a course at Sherburn Hostel.

The electric light plant was not working, however, as there was not enough water in the stream to generate the necessary electricity. Miss Jowett noted that she had written to the Ministry of Works, telling them that something would have to be done once the double summer time ended. It was vital that there was sufficient electricity.

Holden Clough was a low, grey stone house set in the woods of Ribblesdale on the fringe of Bowland. It was a rambling place with many chimneys and surrounded by some of the rarest trees in Yorkshire. Approximately twenty-five girls were billeted here before the hostel closed in April 1944. This hostel housed WLA girls from the mechanised branch and they were trained in tractor driving and handling other farm machinery.

There had been terrible prejudice against the girls working on the farms in Bowland, but when the hostel was closing a local farmer reportedly said, 'Us farmers wouldn't a set a woman on 12 month a gone, but durned in Ah knows what we s'd do without the lassies now!' (*Yorkshire Post & Leeds Intelligencer*, April 1944.)

The Corner House Cafe, Gisburn, near Skipton: In June 1943, Miss Jowett said that the land surrounding the hostel could be requisitioned and part of it ploughed up, as nothing has ever been done with it. However, the hostel closed in 1944 when it was taken over by prisoners of war.

Howden Hall Hostel, Silsden, West Riding, opened in May 1942 and closed in 1947. It accommodated 200 people and there were social amenities such as a games room, where darts and table tennis were played; a busy room, where one night a week an instructor taught craft and leather work; a branch library with over 400 books; and a large concert room with a dance floor. (Bullock, 2002.)

Weeton Hostel, The Limes, Weeton, West Riding: This hostel opened on 16 August 1943, with twenty-six Land Girls and a popular forewoman, Miss Barbara Farnell from Wetherby. Miss Jowett visited the hostel a day later. Mrs Gorden was also there (they had met recently at Cappleside hostel), as she was helping the Warden, Mrs Liddiard, and the Assistant Warden, Miss Firth. The wardens were friends as they had been together at a hostel in Sutton on Trent. Miss Jowett commented that the girls seemed 'a very nice lot – some new recruits and some older girls who had been in other counties and were delighted to come home again.'

The hostel looked most attractive with masses of flowers, and Miss Jowett remarked, 'It really makes a nice hostel.' There was a meal ready for them of cold beef salad, jam tart, cake, bread and butter and tea.

Moat Hall, Ouseburn, North Riding: Miss Jowett arrived at this hostel when Miss Alstaff, the Warden, and Mrs Harris, the Forewoman, were arguing, and 'from the look of the hostel that is all they are doing!' She told them that she did not blame any girl for not staying in the recreation room as it was most unattractive. They needed to group the chairs around the fire and put some flowers there.

After she had spoken to them privately, Miss Jowett found that they each blamed the other. Miss Jowett then spoke to the Welfare Officer about the situation, who maintained that a lot of the trouble started with Mrs Harris, who reported everything that happens to Mr Dowell. It was like having a spy in the hostel, she complained, and this got on Miss Alstaff's nerves. She also had little time for Mrs Harris! Because of these problems, it was thought that the WLA ought to let Mrs Harris go. Miss Alstaff could run the hostel with the cook and a resident domestic, Miss Jowett concluded, as she thought her unlikely to get on with an assistant! She also recorded that Miss Alstaff was suffering from fibrosis and looked frightful.

The Welfare Officer also told Miss Jowett that the food always looked good and the girls were well fed but the hostel is not as clean as it should be.

Moat Hall was a Grade Two listed early eighteenth-century house, incorporating part of a seventeenth-century or earlier house and had later extensions and alterations, being part timber framed. It was occupied by the Women's Land Army from 1943 to 1944, until it was closed as a result of enemy action and the Land Girls were transferred to Arkendale Hostel.

Later, a Canadian plane skimmed the roof and came down very near the house; six airmen were killed during the incident. A Land Girl was billeted at a farm in nearby Grafton, which was lit by candles at night. One evening she thought she saw someone passing with lots of candles, but she learnt later it was the sparks from the engines of the Halifax bomber, which was trying to get home to Linton Aerodrome, but crashed. It badly damaged the top of the roof of Moat Hall. Damage was also done to the church and Georgian mausoleum. The present house is now a private residence.

Brooklands, Selby, East Riding (Known as 'Jumbo Castle'): Miss Jowett took the Warden to the hostel on 24 September 1943 and the Assistant Warden and the domestic were already there. The blackout was up and all the equipment was in place, with the exception of the easy chairs and thermos flasks. Miss Jowett thought the Wardens seemed appalled by the amount of work to be done, but commented that they were both splendid and had promised to have the place ready. Luckily, Miss Jowett had brought them tea and milk and a domestic came armed with tea, cake and honey, so everyone cheered up.

The domestic hot water boiler was working when Miss Jowett arrived, but not the central heating. Everything was on a meter – telephone, gas and electric light – and a great deal of time and effort was taken up with inserting shillings into the meters.

Blois Hall, Sharow, near Ripon, West Riding (now North Yorkshire): Miss Jowett visited Blois Hall at the end of August 1943. She thought the Land Girls and staff appeared happy, apart from one woman, whom the Warden Mrs Ladle said was 'unsuitable to be with young girls'. She was thirty-seven and went out with a different man every night, then arrived back late. This was a bad influence on the rest of the girls. The same woman was also being difficult over food and wanted something different all the time. She liked to choose which farms she wanted to work on and one farmer that week had refused to employ her. Another girl was described as a 'bit simple' and the Warden thought the other girls might 'rag' her.

The hostel had a major water problem and on some evenings there was not a drop of water for washing, lavatories etc. An engineer came and pumped water for four hours from the overflow tank to the house tank, then someone came out from Harrogate and filled up every tank, but this situation could not go on. The water came from a spring to a run (a common way of irrigating a field) and this run was frequently out of order.

Some of the WLA at Blois Hall had not been offered work, as it had already been taken by the girls at Dishforth Hostel and those at local forest camps. During the previous week the farmers had said they did not want the girls from Blois Hall.

The Ministry of Works had sent lots of equipment and the hostel looked very nice, Miss Jowett noted, although curtains for the dining room and linoleum for the dining room were still needed.

Dishforth Hostel, North Hill Farm, Dishforth: WLA official Miss Walker accompanied Miss Jowett when she visited North Hill Farm. Miss Walker was delighted with this choice of hostel, as it seemed as though it might have the best staff quarters in any of their hostels and would be very convenient in every way. The work was going well and she would be arranging for the staffing immediately.

Miss Jowett went with Miss Jacob-Smith to the opening of this hostel on 30 August 1943. The hostel kitchen looked very rough, she noted, and the scullery was untidy. The whole place looked slipshod and blankets were trailed on the stairs and on the floors of the staff rooms. The staff consisted of the Warden Mrs Seymour and her sister, two part-time dailies and a man whose duties the two WLA ladies could not make out, who was sleeping in a small room at the end of the dormitory. Mrs Seymour had put three wardrobes across the end of the dormitory and she had tacked a blanket across them. She alluded to the partition as 'The Wall of Jericho'! There was another entrance to the end, so the ladies presumed that the man did not go into the dormitory at all. The drainage was not working at all, so they are using chemical lavatories.

Sixteen girls had been transferred to Dishforth from The Greens at Masham and twenty from Brompton Hostel. Supper that day consisted of pasties made from sausage meat, tea, rock buns and plums. During their visit, Mrs Seymour kept telling the two visiting ladies, that whoever was warden would have a heavy responsibility, as the Sergeants' Mess was just down the road at the airfield. The road also ran 'absolutely under the windows of the dormitory,' she explained. 'Then there are two hundred Irish navies working for a construction firm at the aerodrome...there are the ENSA entertainment, movies and dances most nights!'

Miss Jowett wrote that she was not at all happy about the way in which the Ministry of Works had completed the hostel. The drying room was far from satisfactory, as both it and the scullery were not properly roofed – there were rafters and no ceiling! There was no linoleum, just cement floors which created appalling dust. The hostel already needed redecorating after all the working harvest holiday camps for people from the towns, and the general impression was one of untidiness.

Miss Jacob-Smith continued to visit this hostel on the resignation of Miss Jowett, and the problems there multiplied over the years (as will be discussed in a later chapter).

Stockton on Forest: (Like Dishforth, this hostel will be discussed at greater length in a later chapter.) At the end of June 1943, Miss Jowett, together with Miss Walker, visited the house. There was still a great deal of work to be done, as most of the upstairs ceilings needed to be replaced. The hostel promised to be comfortable, however. It might have been better if the hut outside had been made larger though, she noted. The hutment addition would be nice, but it only held eight girls.

CHAPTER THREE

Miss Winifred Jacob-Smith MBE:
The Organiser of the Women's Land Army
in North Yorkshire (1939-1945) and
the whole of Yorkshire (1945-1950)

WINIFRED JACOB-SMITH PLAYED A MAJOR ROLE in the Yorkshire Land Army and the records she kept are unique. Amongst them are records kept by Miss Jowett from 1942-3, covering her involvement with the Ministry of Works inspection and selection of suitable houses for occupation by the Women's Land Army. These records were retained by Miss Winifred Jacob-Smith.

Over a period of eight years, from November 1941-1950, Winifred Jacob-Smith, the Organiser of the North Yorkshire WLA, recounted her visits to Land Girls in farm billets and hostels. These were in the form of diaries, handwritten and in various sizes, running to eighty in number. The duplicate copy was retained in the books, as the top copy was sent to the WLA Yorkshire Head Office at Harrogate. Some of the duplicate copy entries are now faded and impossible to read.

On her death, these books were rescued from Miss Jacob-Smith's house by Mr James Stephenson, of Stephenson & Co., Professional Auctioneers and Valuers. The company had been associated for generations with the Jacob-Smith family, who farmed at Humberton,

Winifred Jacob-Smith receives the MBE.
(*Murton Farming Museum Collection*)

between Knaresborough and Boroughbridge. The Jacob-Smith family had a herd of pedigree Ayrshire cattle, which Miss Jacob-Smith continued to keep with her elder sister Dorothy. They also purchased thirty acres at Scriven, near Knaresborough, for this purpose in 1965. It was traditional for the first son of each succeeding generation of the family to be called Jacob, but as the last of the line were daughters their father changed the surname to 'Jacob-Smith' so the tradition would be retained.

Winifred was the last of two spinster sisters to die in 2003, aged ninety-four. James Stephenson went to Somerley, the Jacob-Smith family home, to sort through all the family possessions which should have passed to another generation. He found wartime memorabilia in the attic, including the Women's Land Army records and uniforms. As their intrinsic value was very limited, at his request, the executors allowed these items to be donated to the Yorkshire Farming Museum at Murton, York. Here they could be displayed properly. The information within the duplicate books was concentrated on about eight hostels in the area, and shows the different management styles and the lives of the Land Girls in Yorkshire.

In a recording held by the Imperial War Museum, only half of which has been retained, an aged Miss Jacob-Smith recalls the early days and her involvement with the Women's Land Army. She had been educated at St Margaret's School in Scarborough and later undertook a secretarial course at the Yorkshire Ladies College in Leeds. Winifred's mother was President of the Knaresborough's Women's Institute (WI), in which her two daughters took an active role as well. They published a book of local recipes in 1938.

At the Women's Institute, Winifred socialised with Lady Celia Coates, who asked her in 1937 to 'look after the Women's Land Army if war should break out'. In 1938, Winifred organised for a few girls to spend a fortnight working on a farm as volunteers. Soon after war broke out, on 14 September 1939 Miss Winifred Jacob-Smith joined the Women's Land Army, and her certificate, number 22569, was signed by Lady G Denman and Lady Katherine Graham. She was thirty years old.

After the problems in agriculture that had arisen during the First World War, the Ministry of Agriculture suggested that women should work on the land in 1939, but there were few recruits. Lady Celia Coates became the local Chairman of the North Riding WLA and Winifred, as Secretary, got involved in recruitment and organisation of the few volunteers.

On 16 March 1940, the *Knaresborough Post* newspaper reported, under the heading 'Received by the Queen':

'Miss Winifred Jacob-Smith, younger daughter of Mr and Mrs Jacob-Smith, Somerley, Boroughbridge Road, Knaresborough, had the honour of being selected as one of the Women's Land Army representatives to attend a reception by the Queen in London on Thursday. Miss Smith has been acting as secretary for the North Riding branch of the Land Army.'

On the death of her father in 1941, Winifred also began to manage the family farming enterprise at Somerley with her sister Dorothy. Winifred worked for the WLA from her own home in Knaresborough with two typists. Notes were posted in the Labour Exchanges and glamorous posters were issued. Many girls volunteered in a state of panic and there were more recruits than jobs. The men on the farms had not yet been called up, so there was little demand for extra labour and few farms requiring help. Consequently, many possible recruits decided to join the Auxiliary Territorial Service (ATS) or the Women's Royal Naval Service (WRNS).

Winifred was also the editor of the monthly report called *The Bulletin*, which went out to all hostels and WLA clubs. This magazine itemised news about future and past events, uniform information exchanges etc., poems and songs written by Land Girls and anything relevant to the Women's Land Army.

Materials from the duplicate books Winifred kept are now the major source of information about the WLA hostels in Yorkshire. The author of this book has visited many of the former hostels included in the book to ascertain the state of preservation and to gather recollections from local residents and WLA veterans. In addition, many contacts have been made with former Land Girls from these hostels, in order to record their personal reflections and to compile a photographic library. The existence of over fifty hostels in Yorkshire has been discovered, although Miss Jacob-Smith only visited and recorded information about a few of them.

Winifred was diligent in her daily role of advising, caring for the Land Girls' welfare and criticising the management of the hostels, and she made the best interests of the girls a priority. She did have fixed views on some matters, however, and a few of her comments on the Land Girls reflect this. In her records she gives her views on the reasons why girls might have been billeted in a particular hostel. The following quotes represent a varied selection:

'The wife said to the farmer "Either she goes or I will!"'

'The girl refused to feed pigs so the farmer gave her a minute's notice.'

'The farmer's wife thought that 9pm was late enough for the girl to be out at night!'

'The girl has a reputation so the farmer would not keep her!'

'The farmer's wife was fussy and old fashioned and the cottage was old fashioned and rather isolated in winter, one and a half miles from a bus stop going down a dark lane. The girl wanted more of a social life.'

'The farmer was a typical Dales inhabitant with no sophistication what so ever.'

'The girl did dairy work but she was asked to do housework in her time off and she found it difficult to refuse.'

'The girl comes in at 11pm and the farmer thinks it is too late. She should be in by 9pm.'

'The girl finds the farm lonely and wants to be near her boyfriend.'

'The girl was very thin and delicate and she likes hostel rather than farm billets.'

'The girl quarrelled with the farmer's wife so they did not speak for two years.'

'The farmer does not approve of her going out to a public house at night. He thinks no girl should do this.'

'The girl cannot make any friends on the isolated farm.'

'The girl had an extremely dirty head, lice, so she was sent home!'

Miss Jacob-Smith had to move at least twelve girls from farm billets, because they missed hostel life. Most said they had found the farm too quiet after hostel life and one girl said she had found the farm conversation above her head.

Miss Jacob-Smith kept a record card about every girl and she classified them into types, often adding telling phrases. There were a great variety of girls sent to the WLA in North Yorkshire and Miss Jacob-Smith's reports were generally favourable. In hostels these qualities were appreciated, together with the more grating attributes of some of the girls, such as lack of personal cleanliness, belligerence, coarse or rude behaviour. These were described in the books as follows:

'She is a cheery bright girl still quite happy.'

'A nice girl cheery and red faced.'

'A big strong girl inclined to grumble. Always grumbling she left to work on the buses.'

'Had a queer brother and mother was a bit different too?'

'Had an unstable mother, girl slightly odd, eventually had to marry farm worker.'

'She married a man of 71 years who lived for six months.'

'The girl is always tired through overworking.'

'The girl was always complaining about cutting thistles and says she is sick and tired of the sight of thistles.'

'The girl was always complaining about her bicycle tyres wearing out as the road was dreadful to the farm.'

'She hopes to marry a man with a farm.'

'The girl has now got false teeth to replace two knocked out, when she fell off her bike.'

'She likes racing.'

'She was a delightful girl but got really annoyed as she was sent a great coat with moth holes in it. She always endeavours to look smart.'

'She is inclined to stand around doing nothing.'

'She only appears when the meal is ready.'

'The girl is a bit daft but she hopes to marry a bricklayer.'

'The girl is very happy as she had a wonderful holiday at Butlins.'

'She has lost all her teeth and cannot get used to the false set.'

'The girl says she is getting married in August and then she said May. I am not sure I can believe her.'

'The girl is very hard working and never seems to need anything.'

'She was knocked down by a bull and was badly bruised.'

'She has put on weight since ceasing to be a forewoman, as her new job is less worrying.'

'The girl is a bit fast and collected a boyfriend straight away.'

Miss Jacob-Smith. (*Joan Nicholson Collection*)

'One girl came back to the hostel very upset. A farmer had killed a goose and the girl put it in a copper and started to pluck it. To her horror it stood up and proved to be very much alive. The girl said it gave her a queer feeling.'

'She saved a farmer from a bull.'

'The girl became too lazy...a tiresome girl.'

'She's a nice rather shy girl.'

'This is a nice little thing but dreadfully stupid. She left the door of the chicken house open two nights running and each time the chickens were devoured by foxes.'

'She is far too stupid and idle.'

'She is very fat and podgy.'

'She is a particularly good type of girl.'

'The girl is a rough type and is bad tempered.'

'The girl has gone blonde since I last saw her, but there is no improvement!'

With all the above women living in hostels, Miss Jacob-Smith's records show how hectic and varied life could be in the confines of a house filled with tired, noisy and wonderfully human Land Girls.

When war seemed inevitable, WLA recruits were interviewed to judge their suitability and given medical examinations. It was not hard to get into the Land Army and, although the official starting age was seventeen years, some girls accepted were younger. No birth certificates were required and some deficiencies, such as short-sightedness, might be overlooked. In North Yorkshire, unusual characteristics noted by Miss Jacob-Smith included: a girl with one eye and false teeth; a girl with a squint; a bed-wetter; a girl who was sick on any journey; a girl with a leg in irons; and a girl who had hysterics during the night because of being involved in an air-raid on York Gas Works.

Joan Nicholson (née Lund) was at Thirsk Hostel from 1947-49, and she remembers Miss Jacob-Smith with great affection. She said that Miss Jacob-Smith was always concerned about the welfare of all the Land Girls and sought to make their lives as comfortable as possible. She was particularly kind to Joan when she developed tonsillitis after cleaning some drains on a farm.

When Joan returned to the hostel and fell on her bed, Mrs Keep the Warden was very concerned, so she put her in the sick bay and called the doctor. The doctor told her she must go to the hospital immediately, but Joan refused and said she would prefer to go to her home in York. How was she to get home? Joan said she would go by bus. However, Miss Jacob-Smith arrived at the hostel and said she would take her to York. Joan was feeling terrible and went with Miss Jacob-Smith and her very large dog. Unfortunately, the dog contracted Joan's symptoms and died a few weeks later.

Edna Braithwaite (née Partington) also remembers Miss Jacob-Smith's 'love and concern':

'She was a really lovely kind soul who helped and cared for all the land girls. We never referred to her as "Winifred", but always Miss Jacob-Smith. She was exceptionally pretty, with bright blue eyes and she

Miss Jacob-Smith's invitation to the Farewell Party. (*Murton Farming Museum*)

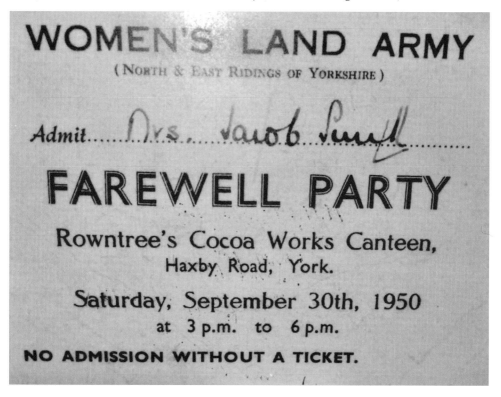

nearly always wore a bluish Harris Tweed style cloak. She was sometimes escorted by a handsome army officer, who might have been killed in the war. She was awarded the MBE for her services to the Women's Land Army. Her mother and elder sister went with her to the palace for the presentation.'

Edna visited Miss Jacob-Smith at her home in Somerley many years later. By then Miss Jacob-Smith had become house-bound and was exceptionally lonely, mainly existing in the kitchen of her large rambling house. She was visited rarely by anyone, which Edna found strange, since Miss Jacob-Smith was well-known and liked in Knaresborough.

For many years after 1950, Miss Jacob-Smith had organised the reunions of the Yorkshire Land Girls and many of them remembered her with great affection. As the last surviving member of the prominent local farming member, she left her land to Harrogate Council for the people of Knaresborough to be made into a park. This thirty-acre park in Scriven, is surrounded by an impressive stone wall and there are many ancient trees within it. The park opened in 2008 and since then a further one hundred trees have been planted.

Winifred Jacob-Smith is buried with her sister in the churchyard at All Saints' Church in Kirby Hill, near Boroughbridge. Her grave is next to that of her parents and can be found in the north-west, near to the outside wall of the Saxon church. Any former Land Girls or their families who might be passing by should be encouraged to visit her rather neglected little burial plot.

A reunion, Miss Jacob-Smith is
standing on the far right.
(*Joan Nicholson Collection*)

In
Loving Memory of
DOROTHY JACOB SMITH
SOMERLEY, KNARESBOROUGH
WHO DIED
ON 26TH APRIL 1984
AND HER SISTER
WINIFRED MARY
JACOB SMITH M.B.E.
WHO DIED
ON 23RD MAY 2003

Grave of Winifred Jacob-Smith
with her elder sister, Dorothy at
All Saints Church, Kirby Hill,
near Boroughbridge.

CHAPTER FOUR

Home Comforts and Living Conditions

Sleeping arrangements at the hostels

Mary Tetlow, a former Land Girl at Catterick Hostel, enthusiastically described her new home:

> 'My bed is comfortable and I sleep deep. Hot water can be had in ten minutes from the copper boiler. There was enough left from my washing for two girls to have a bath. The furniture in my room consists of two beds, 2 chairs and a small dressing table, a clothes cupboard, a rug, curtains and a fireplace with plenty of coal. I send my overalls and dungarees to the laundry and we wash our own underclothes. Soap is sold and we have one soap coupon each Saturday and household soap is fine. There is a double bunk in case anyone turns up.'

The sitting room at Stokesley. (*Eden Camp Collection*)

This account shows real luxury, however, when compared to some WLA hostels in the county.

It should be remembered that not only were the Yorkshire Land Girls of different shapes and sizes and varied personalities, they also came from various social classes and from both the towns and the countryside. In the hostel at Stockton on Forest, in 1944 six Land Girls had formerly been shop assistants, six shorthand typists, four tailors, two waitresses, two labourers, three factory workers, and the rest included: a glass cutter, domestic, a chemist assistant, a farm worker, a children's nurse, a grocer's assistant, a clerk, a foundry worker, a binder's assistant, a button sprayer and a transport driver. Five girls came from Scarborough, three from York, two from Flaxton, two from Leeds, four from Middlesbrough and the others came from Hartlepool, Whitby and Rotherham.

All of these women slept in shared rooms or dormitories, ate together and socialised and so there must have been considerable adjustment in order for them to live harmoniously together!

In some of the requisitioned houses turned into WLA hostels, single beds were a luxury and bunk beds the norm. Before going to Beacon Garth, Hessle, a requisitioned house, Gwen Burkitt had lived in Sherburn Hostel, a hutment hostel near Malton, which she described in an article published in the magazine *Down your Way*:

'The hostel had stone floors, heating was by a coke-fired stove and our sleeping arrangements were wooden bunk beds in a dormitory...The beds were made of plywood with a very thin mattress and a couple of army blankets. The beds always felt damp with perspiration.'

Hazel Driver wrote about the beds at Skipton Hostel, in another account published in 1975. At this hostel the Land Girls slept in bunk beds with one paillasse, one pillow, a pair of sheets and two blankets. The blankets could be used single or double according to the temperature. There was theoretically a surplus of mattresses but they kept mysteriously disappearing. Miss Crabtree confiscated them from any girls who had taken an extra mattress for comfort for a few nights. She denounced the culprits and returned the mattresses to the store. According to Hazel, this was done for the fun of it, as much as the extra comfort. (Driver, 1975.)

Muriel Thornton (née Clarkson) went to Bubwith Hostel in 1943 and she could not remember any home comforts there. Bubwith had wooden bunks with no springs, just a wooden base that was curved to fit the back and straw mattresses. She remembered all the Land Girls being so tired at the end of the day that they just fell into their bunks and slept like logs.

The only entertainment nearby was the village pub, which some of the girls visited for a drink or smoke and to socialise.

Dormitory wooden beds. (*Eden Camp Collection*)

At Skipton Hostel, two large boxes were supplied to the women in which they were supposed to keep all their belongings. These boxes were simply pushed under the bottom bunk. Later, more appropriate furniture was supplied, but their bunks were just pieces of wood drilled for ventilation and paillasses, which were uncomfortable. In 1945, Skipton Hostel was pleased to receive quilts from the USA, each one including the names and addresses of those who had made them, to allow the girls to respond.

In 1941 and 1942 most WLA hostel dormitories were very basic and contained little furniture other than the bunk beds, with a thin mattress and an army blanket. There were no sheets or pillow cases. The Land Girls used their own suitcases to store their clothes. Later, dressing tables or chests of drawers and shared wardrobes were provided. Sheets, when issued, were washed once a fortnight and a pillow case was provided to each Land Girl. As the war progressed, like Skipton, other hostels received gifts from the Canadian and American ladies who sent over quilts to make the Land Girls more comfortable.

The wooden bunk beds were not substantial and the flimsy wooden slats often needed repair. In the middle of the night it was not uncommon for the occupant of the upper bunk to roll over and fall out, causing a disturbance to all. As mentioned earlier, bed cushions, nicknamed 'biscuits' or 'tea cakes', were stuffed with straw. At some hostels in the South of England chamber pots under the bed were mentioned, but Miss Jacob-Smith does not refer to this arrangement in any of the Yorkshire hostels.

Girls would often play pranks on each other in the hostels. When camp beds were provided they would unhook one another's beds so they collapsed, or fold the sheets so they were half-way up the bed and tuck in dead moles, mice or baby rabbits provided by the 'rat catchers'.

At Skipton, Hazel Driver recalled that one Land Girl named May had to be banned from sleeping on the top bunk. She put the whole hostel in uproar one night by taking a flying leap from the top bunk, when she dreamed she was jumping off a runaway tractor! Another woman, Nora, used to go berserk at the sound of a snore, then she demanded that culprit shut up. When this failed, she would aim a slipper in their direction. Further disturbance was caused by Nan, who rocked herself to sleep on the lower bunk and infuriated her partner up on the top bunk, who complained that she was virtually seasick.

Hazel also described how their colleague Mary used to keep her dentures in a tumbler by her bed. In the early morning she would panic, asking, 'Hath anybody theen my teeth? I muth have put them down thome where lath night.' Someone had put them somewhere, for nothing was sacred! It seems that the Skipton Land Girls were a merciless lot! Holly was put into the beds at Christmas and sometimes a life-like rubber mouse made an appearance. (Driver, 1975.)

In some dormitories there was a stove or, as in the case of hutments, several stoves which would be lit in the corridors outside the cubicle. The stoves were usually serviced by a hostel orderly. One orderly used to take a shovel of hot coke from the boiler room and carry it precariously to the dormitory stoves to light them – there was little regard for health and safety! At Skipton Hostel, in a dormitory of ten double bunks there were two stoves, but the Land Girls were not allowed to stoke them after 10.30 pm. At Pollington Hostel, in a small room with two camp beds the orderlies were allowed one bucket of fuel per day for their stove.

At Kirk Deighton Hostel, forty girls slept in the dormitory which housed twenty double bunks on each side. Each bay had a slim small wardrobe on either side of a tiny dressing table. The floor was concrete and the only touch of homeliness was a small mat. The girls were woken by the Warden at 6.30am, when she knocked on everyone's bunk saying, 'Six thirty, six thirty!' One of the girls would always retort, 'Good God another bloody day!' Another girl, despite being the nearest to the washing facilities, would keep a jerry (a type of chamber pot) under the bed.

At Dishforth Hostel, in 1945 there were complaints about the blankets not being washed for two years. At the same hostel, a girl reportedly contracted scabies in 1947. Scabies rash was caused by a tiny mite which was spread by contact or on clothing. The key to getting rid of the mites was to wash anything the infected person had touched in very hot water and then dry the fabric at a high heat. Heat was extremely effective in killing the mites, hence this process, which was known as 'stoving'.

The doctor said the bedding used by the infected girl must be stoved. This upset the other girls who thought all their belongings would also have to be stoved, as the whole dormitory was to be disinfected the following week. The girls complained that their blankets had not even been washed! The Warden had arranged for six to be washed each week and the cleansed blankets were given to the new girls. This meant that some of the older residents had never had their blankets washed. Two other girls had had scabies four weeks before, but the Warden said the girls had borrowed each other's clothes. Miss Jacob-Smith said that this must stop or else the stoving and disinfecting would be in vain.

Standards varied at different hostels. One of the wardens fined the girls if they did not make their beds in a strict fashion. Mrs Keep, the Warden at Thirsk Hostel requested iron beds because she thought they might deter bugs.

In 1947, at Dishforth Hostel, the plywood bunk beds badly needed repairs and there were requests for new ones made of iron. New beds did arrive three months later, but only for the sick bay and the staff rooms, and it was discovered that one of the original beds had mysteriously disappeared.

At Thirsk, there was a problem with 'creepy crawlies' and unidentifiable insects scaling the walls of the dormitory. There was an enormous pile of rotting turnips near the hostel and the smell was terrible. Fumigation was ordered and the smell from that was even worse than the turnips. Several girls became really ill from it!

Two of the most memorable occasions involving the dormitories within the WLA hostels occurred at Stockton on Forest Hostel and Dishforth Hostel. Both of these hostels were old houses which had been requisitioned.

Stockton House was a Georgian house with numerous outbuildings. When the building was prepared for the Land Army, a fire escape was constructed at the rear bedroom. Ex-Land Girls who stayed here tell of how their boyfriends from the Royal Air Force used the fire escape to visit them. This was unknown to the Warden or, indeed, to Miss Jacob-Smith. Near to the house, bats made their home in the outbuildings and some had roosted under the eaves of the house, probably near the fire escape. In the summer of 1947, during the hot weather the bats were flying around in the bedrooms. This was a frightening experience for the girls and more so for the terrified Warden, who had to evacuate her own bedroom. The bats flew quite low and the women instinctively ducked to avoid them, but then they immediately surprised everyone by making a return circulating flight.

Although the bats were tiny, their reputation had been exaggerated by the horror films of the day. Things came to a head when the bats sought refuge in the dining room. Eventually, after a month of complaints the Ministry of Works eradicated the problem. Fortunately for the girls, there was no protection of bats at the time.

Not all accommodation provided such alarming experiences and most of hostels were peaceful and secure places. This was illustrated in war artist Evelyn Dunbar's paintings in 1943. She portrayed off-duty Land Girls from Northumberland. One picture shows the girls going to bed in what looks like a requisitioned house. There appears to be a lot of space in the wallpapered room and a huge window illustrates two sets of double bunks. There still seems to be daylight outside and one of the girls is reading. During the war, the clocks were set at double summer time, so it would have been light during the summer nights even at 10.30 pm. In an article on Evelyn Dunbar, art critic Christopher Campbell-Howes suggests that the painting might have been completed in May. He also deals with the perspective within the painting: 'The lower of the left hand bunks does not match the one above it and the side rail is conveniently obscured by what might be called a chair robe, huge with a pair of shoulder strapped regulation khaki dungarees and a camisole.' Perhaps the lack of true perspective was deliberate emphasising the make-shift nature of the hand-made bunk beds.

The second painting shows the hostel dining room, in which the women are queuing for their evening meal. They have probably come back to the hostel very recently, because they are depicted in their working dungarees, but they have made a little effort to change into coloured shirts. The bright colours give an air of cheerfulness and camaraderie to the meal time.

Lighting in the hostels – Darkness at Dishforth

Dishforth Hostel was in an old farmhouse. It had no electricity supply and often it was so dark in the hostel during the evenings that the Land Girls could not see to write a letter home. In February 1944, Miss Jacob-Smith remarked that sometimes there was only a single oil lamp in the dormitory. The girls had to buy candles and there were no candle sticks, so the girls had to stick the candles to the furniture, including the bunk beds. The habit was exceedingly dangerous and the girls complained about the wax spilling on to their clothes, bedding and furniture.

On 9 November 1944, Miss Jacob-Smith wrote that the lighting at Dishforth was so deplorable that she could hardly see to make her report. The light in the hostel consisted of two hanging lamps. One girl had to light a candle in the sitting room to write a letter. The hostel needed more Aladdin or Tilly lamps, Miss Jacob-Smith noted, but Miss Holloway, the Warden, said she did not have the time to clean and fill the lamps. Some months earlier, the Ministry of Works had taken some Tilly lamps belonging to the hostel for repair and they were never returned. Now only ordinary oil lamps were available.

Miss Jacob-Smith's records show that the situation continued to deteriorate. On 22 February 1945 there were no lights in the dormitories at Dishforth, only candles. The girls complained that this was affecting their eyesight.

On 8 November 1946 Miss Jacob-Smith was asked again about her efforts to get electric lighting at the hostel, as its absence prevented the Land Girls from doing anything in the evenings, especially sewing or knitting. Miss Jacob-Smith asked Mr Whetnall, the new joint Warden who had moved into the hostel with his wife, why there were not more lamps in the sitting room, as it was impossible to see with only two. Disgruntled, he said they had no more, as the girls had broken them at the rate of one a night. She told him to order five dozen more glasses immediately. Previously he had offered the excuse that he had ordered lamps but they had not arrived. It was noticed, however, that there were two lamps in his own room and Miss Jacob-Smith thought that one of them could go into the women's room instead!

By New Year's Day 1947, twelve new oil lamps had arrived for use in the hostel, yet five more were not working. No surplus glasses were supplied and no glasses for the older lamps, which were urgently needed. The new lamps had improved the light, though. On 15 January 1947, Miss Jacob-Smith noted that the lighting in the sitting room was not good and as the Wardens said they were not short of glasses at that moment they were told to use sufficient light. The Ministry of Works had delivered new glasses and mantles, and the Wardens were told to be careful with them, as they would not get any more!

Miss Jacob-Smith was still worried about lighting and so she inspected the walls of the hostel dormitories. She came to the conclusion that it would be difficult to fix brackets on the walls to allow the girls to read in bed. She thought a hanging lamp might be better, but it would not solve the problem of light for the bottom bunks.

Rationing

To cope with shortages during the war which continued until 1954, the British Government introduced rationing for food and clothing. Until 1949, soap and even bread were rationed. In 1946-1948 potatoes were similarly restricted, followed in 1947 by confectionery and sugar, which remained on ration until 1953. Rationing of meat ended in 1954.

On 6 January 1940, the *Knaresborough Post* reported: 'Rationing begins on Monday Jan 8th (per week). Sugar each person 12 oz, Butter 4oz, Bacon/ Ham 4oz.' The rations supplied varied from month to month; sugar and butter rations were gradually reduced, while cooking fat and margarine varied. An egg was rationed at one a week or every two weeks. Tea was set at 2oz per person and milk either three or sometimes two pints a week. Although they suffered the same restrictions as civilians in other cases, WLA girls could claim extra cheese rations.

Marguerite Patten makes the following statement about rationing in her *Victory Cookbook* (2002):

'Wartime food was not exciting but we were not under-fed nor were we hungry, as most people in Europe and other parts of the world. While rationing made it possible for everyone to be adequately fed, there is no doubt that we would all have been unhappy indeed if we had known in 1945 that rationing was to continue for many years to come.'

In 1946 rationing became more stringent. There were cuts to the already meagre rations and in July bread was rationed for the first time. This must have affected the hostel lunch boxes.

Fuel supplies were also bad and fuel cuts caused anxiety for the hostels. This was shown at Easingwold Hostel when the boiler man was suspected of taking away coal in his sock! In the exceptionally cold winter of 1946-1947 transport became a problem for making deliveries of fuel and food to the hostels. This meant that catering in the hostels was badly stretched, with few fresh vegetables supplied.

After the dock strike at Southampton, the meat ration was cut to just 6d and there were many reports of black marketing. (Patten, 2002.) By 1949, the food situation was less grim and there was great enthusiasm amongst Britons for bottling and canning fruit. Many of the hostels were involved in this, especially Stockton and Easingwold.

The food in WLA hostels was reportedly variable, from very good to dreadful. When the daily menu of recruits was raised in Parliament, the Minister of Agriculture replied that 'a cooked breakfast was provided...a packed morning snack, a packed luncheon consisting of sandwiches or pasties and a drink; a main meal on return at 6pm consisting of a meat course with pudding and finally a light supper of cocoa, biscuits, bread and jam or cheese.'

At Skipton Hostel the inhabitants enjoyed a substantial cooked breakfast, which was passed through a hatch from the kitchen. Afterwards they went to the kitchen and packed their own lunch boxes with sandwiches containing meat paste or beetroot. The fare was solid and dull, common to most households in the war years. They always got a bit of cake, but it was usually a square cut from a large dripping tin, usually plain or chocolate. At the beginning of the rationing period there was sometimes a thin layer of jam. The main evening meal was always gratefully received, as working outdoors gave the girls enormous appetites.

The Warden of Skipton Hostel, Mrs Rolston, often had brainwaves which the girls knew could go badly wrong, and one of these occasions became a long-standing joke. Mrs Rolston had cajoled a farmer into letting her have a tin of molasses. She made a huge sponge pudding and topped it with the molasses, but she did not realise that the farmer's molasses was used to top the silage and was not like the type used for cooking in her native Canada. What had promised to be a treat for the girls was sent straight back to the kitchen, as it tasted and smelled like burnt tar!

On some of the farms at Skipton, their 'drinkings' (tea or a drink provided by the farmer during their lunchbreaks) came out in a basket. These sometimes also contained egg sandwiches, crusty scones and a jug of tea. (Driver, 1975.)

Recruits who transferred to Settle Hostel found food scare there. One girl collected mushrooms for her breakfast and another started to smoke because she did not receive enough food. She often took her sugar ration home to allow her mother to bake. Recruits often supplemented their meals at the Naked Man Café in the town. (Bullock, 2002.)

Food at Pollington Hostel, served up for 130 Land Girls, was excellent but it was kept within the rationing, as everything was weighed meticulously in the large ex-WAAF kitchens. Unlike most hostels, the girls did not make their own sandwich lunches at Pollington, as dedicated orderlies were employed to prepare their sandwich tins. At Kirk Deighton also, the Land Girls' lunches were prepared for them, consisting of three half-sandwiches of cheese, spam and beetroot. They were also given half a tea cake and piece of fruit cake known as 'NAAFI cake'.

Mary Tetlow, who was based at Catterick, recalled that her evening meals were well-cooked and plentiful, and she marvelled at the contrast to meals at home. She wished she could have eaten like that at midday when she was working, as her sandwiches seemed inadequate. However, she had many of the privileges of the servicemen in being able to use the NAAFI canteen, which was usually forbidden to Land Army girls.

Concern for the welfare of WLA recruits was occasionally expressed in the House of Commons. The majority of the questions on welfare related topics asked between 1941 and 1943 were about the use of canteens by WLA members. It was extremely important to the girls, for they felt humiliated and ostracised by the other services. Many were billeted a long distance from home. For example, Land Girls from Yorkshire served in the South of England and coming home on leave necessitated changing trains or travelling overnight. Even travelling from one side of Yorkshire to the other would involve long waits for trains in wartime conditions. On these occasions, however, they were prohibited from using the canteen facilities available to servicemen and women. This had the effect of depreciating the standing of the WLA compared to the other services.

The explanation given for this prohibition was that Land Girls were civilians and not service personnel. However, due to constant lobbying WLA personnel were finally allowed to use service canteens run by the voluntary organisations, but they still could not use the NAAFI canteens. A bureaucratic exercise made the WLA organisation state details of every canteen where admission was desired

Dining room hatch at meal times at Sherburn in Elmet. (*Eden Camp Collection*)

and the number of girls employed in the area who were likely to use the facilities. By late 1944, nothing had been resolved and the Ministry of Agriculture emphasised that it was 'Highly unsatisfactory, especially in view of the admirable work which members of the WLA are doing and the existing absence of facilities.' (Bullock, 2002.)

Miss Jacob-Smith also recorded more domestic gripes about food within the hostels she visited. On 8 August 1944, she reported that at Blois Hall, the Forewoman and the Warden told her the girls had quarrelled about the sandwiches, as they had suggested that the meat in them was bad. Mrs McLeod, the Warden, said the food was very good, but there was no cook in the hostel and she was doing the cooking.

At Howden Hostel in the East Riding, the women queued patiently for their meals in the dining room. However, former inhabitant Muriel French can remember strikes by girls refusing to go to work in protest against the loss of rations (sugar etc.), which they believed had been taken by the wardens and sold. Food was also allowed to go mouldy and the Warden was accused of making Christmas cakes with the girls' rations, and selling them in the local pub. These strikes brought the WLA's Yorkshire Vice-chairwoman Lady Dunnington Jefferson over from York to see what was going on.

Dorothy and friend working hard. (*Dorothy Buckton Collection*)

At Moor Park, Beckwithshaw, the Land Girls went to the local WLA office to complain personally about the standard of food, amongst other issues (see the section on Moor Park for details). They emphasized that the breakfasts provided at the hostel were insufficient. For example, they had very small helpings of cereal, one sausage or beans without toast or one pilchard, and a very small ration of jam. By lunchtime they were starving and they had also been given an inadequate and boring packed lunch, with just three kinds of sandwiches: pilchard, fish paste or jam. There was no variety, except the occasional meat pasties which they described as inedible. They asked if they could have meat pies and sausage rolls instead.

For their evening meal there were not enough green vegetables and vegetables were not always served with every meal. The potatoes were never peeled and were served baked, steamed and mashed with their skins on. When mashed they were very brown and unappetising. Miss Yate Lee, the Hostel Warden had said that they could not have them peeled as there was no one to peel them and no potato-peeling machine.

After the war, there was a shortage of cups in the hostels. Many had one for each person only, which did not allow for breakages or for any new recruits.

A sample WLA menu

Due to the fact that the girls were working hard outside, they had enormous appetites which could not always be fulfilled and many complained that they were always hungry.

Like everyone else in the country they suffered deprivations. In a good hostel, however, meals could be an improvement on family catering because everyone's rationing coupons were combined. Thus meals could be more adventurous and many girls felt sorry for the lack of food in their own homes when they visited their families at weekends.

Yet, in a hostel where catering was poor, Land Girls often felt a real grievance against the management, as evidenced at Beckwithshaw and Howden, and perceived the wardens as depriving them of their rations!

Clothing

Since many existing books have already covered the subject of WLA uniforms, these will not be described in detail, except to note the worries Land Girls in the hostels experienced about supplies. Miss Jacob-Smith and the other reps were regularly asked about uniform ordering on almost every visit to the hostels.

The girls had to submit all their clothing coupons to the WLA for their uniform, which left them without any coupons to buy other clothes. Some uniform items were replaced after two years. Even when they had been given no additional uniform items during this time they still had to hand in their coupons, and this often caused dissent. At Easingwold, on 23 August 1944 the Land Girls rebelled against the collection of their clothing coupons. They had given up thirty-six coupons for the first year, twenty-four last year and now the WLA Office wanted twenty-four coupons this year, although they had not been given any replacement uniform.

One Easingwold Land Girl thought about this problem and gave her opinion to Miss Jacob-Smith. If a girl has taken care of her uniform and requested no replacement why should she have to give up her coupons, she asked? This only encouraged Land Girls to be careless with their uniform, so they could apply for a complete new uniform whether they required it or not. It might even encourage them to sell surplus uniform to other agricultural workers or other Land Girls.

Underclothes and sanitary towels were not provided to Land Girls, unlike the other female services. They used their own blouses, scarves, gloves and socks when working in the fields and this caused resentment. Frequently, Land Girls asked for second-hand uniform items because those did not require coupons. The items in most demand were stockings and slipper socks.

In addition to shortages, quality was also a problem. Often uniform items were inferior, especially the macs and boots which leaked. Wrong sizes were often sent, too. The quality of the towels issued to one hostel was criticised. After one girl left the service a demand was made for her towel and she wrote back, saying that it was so old that she had used it for a floor cloth at home!

After the war, it was almost impossible to get stockings, even second-hand ones. The Warden at Stockton asked at the WLA Office for any old hats, so she could use them to show the girls how to make slipper socks. When a Land Girl left the service for any reason she was supposed to surrender all her uniform, even darned socks. After the WLA was disbanded, most of the uniform, except the coats, were supposed to be collected up, even the Land Girls' badges. Unlike the other women's services, they were not eligible for a demob outfit. The girls had few souvenirs of their life in the Land Army, except their memories!

CHAPTER FIVE

Stockton House

The following section has been compiled from an interview with former Stockton House Land Girl Dorothy Buckton, undertaken by the author in 2012.

THE HOUSE (NOW A LISTED BUILDING) was situated in the centre of the ribbon development village of Stockton on Forest, about four miles from York. There was a public house opposite and three others within the village. The Methodist Chapel was part of the house and the Holy Trinity Church was about 1,000 yards away. The farming area was mainly arable but there was also some mixed farming. The property has an interesting history, as it was built in

Stockton House as it is today.

The annex built at the back of Stockton House. (*Dorothy Buckton Collection*)

about 1790 and had been used subsequently as a merchant's holiday home, school and chapel.

The main house, including the integrated schoolroom and the garden, was used by the Women's Land Army during and after the Second World War, until 1950. The Ministry of Works erected a hutment, which was attached to the rear of the building, to accommodate further girls and staff. The chapel, however, was not requisitioned and still functioned independently.

Today, Dorothy Buckton (née Dale) lives in Stockton on Forest. During the Second World War, she was a Land Girl billeted at Stockton House. Dorothy was from Scarborough, where her parents owned the waxworks on the seafront. After leaving school, she took a job in a lady's outfitters in Scarborough. When she first joined the Land Army in March 1944, aged eighteen, she was sent to work at a remote farm in the Yorkshire Dales. The work was not familiar and Dorothy found it hard. She was lonely without the company of other girls and this made her most unhappy.

The support staff for the Women's Land Army ensured that the girls always had someone to talk over their problems with. Consequently, in 1944 Dorothy was sent to Stockton House. Whilst some information about the work to be expected there had been divulged in the form of glamorous posters, it must have been a terrible shock for a former shop-girl, to have to work in the fields for long hours in all weathers.

Dorothy Buckton (née Dale) working with her friend in the field.
(*Dorothy Buckton Collection*)

Dorothy Buckton outside the Fox Inn, Stockton. (*Dorothy Buckton Collection*)

At Stockton Dorothy was issued with the WLA uniform: a green v-necked, ribbed long sleeved jumper (which, when worn out could be cut up to make socks), three green aertex shirts, a tie for formal occasions, two pairs of baggy, brown corduroy breeches, knee-length fawn socks, brogue shoes and a porkpie brown felt hat. A three-quarter length waterproof coat finished the uniform. During working hours, Dorothy wore wellington boots or a pair of ankle boots. An additional two pairs of brown dungarees and a jacket was the norm. Two towels and a green armlet were also supplied to each new recruit. In winter, extra gloves were made from old socks cut down and sewn up and the Land Girls would resort to tying old brown sacking around their waists to protect them from the cold and mud.

After six months of satisfactory service a Land Girl would receive a half-diamond to be displayed on her armband. A special armlet would be given after two years' service and a scarlet one was issued after four years. The uniform was provided free of charge but, as previously mentioned, each girl had to surrender her clothing coupons.

Many Land Girls found the porkpie hat a nuisance but it did give them some individuality, since it could be pulled into different shapes with the help of a steaming kettle. In 1944, there was a shortage of the hats, so one Land Girl used her husband's trilby, simply turning in the crown, steaming the trim up and putting around eighty stitches on the brim.

Dorothy was happy to join other girls of a similar age to her at Stockton House in 1944. In the house were upwards of thirty-five Land Girls, with eight housed in the hut outside. Dorothy was billeted in the annex Nissen hut, which had been erected in the garden. The rest of the garden was dug up for the war effort and vegetables were grown there for use in the house.

Hilda Preston (née Skelton) in the middle on tractor. On her right is Sylvia Sawdon. The forewoman, Miss Page, is driving. (*Hilda Preston Collection*)

North Riding girls shovelling snow, winter 1947.
(*Eden Camp Collection*)

The Nissen hut was equipped with electric lighting, a bathroom with hut running water, one bath, three sinks and toilets. Each girl had a kit box and she shared a wardrobe with another, together with a chest of drawers. There was constant source of heat from a centrally placed iron stove, which was stoked with coke. The girls slept in double height bunk beds, with four per room. There were eight girls in the annex, plus a small room for the Warden and another for the visiting inspector, Miss Jacob-Smith.

In the main house, about thirty-five Land Girls were accommodated in bunk beds within the numerous rooms. There was also a cook and a helper working in the kitchen to cater for them. The left-hand room within the main house, the former parlour, became the dining room as it was linked to the kitchen. The girls' sitting room was in the former schoolroom, which was furnished with a radio for evening listening. In this room beetle drives and film shows organised by the RAF were held for the villagers.

The Stockton Land Girls went everywhere on heavy black bikes, which were virtually thief-proof. They hired these out at one shilling a week in the stables and the old chicory factory. Some girls had to ride for several miles to work on outlying farms and on dark early mornings the journeys must have seemed treacherous and frightening. The bicycle lights had a black mask halfway across the top, so the rider had just enough light to see where she was going. There was a regulation white patch on the mudguard. The rear lamp had one aperture no bigger than an inch in diameter, which must be clearly visible at thirty yards but not at 300. Batteries were hard to get and expensive, so only the first and last riders had their bicycle lights switched on when they went out in a gang.

On Fridays, there were dances at the nearby village of Gate Helmsley, so the journey home by bicycle was often hilarious, with noisy, excited Land Girls trying to find their way down the country roads in the blackout. Mr Wilson, from the neighbouring property to Stockton House, had a young family and he was not pleased by the frequent sound of giggling.

Stockton on Forest Girls on a day trip to Scarborough (*Dorothy Buckton Collection*)

Stockton on Forest Girls on a trip to Whitby Abbey. (*Dorothy Buckton Collection*)

Miss Rabjohn. (*Dorothy Buckton Collection*)

One such dance at Gate Helmsley in January 1947 was very successful. It was organised by Paddy Fawcett and Muriel Thompson of the Stockton House Hostel and raised £21.3s 6d for the WLA Benevolent Fund. The dances were popular with all the girls. Many had come from busy towns and, as they knew all the modern dances with their complicated and showy dance steps, they were an instant hit with locals and service personnel. This did not always endear them to the local girls, though. However, Land Army brogue shoes were adequate protection from the local lads' farm boots.

Although they enjoyed their nights off, the Stockton Land Girls worked extremely hard. Gangs of the girls were employed for the potato harvest. The farmer might pick up the gang from the hostel early in the morning and later return them, of course claiming the necessary petrol allowance. Many girls returned to their family homes at the weekends. Dorothy looked forward to the enthusiastic welcome when they returned by taxi back to Stockton, as all the lads from the village would be waiting outside the Fox Inn, opposite the hostel.

The wedding at Stockton Church. (*Dorothy Buckton Collection*)

The wedding reception at Stockton Hostel.
(*Dorothy Buckton Collection*)

The work the Stockton Land Girls undertook in the fields was very hard, often cold and dirty. For most of the day they might be bent double, ankle-deep in mud, with icicles forming on the ends of their noses as they battled with the bitter winter weather. Tractors had to be drained at night because of the cold. In 1947, towards the end of Dorothy's stay at Stockton, there was a hard punishing winter. After a heavy snowfall all the roads were blocked. The snow froze solid and the transport was at a standstill. The girls, together with the POWs from nearby Eden Camp, had to shovel the snow to open the road to York. They also ensured that the locals had supplies of food, potatoes and milk.

Land Girls were not allowed to work longer than forty-eight hours in the winter and fifty hours during the summer. In 1945, farmers were given special rates for hay-making, corn harvest, threshing, sheep shearing, lambing, hoeing and the shingling of roots, in addition to seasonal rates. Extra allowances were also granted to farmers to enable them to provide two hot drinks per day for each worker. Around 4-5oz of tea, 1oz of sugar and half a pint of milk per worker per week were allowed.

As in most hostels, at Stockton there was occasional unrest. Some girls objected to the close supervision of the Warden, saying they were treated like children; one group in another hostel said that the Warden would sneak up on them so they did not feel the hostel is their home. Certainly, there was some disagreement between the wardens and the catering staff. In 1947, a letter was sent by Miss Jacob-Smith to Miss Spiers, who was then the Warden at Stockton Hostel, supporting her in her complaints. It was agreed that she should have some say in what the girls had for meals. Fish should be served and certainly not something called 'fish and shape'.

The Warden during Dorothy's time at Stockton, Miss Maisie Rabjohn, was very short and she seemed to Dorothy to be aged between forty and fifty. She was also extremely stern. From records held at the National Archives, it appears that before the war Maisie Rabjohn had worked in tailoring, in Leeds. In October 1948, she transferred from Stockton House to Bedfordshire and she was released from the WLA in June 1949, on medical grounds.

In March 1945, a bring and buy sale was organised at the Stockton Hostel, together with dances and whist drives, as there was an urgent need to raise £1,000 for the Benevolent Fund, which helped to support any Land Girl who became ill, had an accident or needed financial help. A local farmer donated a calf for sale, which certainly showed the goodwill in the village towards the work of the WLA. The Land Girls, in return, organised tea parties for village children. A picture of one of these appeared in the local paper, showing the children, together with a warden Miss P D Smith and the local rector Reverend W R Davis.

There were also various individual fundraising efforts. In December 1945, Dorothy Dale also received an award for collecting the greatest amount of money for the Benevolent Society. Another girl, Lucy Bonner had collected the same amount and was also given a prize. In May 1946, Miss Rabjohn participated in a handicraft competition organised by the WLA in North Yorkshire, which was held in the Thirsk Hostel. Bringing glory to her home hostel, she was presented with the first prize for a piece of embroidery in wool and first prize for a handmade garment.

Dorothy working in the walled garden, Stockton House. (*Dorothy Buckton Collection*)

In 1946, a recruitment drive was organised in York and the Stockton Land Girls helped out, as they were the nearest WLA hostel. A farmyard was created in a bombed arcade in Coney Street and cows, sheep and lambs, pigs and chickens helped to set the scene, together with farming implements and tractors. Many girls gave up a half-day's pay just to riddle potatoes in the centre of York.

Miss Rabjohn was praised for organising the successful beetle drives and whist drives for the villagers to raise money for the WLA Benevolent Fund. In addition to dances and fundraising efforts, Miss Rabjohn organised many trips to the seaside for the girls. Twice a year, they were taken to Bridlington, Scarborough or Whitby. In 1947, the first trip was to Scarborough, the second to Whitby and both days were fine with plenty of sunshine.

The local RAF boys also organised lantern slide talks for the villagers in the front room of the Stockton WLA Hostel. Concerts were arranged for the girls too, together with Land Girls who had billets nearby. In 1945, a tour of the WLA hostels was made by the actress Miss Elspeth Douglas Reid. This was sponsored by The Council for the Encouragement of Music and Arts (CEMA), which organised entertainment for troops and service personnel during the war years. After the performances, a collection was made to defer expenses. In 1947, Miss Theresa Carroll, an impressionist, and Miss Howard a Celtic harpist, also entertained the girls. In the same year, a series of talks were organised on 'Beauty' by the Pears Company and Mrs Godfrey Phillips spoke on the subject of 'Health and Happiness'.

Parties were another source of great pleasure, particularly at Christmas time, when special meals were given and everyone became involved in making decorations. The Stockton Hostel became the centre for Christmas activities for all the Land Girls working in the area. A wedding was a special occasion.

On 2 October 1949, the Stockton Hostel represented the WLA in North Yorkshire at the County Harvest Festival at York Minster. In the *Land Army News*, (November 1949, Vol. 3) it was stated that thirty seats in the Minster had been allocated to the WLA: 'Most impressive were the Young Farmers in white coats followed by the Land Girls from Stockton House Hostel who walked in procession up the aisle carrying their gifts to the altar.'

Most Land Girls received twenty-five shillings in pay each week. After the deductions for her keep, Dorothy says she was left with nine shillings a week. Dorothy worked on a farm off the Malton Road. It was here that Dorothy met her future husband, who was the son of the farmer. They married in 1953, and came back to live in the village. Like many of the Land Girls she worked hard but had a happy and memorable life during the war. There was further romance at Stockton, as Mr Thompson, who owned Glaisby Farm next door to the hostel employed two very handsome blonde German prisoners of war. Dorothy recalls a lot of giggles and sighs among the girls in the annex when they saw these personable men. One of the girls from the hutment was lucky enough to work on that farm.

Dorothy was demobbed in November 1948, but she still remembers her friends from the Stockton Hostel. Dorothy's best friend was Norah Darling. Norah married her boyfriend, who was a Belgium soldier billeted in one of the Nissen Huts at Stockton Hall, and went to live in Belgium. The other girls in the hut were: Margaret Donald from Castleford. She had been a tailoress and was twenty-one years old when she joined. Due to medical grounds, she left in December 1945. Nellie Wortley, who was over 6ft tall, was twenty-three years old when she enlisted, and a former glass worker from Rotherham. She also left in 1945 because of medical grounds.

Joyce Duxbury came from Leeds and she had joined earlier than the other eight girls, having enlisted in August 1942. She was nineteen when she enlisted and had been a shorthand typist. She was demobbed just before Dorothy in August 1948. Joyce Thornton was a typist in Northallerton and she joined in February 1944, aged nineteen. Audrey Atkinson was from West Hartlepool and she had already worked as a labourer before, at eighteen, she joined the gang at Stockton on Forest. She resigned on medical grounds in 1946. Olwyn Hill, a shop assistant from Whitby, aged seventeen, joined in April 1944.

Hilda Preston née Skelton turned out in her uniform. (*Hilda Preston Collection*)

Girls outside Stockton Hostel. (*Dorothy Buckton Collection*)

Other former Land Girls from Stockton were also interviewed by the author. Rosalind Wadsworth (née Hodgson), now sadly deceased, also stayed at Stockton. She remembered working very hard work and sleeping soundly at the hostel. Hilda Preston (née Skelton) said that her dormitory room was at the front of the house, where she overlooked the open fields and the pub. She was one of the few who got on well with the strict warden, Miss Rabjohn. Often Hilda did not agree with Miss Rabjohn and she told her so.

The work of the Land Army girls in Stockton on Forest, and throughout the whole service, was perhaps best summed up by Vita Sackville West in 1944: 'It is a plodding story of endurance, rather than heroics and she should be richly honoured for having chosen her vital and exacting role so thoroughly away from the limelight.'

The work of the Women's Land Army at Stockton on Forest made a deep impression on the history of the village and Stockton House is still fondly remembered by the locals.

Winifred Jacob-Smith's visits to Stockton House

(This record has been compiled from eighty of the duplicate books written by Miss Jacob-Smith. To protect personal information about individual Land Girls, their names have been omitted. The notes have been transferred into the past tense for the ease of reading and, where appropriate, to clarify a statement the author has added an explanation in brackets. Each entry was punctuated with notes about Miss Jacob-Smith's visits to individual farms and other hostels. Some of the more mundane comments about ordering uniform, travel warrants and other miscellaneous details have not been included.

Where there is a gap in the chronology, Miss Jacob-Smith has probably used another representative to make the visits.)

On 28 May 1944, the Women's Land Army Hostel at Strensall was closed and all the thirty-five girls formerly based there came to Stockton House. Later, when other hostels closed nearby, such as Brompton and Terrington, some of the girls may have come to the Stockton Hostel.

A Miss Donaldson was appointed the Warden and on 27 June 1944, the first party was held at this new hostel. In September 1944, the *Women's Land Army Newsletter* stated: 'All the girls have settled down in the new surroundings and enjoy living in a house instead of a hutment!'

During 1944 and 1945 Miss Jacob-Smith's visits to Stockton Hostel were not frequent and she mainly seemed to be greatly concerned about the then Warden, Miss Rabjohn.

1/6/44 Miss Jacob-Smith called to collect the uniforms from Land Girls who had departed. Miss Hardy showed her round. She described the sitting room and dining room as very nice, also the stage and larger room as adequate. Bike sheds were available and the girls were delighted to have bedrooms, rather than the dormitory of the hutment. Miss Donaldson, the new Warden from Northumbria, was anxious to work in the hostel.

25/9/44 Miss Hardy commented that she found it difficult to see all the girls, as they worked late and so felt she did not really know them.

Land Girls were not coming back to the hostel on Sunday nights, after spending a weekend away. Since then, however, Miss Donaldson had spoken to them and after this they all came back on Sundays. She thought they had not realised that they could not stay until Monday morning. However, the last bus on Sundays left York at 8.20 pm, which meant that to be back in York by then the girls had to leave home during the mid-afternoon. A taxi from the station cost 5s and it was often difficult to find one. It was four miles from York and a long walk from the bus at the Malton Road.

Miss Rabjohn is seated centre front. (*Dorothy Buckton Collection*)

13/2/45 There was a query about bringing the girls back to the hostel on Sundays, but there was no van allocated to the hostel. One of the girls suggested that they could leave a vehicle in York on Saturdays and drive it back on Sundays.

21/2/45 A van was subsequently allocated to the hostel and, as it could provide transport for seven girls, each Stockton Land Girl might expect a lift once in five weeks.

23/3/45 – 9/10/46 During this time there were various ailments and injuries among the Land Girls of the hostel. One girl broke her ankle, while her colleague had a pierced ear drum; another had quinsy and was off for a month; tonsil problems resulted in a further girl being on leave for a month and ten days; yet another was operated on for mastoids; and Miss Rabjohn twisted her ankle!

One of the girls had ringworm and the doctor said she was fit for work but she could not remain in the hostel. She had been living at her home in York and

83

returning to the hostel for her meals. The Doctor and Miss Jacob-Smith both thought this was a silly idea. Another girl went home with a poisoned hand. She may have had all her sick pay but, as her family was badly off, arrangements were made for Mrs Bottomley from the Welfare Department of the WLA to visit her home.

Nosebleeds were a problem with one Stockton girl. The Doctor thought it was from bending down, but she was still offered a job as a tractor driver by the WASC District Office. However, she planned to leave the hostel to live at home. Another Stockton Land Girl failed to return to the hostel after an accident falling off her bicycle.

Two trips were arranged for the Stockton girls, to Scarborough and Whitby in 1946, and Miss Jacob-Smith commented on how lucky they were!

In September 1946, Miss Wilson, the Deputy Warden at Stockton, went to help out at Easingwold Hostel and she claimed the 2s 4d bus fare. She hoped to stay a little longer there, as she had enjoyed it so much, but Miss Rabjohn wanted her day off and Miss Wilson was too scared to return, as Miss Rabjohn had made such a fuss.

10/10/46 Two lectures were organised at the hostel. Miss Jacob-Smith collected Mrs Browne, who gave a talk on 'Health and Happiness', but it was judged not as good as Mrs Phillips' lecture. She then took Mrs Browne to Easingwold Hostel. The talk did not start until 9.00 pm and only fifteen girls had stayed in to hear it. Miss Jacob-Smith decided that two lectures a night was too much.

15/10/46 The girls began complaining about insufficient sandwiches, which were also monotonous, consisting of only cheese and beetroot. However, Miss Jacob-Smith thought Miss Rabjohn was too domineering to have any effect, and most of the complaints came from the Hostel Forewoman. Miss Rabjohn had worked very hard when she first arrived and had pulled up the hostel very well, but since then she had become very dogmatic. Miss Jacob-Smith asked the advice of the WLA Office in Harrogate as to whether she ought to speak to Miss Rabjohn or offer her a transfer.

There were various requests for uniform, and no best shoes were available. Slipper socks were always being required, as well as gum boots.

Miss Rabjohn continued to be dictatorial, but it was hoped that her break at Christmas might be for the good of Stockton. She had not been too well and illness was believed to be the cause of her abrupt manner with the girls. She had organised a series of whist drives and beetle drives, which the girls had enjoyed but did not want any more of.

Miss Jacob-Smith attended a meeting between the Stockton girls, Miss Rabjohn and Miss Wilson. A member of the Hostel Committee made the following points:

Whist drives: Land Girls who attended the whist drive got a better supper than those who did not. The supper given to those attending, both for girls and outsiders, was excellent – in fact too good! The girls objected to their rations being used to feed outsiders, while Miss Rabjohn pointed out that the whist drives were being held to raise money for the hostel funds. The outsiders' money helped them all. However, the girls said they were tired of these events and did not want any more, saying the outsiders were gluttons! They would prefer to give 6d a week instead. Miss Jacob-Smith thought this was hard on Miss Rabjohn, who had only been trying to help.

Second helpings: These were not always available, apparently due to the Cook always thinking about her boyfriend. It was suggested that perhaps when she left things might be better. Miss Rabjohn was accused of being sarcastic when the girls asked for more food. She said they were gluttons. Miss Rabjohn said that this comment was meant to be funny but the girls had taken it the wrong way.

Sandwiches: More sandwiches were required. Miss Rabjohn said she would look into this. Someone suggested more cakes and she was told that this was impossible. The point about whist drives suppers was raised again.

Daily papers: Miss Rabjohn spent her own money on the Sunday newspapers for the girls to read and now the girls now wanted daily papers as well!

Boyfriends were only allowed in one night a week. Miss Jacob-Smith thought this very little. Miss Rabjohn would not even allow them to wait in the hall on other nights, forcing them to stand on the doorstep even when it was raining. Miss Jacob-Smith thought that was a bit hard.

Electric Light Bulbs: The girls asked for larger light bulbs, as the present bulbs give poor light. (A month later, Miss Jacob-Smith reminded the Ministry of Works to provide larger bulbs as the lighting at the hostel was very bad.)

Piano-tuning was required for the forthcoming concert. Miss Rabjohn intended paying for it out of the hostel funds. But Miss Jacob-Smith intervened and said she would pay. Other points discussed were late passes, the waste of bread, noise outside the hostel at night and the holding of a hostel dance.

10/11/46 Miss Wilson had been in charge in Miss Rabjohn's absence and she appeared to have managed well. The Cook gave in her notice and a hostel orderly had taken her place.

Miss Rabjohn made the girls go home at the weekends to save on extra work for the staff. Miss Jacob-Smith objected to this arrangement and told her there should be no limit to the number of girls allowed to stay at the weekends. Miss Rabjohn had justified this by saying that girls went home at weekends at Guisborough Hostel.

An electric fire was required in the Forewoman's room. The stove in the annex was not usually put on until the afternoon, but Miss Wilson had put it on especially as she thought it might appear damp to Miss Jacob-Smith. She was too frightened to say that it was not on all day.

(From this point Miss Jacob-Smith's visits became increasingly frequent, perhaps because of the issues with the Warden.)

2/1/47 Miss Rabjohn, it was noted, appeared to dominate the girls, using compulsion rather than persuasion.

14/1/47 A public bus service was now running from York each evening and on Sundays at 9.00 pm. The question of transport to the cinema no longer existed.

Miss Jacob-Smith commented that she was very worried about the internal management of the hostel. Various repairs were urgently required, such as locks on the outside doors, dining room and kitchen and the linen cupboard. The local man who did repairs was very slow and, according to Miss Rabjohn, he was too busy building houses to do any work in the hostel. However, the linoleum had been laid in the dining room and the hostel looked better for it.

Sandwich tins ordered some time ago had not arrived, so Miss Rabjohn had made the girls buy green tins. The Warden was very keen on handicrafts and she had persuaded every girl to make at least one article for the WLA handicrafts exhibition.

11/2/47 Miss Jacob-Smith saw Miss Rabjohn and told her she must not dominate the girls. The hostel had encountered some difficulty in getting dishcloths, but they found that old aertex shirts made good dishcloths. Stockton made a request for old aertex shirts from other hostels.

24/2/47 The supply of coal was getting low and they only had enough for three to four weeks in stock. In view of this, Miss Jacob-Smith recommended that the sick bay fire should only be lit once a week to keep the room aired, unless it was exceptionally cold and damp. The wood supply was exhausted and enquiries were made to see if they could buy some from the next door property.

6/3/47 Everything seemed to be fine at the Stockton Hostel when Miss Jacob-Smith visited. Miss Rabjohn was reminded once again not to be so domineering and Miss Jacob-Smith hoped the warning would have the necessary effect.

10/3/47 One of the girls wanted a transfer to Kent, to be near her boyfriend's home. He was then serving abroad. Her mother and father did not live together and she had made her home with her grandmother, but she was not happy with this arrangement. Miss Jacob-Smith warned her that if she moved south then she could not move back north.

The girls complained again about Miss Rabjohn's domineering attitude, and Miss Jacob-Smith informed the WLA Office that something would have to done. They also said that the Assistant Warden Miss Wilson was as bad, but Miss Jacob-Smith doubted it.

18/3/47 A girl complained to Miss Jacob-Smith about how unhappy she was and, in particular, about Miss Rabjohn's manner. Providing this was improved, Miss Jacob-Smith felt that the girl would settle down at this hostel.

19/3/47 Miss Jacob-Smith wanted to know if the hostel had bought a gramophone out of hostel funds and, if so, whether the WLA Office could make a contribution. The last one she had taken had lasted only for a short time.

One of the girls spent a day's leave visiting Durham Prison to see her boyfriend, who was serving a sentence for stealing cars.

There was a shortage of second-hand stockings for the girls to purchase. In view of this, Miss Rabjohn decided to show the girls how to make slippers out of old hats. She made a request for the WLA Office to supply the hostel with old hats for this purpose.

27/3/47 An orderly had been acting strangely and Miss Rabjohn thought she was affected by the new moon. The Forewoman wanted one of the girls to be sent to Leeming Bar Hostel, because after the Easter holiday she had not returned until 9.45 am on the following Monday. The girl said she had been late because of the floods near Burythorpe. Miss Jacob-Smith wanted the WLA Office to check whether the girl could have travelled on the Sunday evening before they removed her to another hostel.

29/3/47 There were further complaints about Miss Rabjohn's dictatorial manner. She said the complaints were unjustified, as she worked hard and did not intend to be domineering. The hostel had won the handicrafts completion, she claimed, entirely due to her interest and influence.

21/4/47 One of the girls was recommended to go to a Respite Hostel. Another, who was described by Miss Jacob-Smith as a sensible girl but not exactly pretty, had gained a pen friend in Singapore.

The radio was not working. Miss Rabjohn claimed that the girls were deliberately breaking the wires and then did nothing to pay for the repairs. She suggested that the girls should buy a second-hand set but Miss Jacob-Smith could not see why. Miss Rabjohn wanted to use the money from the handicraft purse for this purpose, but Miss Jacob-Smith felt that the WLA Welfare Office might not agree.

Miss Rabjohn complained said that she no longer wanted to organise whist drives and the girls must organise activities themselves. She had organised a raffle for the girls and when two of them had refused to buy tickets Miss Rabjohn summoned them to her room and talked to them about being uncooperative. She had also booked a bus to go to Scarborough in May for a day's outing for the girls, but they were no longer interested. Miss Jacob-Smith suggested that she should no longer bother with such trips until the girls wanted them.

The daily cleaning woman had been off ill and Miss Rabjohn complained that she also interfered with the girls' activities and she did not like working in the hostel whilst the girls were in. Miss Rabjohn made the girls do the chores then, as she said 'the Daily wants pampering'.

22/4/47 Some girls came in drunk after going to a birthday celebration. Two apologised but a third girl had not, yet Miss Rabjohn did not appear to have made any comment. When a fourth girl came in late Miss Rabjohn accused her of being the ringleader and of also being drunk. She admitted she had been drinking but was not drunk and had easily put herself to bed, as verified by a reliable girl in the same dormitory. Miss Rabjohn did not listen to the other girls' accounts, even though they were not on speaking terms with the fourth girl and she had not been celebrating with them.

1/5/47 The local joiner had still not mended the locks, including the sick bay and windows. A whist drive was held in aid of the Food Relief Fund.

9/5/47 Miss Rabjohn wanted to distemper the sitting room and dining room, if the distemper and brush could be provided by the Ministry of Works. The old gramophone could be repaired for 18s 6d and she would like to take the money for it from the hostel accounts. Miss Rabjohn wanted some tins for canning fruit. The local WLA Office would need to be told about this, to account for the purchasing of large quantities of fruit.

A girl was suffering from warts due to working with cows and it was noted that she should have compensation. The girl was sent home ten days later.

12/6/47 A Land Girl had had a row with Miss Rabjohn, seemingly for no reason. Miss Jacob-Smith noted that the girl had a rude manner and was obviously not one of Miss Rabjohn's favourites. She was claiming her towels had been stolen at

Stockton and, as she had been in the WLA for three years, had asked why could she not have some more?

13/6/47 The windows and the clock at the hostel had still not been repaired. The clock seldom went and had to be wound up several times. Five girls have asked for a transfer, as they were fed up. Another girl said Miss Rabjohn was leaving! Miss Jacob-Smith commented that something would have to be done, as there appeared no hope of improvement in the hostel whilst Miss Rabjohn and her assistant Miss Wilson remained.

15/6/47 The library books at the hostel had not been changed for a year. (They were eventually changed a month later.) The bread machine needed the safety catch attending to and a slate had come loose from the roof.

16/6/47 Miss Rabjohn went on holiday and a Miss Spiers came to take over as temporary Warden. She thought that the hostel was run on military lines, without any thought as to the girls' comfort. Considerable thought had been given to the cleanliness of the hostel though, she said, and most of the work had been done with the least effort. Miss Spiers thought it was an easy job being a warden or an assistant warden and told Miss Jacob-Smith that Miss Wilson appeared to go out a lot in the afternoons and evenings. Miss Spiers was not allowed to interfere with the catering but she was mystified by the meat content of a dish known as 'fish and shape'.

20/6/47 Miss Spiers reported that the girls were not at all bad but they seemed to have been badly treated. It appeared the Cook and the Forewoman had been forced to copy the Warden's strict example. Miss Spiers was sorry for the girls and thought that what they wanted was an older person who would mother them, even though the place might not be so clean!

4/7/47 Miss Spiers telephoned Miss Jacob-Smith to ask if she was going anywhere near Stockton could she call. In the ensuing meeting Miss Spiers recounted her conversation with the girls on the previous evening. She had been horrified by their stories of how they had been treated by Miss Rabjohn. She refused to go into details on the phone but said one girl had had her ears boxed and another had been called a swine!

Miss Spiers telephoned later to say a girl had been sick. Miss Wilson said the girl was drunk and should be removed from the hostel but Miss Spiers found that, although the girl had been in the pub, she had eaten a lot of cockles or mussels. She was sure that it was these that had made her sick and she was not drunk. She had a long talk to the girl about going into pubs and another girl promised to look after her sick colleague. As the girl in question was apparently hated by Miss Rabjohn, Miss Spiers thought the incident might mean her removal to another hostel. She wanted the office to know the story and to take notice, as she was sure the girl had learnt her lesson.

7/7/47 Whilst Miss Spiers had been acting as a relief warden things had seemed much better at Stockton and the hostel had appeared to be well kept.

(Miss Rabjohn and Miss Wilson left the hostel on 8 August 1947 and they were replaced by Miss Gregory, who also proved unsuitable. The food was very bad during this time. As a result of the inadequate food the girls held a one-day strike. Miss Gregory was distraught.)

23/8/47 The office papers had been left in splendid order when Miss Rabjohn left. Although Miss Gregory appeared to have taken over the hostel, she had not filled in the daily reporter book, Miss Jacob-Smith noted. Miss Smith, the new Warden would have to make it up from the Forewoman's lists. The memo book had also had some of its pages torn out.

25/8/47 The new Cook appointed was most satisfactory and her cooking 'was smashing', according to Miss Jacob-Smith. There were complaints about the new Warden, Miss Smith, who appeared to have no interest in the girls' work or their personal lives. If the girls met her on the stairs, they claimed she said nothing to them. When they had asked if they could organise a whist drive she said it was too much trouble. Many things seem to annoy her, like too much noise. She said she was tired of them and the girls wanted to know why she should be.

The girls wanted to know why Miss Smith did not simply go and leave them with another warden who would take an interest in them. Two girls who had been at Thirsk Hostel wanted to know why they could not have someone like Mrs Keep, Thirsk's Warden, to look after Stockton. They also suggested that Miss Spiers should come back.

The girls asked for: wireless repairs; piano tuning; net for the back windows, as only the front windows had curtains; ashtrays; pokers; a wardrobe each; flower vases; a new gramophone; a dart board and darts; table tennis balls; a pack of cards; Monopoly; and a set of draughts. A large wooden badge was also required for the outside wall of the hostel.

[Here, another WLA inspector seems to have taken over visits to Stockton for some months.]

30/7/48 The pigswill needed to be collected as soon as possible, as the smell was bad. The bats had been in the bedroom and Miss Smith's bedroom during the night. The girls and Miss Smith were frightened of them. Two had been killed and the others had disappeared. They were thought to have come down the chimneys.

Miss Smith was sleeping in the sick bay, as she said her bedroom is too small.

31/7/48 Bats were still a problem. Seven of the girls chosen to go to the Royal parade had stayed at Stockton.

28/8/48 The bats were still reportedly troublesome. They were coming into the dining room in the hot weather, even though the Ministry of Works had dealt with them. The decorators were badly needed.

Things had improved with the hostel staff. The Assistant Warden and Cook were noted as excellent and the Cook had trained her staff to be efficient and clean. She was very popular with the girls. The Daily woman scrubbed the floors each day, yet Miss Smith thought that every other day would be sufficient.

Miss Jacob-Smith observed:

> 'Mrs Leng and Miss Colling do not get on. Mrs Leng is very slow but she is kind and thoughtful to the girls. Miss Colling is quick and efficient but rather too efficient NAAFI style and an excellent cook. When Mrs Leng serves the meal she is very slow Miss Colling gets annoyed by this and says so in front of the girls. Miss Smith tries to keep them working apart and thinks Miss Leng will want to move to another hostel. I must admit Miss Colling does look fierce.'

The hostel orderly had been in late for three nights. Miss Smith thought she had poor understanding and wanted her to stay only until the others had had their holidays.

The village gossip, according to the joiner was that the local vicar wanted to live at Stockton House, as he would not consider coming to the village if he had to live in the present vicarage. Miss Smith said she wanted to go to Stokesley, as she found Stockton dull, with a poor bus service.

11/9/48 The garden wall fell down and the girls feared that people might roam round the hostel at night!

29/9/48 Miss Smith had received visits from the Parish Council and the local police, during which it was claimed the noise from the hostel was excessive.

24/11/48 Miss Smith had told the girls that they must go home at the weekends, but Miss Jacob-Smith said she could not demand this. Miss Smith replied that unless she had more staff she would find the catering a problem. The Assistant Warden, Miss Leng, was having her meals in the kitchen to avoid Miss Collings, as they were still not getting on, but she got on well with the girls. Everyone now seemed happier since Miss Smith has become Warden. There were no more complaints from the villagers about the noise.

29/11/48 One of the girls refused to work as she had got drenched in the rain and all her clothes, including her coat, had been soaked but they had failed to dry out in the drying room.

31/1/48 The Assistant Warden, Miss Leng wanted to transfer to the West Riding. The hostel was well kept, despite the absence of the Daily due to illness.

24/2/48 Miss Smith had trouble with a girl who came in late on her first Saturday and again on the following Saturday. Some money had gone missing since her arrival and she was generally annoying. Miss Smith thought she should be removed.

21/4/48 No one from the Ministry of Works had been to see about the decorating. Miss Smith told Miss Jacob-Smith about three orderlies who were very bad about getting up in the morning. Miss Jacob-Smith also became aware that Miss Smith did not go down to breakfast either, as since the Assistant Warden left Miss Smith had done all the night duties. Miss Jacob-Smith asked the office whether she should tell Miss Smith to get up earlier.

4/6/48 The rain was coming in badly, even though the gutters had been cleared earlier in the year. It was essential that re-plastering was carried out before any decorating took place. The sitting room carpet was badly worn and a request had been made to get it replaced or have mats instead. The dressing table locks did not work and should be replaced, especially as some money had been reported stolen recently. The sitting room looked deplorable: some of the girls were not working and they had been sitting on cushions on the floor; the dirty walls did not help.

The new Forewoman had taken girls to see the doctor, meaning a 3d bus fare each way, which was expensive, especially if she went three times a week. Who will pay for this, asked Miss Jacob-Smith? The sewing machine needed repair and although the wireless had been repaired out of hostel funds, costing £5 5s, it still did not work well.

The girl mentioned on 24/2/48 had gone home with a suspected stomach ulcer. She had needed to be removed from Stockton in any case, as she was a very disagreeable type of person. The other girls had suspected her of stealing and a bedspread had gone missing from the sick bay. She had been on light duties but she had still been going out in the evenings. When she had asked for a late pass to go to the theatre Miss Smith had refused it. Miss Jacob-Smith had spoken to the girl but she had the impression that she would still go to the theatre and then go home. One of the girls asked for a laundry boiler, as it was difficult to get stains out without boiling clothing.

30/6/48 The hostel needed redecorating; the chairs wanted re-covering and the sitting room had a bad appearance. Part of the hostel could have been kept better, Miss Jacob-Smith thought, but this might have been due to the lack of cleaning staff. There had been no social events. It was suggested that the village hall could have been used for film shows or dances. Miss Leng the Assistant Warden had left and Miss Cooling had taken her place.

13/8/48 There were only eighteen girls left in the hostel and there was a request to recruit some more for Stockton. The Forewomen said that some drainage men had been working in the adjoining land and disturbed a prop which held up the wall, which had fallen down.

25/8/48 The sitting room wall was leaking badly and the level of tidiness in the hostel needed improvement. A laundry boiler was requested again.

18/9/48 Miss Smith asked the WLA Welfare Office if they would give a talk at Stockton on haircare, as there had been several 'nit heads' recently. There was a demand for single beds but Miss Jacob-Smith could not see how the hostel could accommodate more than twenty-one single beds, as well as two for the Orderlies at the end of the annex, two for the Assistant Warden and Cook and two in the sick bay.

1/10/48 The staff was well disciplined under Miss Cooling. Decoration was badly needed and the roof still needed repair. A film show was being organised in the village hall.

12/10/48 The repairs had been completed at the hostel. The village hall film show was a great success and the hall was almost full. Yet, only five Land Girls went and Miss Colling. Miss Smith did not go.

Miss Smith was in York on Tuesday, 5 October, she had a half-day on Wednesday, 6 October and on Thursday, 7 October she was back in York. She was out again when a policeman called, although she said she had been at the Food Office. The policeman had wanted a statement from her about a lorry coming out of the farm which had run into the side of her van. Her head had been cut and her arm bruised.

10/11/48 For once Miss Jacob-Smith seemed to have run out of things to say. Most of the following weeks' comments consist of repeated complaints about leaking roofs and bad decoration at the hostel. Buckets had to be put on the landing, which was badly cracked and might fall down.

1949 Single beds arrived at the hostel in February 1949, but by then there were only sixteen Land Girls at Stockton. There were few social activities, except for a party in February. The vicar and his wife had taken a great interest in the hostel and the girls were invited to all the church functions. Three girls were confirmed.

In August 1949 the Stockton girls were informed by Miss Jacob-Smith that the hostel was closing. In December some of the equipment was sent to a new hostel at the Croft.

CHAPTER SIX

Dishforth Hostel

(This record has been compiled from eighty of the duplicate books written by Miss Jacob-Smith. To protect personal information about individual Land Girls their names have been omitted. The notes have been transferred into the past tense for the ease of reading and, where appropriate, to clarify a statement the author has added an explanation in brackets. Each entry was punctuated with notes about Miss Jacob-Smith's visits to individual farms and other hostels. Some of the more mundane comments about ordering uniform, travel warrants and other miscellaneous details have not been included.

Where there is a gap in the chronology, Miss Jacob-Smith has probably used another representative to make the visits.)

DISHFORTH NORTH HILL HOSTEL was opened in November 1943 (as reported in that month's issue of the *Land Girl*). The hostel was situated on what is now known as Dishforth Airfield. It was demolished when the RAF moved in after the war and the sergeants' mess was built on the site. Edna Braithwaite (née Partington) remembers living in the hostel, which was an old farmhouse without electricity. It was then opposite the airfield and there were always plenty of social activities, including dances.

The two spinster Wardens who were in charge of the hostel were said to be 'laid back in their attitude to the girls'. Although the Land Girls were expected to be in the hostel by 10.00 pm, a door was always left open by the last girl to enter.

The following transcript continues on from the earlier details given by Miss Jowett of her visit to the hostel on its opening day.

24/2/44 The Young Farmers Club came to speak to the Land Girls and eighteen of them said they would join if a local branch was formed. There were complaints from the girls about conditions in the hostel having deteriorated considerably. The food and cleanliness had become excellent shortly after the new Warden, Miss Liddiard, had arrived and they realised how lucky they were. However, they could not come into the hostel in their boots and walk in through the kitchen in their stockinged feet. As the door was locked, they had to walk across the path in their socks to the dormitory.

The Forewoman used the room at the end of the dormitory as her office, where there was an outside door. The Forewoman had asked if she could have a key to this door from 9.00 am until 5.00 pm, but she was refused. Farmers, thus, had to be interviewed in the recreation room and this was difficult if they wanted to complain about a girl when others were in the room.

No tea was provided on Saturdays, so the girls had to go out and buy their tea. The Forewoman had forced the girls to go to church on Sundays. She also denied having told the girls to go directly to the Doctor, rather than the Warden. The Warden said she had no right to do so.

The Warden was said to decide on which nights the girls were allowed to come in late each week. The Warden denied this. On ordinary night, the girls had to be in by 10.00 pm, but concerts finished at that time, so they had to leave before the end. If the time was extended to 10.10 pm, then they could see the end. Lights were put out at 10.00 pm, so they had to go to bed in the dark.

The Land Girls' complaints continued. They were not allowed to use the gramophone, even on Saturdays and Sundays. The Warden would not allow boyfriends in the recreation room and she did not like the wireless. She had promised to buy one but had not done so. She disapproved of a hostel committee being formed unless she was on it. One had been formed but the Warden did not recognise it. Sometimes there was only one light in the dormitory, so the girls had to buy candles and there were no candle sticks. Candles were stuck on to the furniture and were exceedingly dangerous, with wax also spilling onto the girls' clothes.

The girls had gone to a meeting the previous night of the War Agricultural Executive Committee and had not arrived back until 9.45 pm. They asked if they might have something to eat, as they had missed dinner, but the Warden refused. The Warden apparently did not listen to the girls' reasonable requests and she dressed down the Forewoman in front of girls. The girls were not allowed to sit in the recreation room when they had no work. It was frequently locked until midday, so they had to sit in their dormitories.

Mrs Liddiard asked if the girls had complained about her, saying that none of them told the truth and they were a terrible set. She and Miss Firth did not intend to be such 'mugs' to these people. They preferred to make a full statement to the Welfare Officer Miss Waller, not to Miss Jacob-Smith, which was the correct procedure. Miss Liddiard stated that candles were necessary, as many of the lamps did not work. Wicks were difficult to obtain and the girls burnt them down. All these points were to be taken up, but Miss Jacob-Smith did not think that Mss Liddiard was doing all that she could to help the girls.

5/3/44 On a local farm, one of the Land Girls made breakfast for the farmer and his wife and did the housework on wet days. This must stop, noted Miss Jacob-Smith, even though the farmer said she was the best Land Girl he ever had!

The Forewoman had said that she was going to see her farmer, but instead spent the day in York.

8/3/44 Miss Liddiard was in bed ill with overwork. She complained about the Forewoman, who, in turn, complained about her, saying she was impossible to work with. Miss Liddiard and her assistant had threatened to walk out but, as Miss Liddiard was now ill, she intended to leave after the weekend. Miss Jacob-Smith hoped to try to persuade them to stay until the end of the month, as the only other member of staff was a fifteen-year-old domestic. The WLA Office now had the problem of deciding who could be sent to Dishforth as the new Warden!

29/3/44 At the Warden's request, Miss Jacob-Smith called in to a shop at Ripon for a wireless, but found that they were sold out and another would probably be available the following week.

Miss Liddiard questioned whether the weekly amount paid by private farm girls should be 22s 6d and not the £1 paid by WAEC workers.

The Assistant Warden's sister was staying at the hostel that week and she was working as a general help. The Forewoman said that Miss Liddiard had been better over the last three weeks and seemed anxious to do all she could for the girls.

13/4/44 Miss Jacob-Smith went to collect the Forewoman for a meeting and she was surprised to find that Miss Liddiard had left without warning.

18/4/44 Miss Jacob-Smith was surprised to find that Miss Liddiard knew the new Warden. The Warden and Assistant Warden Miss Holloway and Miss Bell appeared quite nice, she concluded. They had already developed good social activities and suggested a hostel social soon. Both had come from the WLA, not a YMCA hostel. The Forewoman said she too was impressed by Miss Holloway.

29/4/44 Former Warden Miss Grace said she appreciated Miss Jacob-Smith's help as the YMCA had given her none at all.

4/5/44 There was conflict about the price of laundry.

2/6/44 Miss Holloway had been to Boroughbridge laundry and found there was no maximum price for the washing of dungarees or overalls.

16/6/44 The theft of a lipstick was reported.

13/7/44 A box of Ryvita was taken to Miss Holloway.

19/7/44 The Warden and girls had agreed to late passes until 10.00 pm and one late pass to 12.00 am each fortnight. As a special concession, they had been allowed two late nights in the last fortnight, but now they wanted a third within three weeks. Miss Holloway had refused.

Miss Holloway was very glad that the hostel had been distempered and said it looked much better. A large boot rack had been obtained and the hall looked cleaner.

21/8/44 The daily girl had developed measles and now the Warden had no help. A new domestic from Ripon Hostel was sent to Dishforth for one week, to help present staff shortage.

20/9/44 The hostel looked very much better since curtains and linoleum had been supplied. A girl who had now left the WLA said that her two, very worn, WLA towels would not be returned as they were being used as floor cloths in her new home.

October 1945 Dishforth celebrated its second birthday with a most enjoyable party. The first part consisted of a concert given by the Concert Party from Baffarton RAF, including a performance by Jennie Bannister, a WLA member from the Easingwold Hostel. This was followed by refreshments and a dance. During the evening Good Service Awards were presented, including the WLA five-year award to Miss M James, who was now in the Hostel Orderly Corps and the Warden of the hostel.

Much of the success of the party was due to splendid organisation. Every girl from the hostel had been given a special job to do at the party. This made a memorable evening for all the farmers, their wives, and the girls' friends.

5/11/44 One of the Land Girls was unwell and her mother had suggested taking her home to see her own doctor. The Warden had suggested the hostel doctor, but then the girl had gone to walk her mother to the bus stop and she was not seen again. Miss Jacob-Smith suggested that she should leave the hostel.

Two girls lost their macs, so they would not work when it was raining and needed replacements. They would not get paid. Other girls' macs were leaking through the shoulder seams, so they were getting wet through.

9/11/44 A bring and buy sale for the WLA Benevolent Fund was organised and on 25/11/44 a mile of pennies was formed. Benefit Fund collection boxes were needed.

The Temporary Warden Miss Hardy had spent the night at the hostel and said it needed better lighting. The Tilly lamps had been taken away by Ministry of Works for repair and not returned before the present Warden arrived. Only ordinary oil lamps were now available.

Help was needed for a pregnant Land Girl. She might get grants for the baby when it was born, Miss Jacob-Smith said, and help would be given to get work for her. The Forewoman also asked about a girl who appeared to be too delicate to work. She had already had two periods of sickness since coming to the hostel and complained of pains. She could not ride a bike and was not trying very hard to learn. She admitted to having kidney problems but said she really enjoyed hostel life. This case needed further investigation, Miss Jacob-Smith decided.

The lighting at the hostel was deplorable and Miss Jacob-Smith could hardly see to write her report. The lights consisted of two hanging lamps. One girl who was writing a letter had a candle to help her to see. Miss Holloway was always saying how long it took her to clean and refill the oil lamps.

The staff now consisted of Miss Holloway and Miss Bell, the Assistant Warden who did all the cooking, and a resident domestic and a daily girl.

10/1/45 The girls were indignant, Miss Holloway said, as they had been late in on the previous night, although they were supposed to be in bed by 9.00 pm. The girls said they were only about ten minutes late, because it was snowing and so they knew they would not be able to work the next day.

The linoleum in the recreation room had worn badly. Miss Holloway had taken it up to be replaced.

24/1/45 The Hostel Forewoman complained about the Warden being mean in many little ways. The girls were not allowed to stir the fire, as Miss Holloway kept the poker and poked the fire only when she thought it necessary. No fires were allowed in dormitories on Saturday nights and there was only one fire in the recreation room for thirty-two girls. The evening meal was supposed to be ready for 5.30 pm but often was not ready until 6.00 pm.

Miss Jacob-Smith left some wool for the girls to knit for Liberated Europe.

13/2/45 Miss Jacob-Smith collected eighteen pairs of leaking gum boots and replaced them with six pairs.

14/2/45 The Forewoman stated that things were a little better since Miss Hardy was last at the hostel. Miss Holloway was still not very cooperative as she blamed the Forewoman for all the complaints. Blankets seemed not to have been washed since the hostel had opened, but this was difficult to check because of the various changes of staff.

Swine fever was prevalent in the area and some girls were losing work, as pigs were being sold.

22/2/45 There was not one light in the dormitories, only candles. Miss Holloway said she had no time to bother with the lamps. The girls said the lack of light was affecting their eyesight. There were no fires in the dormitories on Saturday nights. Coats left around the hostel were being collected by Miss Holloway and apparently she was wearing them.

27/2/45 Miss Jacob-Smith called at hostel and she was prevented from speaking to any of the girls.

15/3/45 One of the girls wanted to transfer to 'Pests'. Miss Jacob-Smith noted that she was 'only C-type' and always had a 'grouse', as she always thought that everyone was better off than herself. She was not really a 'proper type' for the WLA.

23/3/45 The hostel orderly said a letter had been written by the girls at the hostel, complaining about the conditions since Miss Holloway and Miss Bell had returned. The Forewoman was unwell and she had complained that Miss Hardy had not let her have the weekend off as arranged. Another girl had been off work for nine weeks. In the first week she had received 17s 6d, the second week 2s 6d, but then had used up all her allowances. Her father was a pattern maker paid £4 a week, but he was apparently 'inclined to be thirsty', and the girl had spent £23 of her savings on helping her mother. Could the WLA Welfare Fund help this girl, wondered Miss Jacob-Smith?

4/4/45 A girl's dungarees had shrunk and another had her coat burnt while at work. She was burning thorns when suddenly the wind changed and blew flames on to her coat. Another girl was badly injured while cycling, when she became involved in an accident in which a milk van came out of the Boroughbridge Road and ran into the army lorry.

27/7/45 Miss Jacob-Smith took three Aladdin lampstands and about ten miscellaneous lamps to the hostel.

9/8/45 The girls at the hostel needed twelve more combs.

24/8/45 An orderly was needed urgently. Further staff were threatening to leave if the hostel did not get electricity.

2/10/46 A girl complained of pains and back ache and when the doctor come to the hostel he discovered that she was pregnant. She should cease work immediately, he advised, and a certificate was issued. The girl's husband was a sergeant at Fulford Barracks in York, but she said that they were 'finished with each other' and she would be going to her parents' home. She maintained that her husband was the father, but was very 'elusive' when Miss Jacob-Smith suggested this was not true.

Miss Jacob-Smith thought it would be a good idea for the office of her home county WLA to be told that she was returning home and to also ask them to visit. If her husband did not continue her allowance, then she may need help from the Benevolent Fund help.

November 1945 The hostel's second birthday party involved local farmers and their wives and a concert was also given by the RAF in which a WLA member took part. There were presentations of arm bands, followed by a supper and dance.

(There is a break in Miss Jacob-Smith's records here.)

October 1946 Mr and Mrs Shaw who had been at the Dishforth Hostel for a year were to leave at the end of the month. Everyone was sorry that they were leaving but, as they were going to live in Dishforth village, the girls would not be losing them altogether.

4/10/46 Miss Jacob-Smith collected Mrs Phillips from Thirsk and took her to Dishforth. Twenty-three out of twenty-six girls attended Mrs Phillips' lecture on 'Health and Happiness'. The girls enjoyed it. Various uniform items were ordered.

9/10/46 Miss Jacob-Smith took the new Wardens Mr and Mrs Whetnall to see Dishforth and they thought it was nicer than they had anticipated. Mrs Shaw said she would help them when she had left.

11/10/46 A girl's laundry came back after she had left. As it was her WLA uniform, Miss Jacob-Smith kept it.

The girls still talked about Mrs Phillips' lecture in July, which they said was the best lecture they had ever had. Mrs Shaw needed telephone money and small envelopes and said the dormitory stoves were worn out. Gum boots were needed. Could all recruits from the North Riding be issued with gum boots and slipper socks, Miss Jacob-Smith wondered? It would save sending them when they arrive at the hostel.

22/10/46 Two girls had made orders for stockings and short-sleeved shirts. Four badges were also required. One girl returned her oilskin but now found she had no waterproof coat. Could she have a second-hand one? There were further queries over coats, gum boots and slipper socks. The Cook was going home, as her grandmother was dying and she intended to remain at home until after the funeral. She would be away when Mr and Mrs Whetnall, the new Wardens, arrived. The domestic had to go to Highgate Hospital for an overhaul.

28/10/46 A Ministry of Works official Mr Hall came to look round the hostel with the view to deciding its future.

5/11/46 A girl was ill in bed and hoped to go home for a rest, but her home was in South Scotland and it was expensive to travel there. Miss Jacob-Smith enquired whether she could have a warrant, as her father was in the regular army.

The Whetnalls seemed to have settled in but they thought that the girls were very untidy. Mrs Whetnall had already introduced a system of fines and she had undone several bunks, which she said were not properly made. She said she would deal with the girls when they came in. She was worried about the number of girls with scabies and had bought some lotion from the chemist.

A girl had applied for transfer to Guisborough Hostel but now she had settled at Dishforth and wanted to stay. The Hostel Orderly wanted to join the Hospital Scheme. Twenty Christmas cards were ordered.

6/11/46 Mrs Whetnall said that she thought most of the staff were due a holiday. Miss Jacob-Smith told her that before these people went on holiday she hoped they would clean the dormitory. Mr Whetnall said they were short of cleaning staff and appeared disgruntled.

Miss Jacob-Smith asked Mr Whetnall why there were not more lamps, as there were only two and it was quite impossible to see. Mr Whetnall said they had no more and the girls had broken the lamps at the rate of one a night. He had the appearance of not caring. Miss Jacob-Smith told him he must order five dozen more immediately. Miss Jacob-Smith enquired at the WLA Office to see if the order could be hurried up. She had noticed that there were two lamps in the Whetnalls' accommodation and said that one of these might be put into the girls' room.

There seemed to be some dissatisfaction among the staff. The Cook wanted a transfer, as did the two orderlies. This meant that all the resident staff members were requesting transfers – something was definitely wrong in the hostel!

8/11/46 The girls were very anxious to know the results of the efforts to obtain electric lights for them, as its absence prevented them from doing anything in the evenings, especially sewing or knitting.

Miss Jacob-Smith thought that Mrs Whetnall was full of enthusiasm. She wanted to give girls a hot drink at midnight when they returned on late nights and also at 10.00 am and 3.00 pm when they were not working. She said she found the Cook difficult when she wanted to change the menus. At the moment there was too little variety. Miss Jacob-Smith suggested that she should not be too enthusiastic at first. Mrs Whetnall had also been to a dance at the aerodrome with the girls.

One of the girls did not want to go home. Her father had died some time ago and her mother had married again almost immediately. Then the girl found out that her father had committed suicide. She hated her stepfather and he did not like having her at home. She would do anything rather than go home and would be glad to go to Thirsk as a domestic instead. The Dishforth Forewoman was going to Thirsk on 11/11/46, so it was decided that she could go with her.

Two girls were asked to move from Leeming Bar Hostel to Dishforth, so they sent their home belongings by rail but only stayed in Dishforth for two weeks before claiming release. However, they now had to go back to Leeming Bar in two weeks' time and needed to claim money for cost of transporting their luggage.

13/11/46 The petty cash seemed somewhat confused. Mrs Shaw had agreed to go to the hostel on 15/11/46 to explain how to manage the accounts.

14/11/46 Mrs Whetnall had to take a taxi into Ripon, costing 10s, as the forewoman was using the van to go to the forewomen's meeting. The taxi fare was taken from petty cash. The blankets needed to go to the laundry, so the next bill there would be higher. Mrs Whetnall wanted to revive the saving group.

15/11/46 There was a request for a table tennis set, some packs of cards and dice.

27/11/46 Mrs Shaw had not come to explain the petty cash. Mrs Whetnall had bought three dozen eggs at the packing station and wanted to get more. Miss Jacob-Smith enquired of the WLA office if she could pay out petty cash.

29/11/46 Mrs Whetnall and the Cook had a 'few words'. The cook said she would hand in her notice and leave on 4 December, however no more had been mentioned about this. Miss Jacob-Smith saw the Cook but she said nothing to her about it. If she did go then Mrs Whetnall had a relative who might take the job. Miss Jacob-Smith stressed that before this was done there must be an interview and the WLA Office must approve her.

Mrs Whetnall had ordered two geese from Severas Farm for the Christmas dinner. Mr and Mrs Whetnall had settled down well, although they were inclined to fuss at times, Miss Jacob-Smith felt. They were trying to improve the hostel, but it was difficult without redecoration. A social was organised by Mrs Whetnall and the girls' committee and all the girls seemed to enjoy it. The stoves in the dormitory and sitting room needed attention. The petty cash still awaited explanation but a savings group had been started.

16/12/46 One Land Girl whose sister was also at the hostel had not returned after the weekend. Mrs Whetnall gave her wages to her sister to take home but had no receipt. Mrs Whetnall was worried about having given this money as she wanted a transfer. When Miss Jacob-Smith arrived, three girls were talking to two prisoners of war from the nearby camp. She told Mrs Whetnall that this should not be encouraged. She collected the petty cash and said that the laundry should definitely be paid for from hostel funds.

Miss Jacob-Smith had asked for soap to be delivered but it had not yet arrived. Mrs Whetnall had telephoned to say the Ministry of Works was only providing linoleum for the sick bay, not the dormitory.

Ten tons of coke had been ordered by Mr Whetnall some time ago but it had not yet been delivered. The lamps and glasses ordered had also not yet arrived from the Ministry of Works.

Miss Jacob-Smith found that a WLA girl had been employed to do additional duties in the hostel and she told Mrs Whetnall that that must stop. Miss Jacob-Smith suggested to the office that a notice should be sent to all wardens telling that they could not employ a WLA girl to do hostel duties without first asking permission. If everyone was away for Christmas, she told them to make sure that someone would look after the boiler in case there was a frost.

19/12/46 Miss Jacob-Smith collected £4 for the order of milk of olives and shampoos, which were urgently needed, also Ponds cream. There was a request for a one-gallon paraffin container with a lip so that the paraffin could be poured into the lamps.

1/1/47 Twelve new lamps had arrived but five more were not working. No surplus new glasses were supplied and no other glasses had been supplied for the older ones. The firewood had not yet arrived.

2/1/47 Mr and Mrs Whetnall appeared to have made improvements and the girls appeared to like them. The new lamps made the light in the hostel better but new glasses and mantles were still required.

13/1/47 A Land Girl had been away since Christmas and, according to the other girls, she had gone into hospital. Miss Jacob-Smith wanted to know what was the matter with her. Another girl wanted a transfer to the Skipton Hostel or to a market garden in the Skipton area. She was a 'B-type' and had never been any bother. Miss Jacob-Smith called her 'a nice girl but not outstanding'. Her father was in the army but he had cancer and, as her boyfriend lived in Keighley, she wanted to move to Skipton to be nearer him.

15/1/47 Miss Jacob-Smith called to collect a pair of sewing machines which had been in the process of being repaired for months. She found the girls very upset about Mr Whetnall's language and general attitude, as he was said to have made rude remarks about their hostel friends and boyfriends. They also complained that he did not get up until mid-morning. Other, more minor complaints were that they wanted tea after their evening meal. There were no complaints about Mrs Whetnall, except that she came down to the sitting room and told them not to make so much noise as Mr Whetnall was feeling ill. The girls did think he was always ill. They also said Mr Whetnall was always rude to Mrs Whetnall.

The light in the sitting room was still not good and Miss Jacob-Smith spoke to Mr and Mrs Whetnall about it. They said they were not short of glasses at present, so she told them they must use sufficient lamps to give adequate light. The Ministry of Works had delivered glasses and mantles, but told them that they must be careful with them as they might not get any more. Miss Jacob-Smith told them that an order for four dozen should be made and if they became short, then they must buy locally as there must be sufficient light.

The soap and the buckets had not arrived and were required urgently.

22/1/47 A girl wanted to move to a farm, as she had never really felt at home in the hostel and felt she would be better on her own. Another had been sent a second-hand uniform but found it was dirty.

22/1/47 Miss Jacob-Smith spoke to Mr and Mrs Whetnall about the bad language Mr Whetnall had allegedly been using. Mr Whetnall denied this but afterwards his wife agreed and said it would not happen again.

There were mice in the hostel. The two hostel cats had disappeared and the mice were increasing. If the office knew of another hostel with kittens to spare, Mrs Whetnall asked that they would let her know. If the girls sold the piano, they asked, could they put the money towards a gramophone? They had an old one which had been at the repairers for some time.

3/2/47 Two of the new dormitory stoves had been fitted and the other two would be fitted as soon as the weather got better. Mrs Whetnall still did her best to improve the hostel and remained contented and happy. All the girls had thoroughly enjoyed Mrs Browne's lecture on 'Health and Happiness' and were anxious to know when she would return for the third in the series.

The Cook was worried that she had not received her PAYE code. A Land Girl had some problems with an irritating rash, which the Doctor said could be an occupational disease but he would not say exactly what had caused it. If it was occupational, then the WLA office needed to know the cause, so she could consult a specialist. Another girl did not want to leave the hostel but she preferred to have her release and she was willing to stay in the hostel until then. She was prepared to work in the hostel kitchen instead. Mrs Whetnall was delighted, as she was an orderly short.

Mrs Whetnall and the Cook both said that the domestic on loan from Stockton was a good cleaner when told what to do, but did not use her initiative. They said they would like to keep her until Stockton wanted her back.

Money for cosmetics was given to Miss Jacob-Smith by the Forewoman, in particular for more shampoo.

11/2/47 A girl went to the local infirmary and saw Dr Ingram, who said the girl had eczema not dermatitis and gave her some ointment, telling her to keep her hands dry. She had taken a taxi back to the hostel as she would have had to wait four hours for the bus from Boroughbridge. This cost 5s from the hostel welfare fund.

16/2/47 The hostel wood supply was exhausted and they had to order some from Waddingtons and the coal supply would also only last seven to ten days. They had been cooking on the stoves and could manage, but coal was needed for the heating. The hostel had also been warned by the Ministry of Food that they must use a few less potatoes. Mrs Whetnall was trying to do this but vegetables were scarce and only cabbage and turnips were available. Miss Jacob-Smith said she must tell the girls about this.

One girl at the hostel had scabies. The Doctor did not have time to give her a medical certificate but said her blankets must be stoved. Mrs Whetnall said the girls borrowed each others' clothes and Miss Jacob-Smith told her to tell them that this must stop, or else all the stoving and disinfecting would be in vain.

As regards the decorating, the contractors had received no instructions to decorate the ablution block or the Warden's rooms. Could the Ministry of Works include these, Miss Jacob-Smith asked? It seemed to be a waste not to do them at the same time.

21/2/47 There were orders for slipper socks and an exchange of breeches for a smaller pair and stockings. Six armchairs had arrived some time ago, also green material for curtains and sandwich tins. A further order was made for twelve chairs and lamp glasses urgently. Only six lamps could be used, as all the rest wanted glasses. The clock needed to be repaired and they also demanded paint for woodwork.

3/3/47 The Warden had found a shop in Northallerton which sold lamp glasses, so she bought twenty-four and paid £2 14s. She would have bought more but she had no money.

4/3/47 There were further orders for clothes. One girl had no receipt for the clothes that she had sent to the WLA Office. Shampoos were needed.

6/3/47 The hostel had been improved with the decoration in the kitchen, recreation room, and dormitory, but the ablution block and Warden's quarter still needed doing. Unfortunately, in a recent blizzard, some snow on the roof had come into the dormitory and it had left wet patches on the recently decorated ceiling. The general atmosphere in the hostel was good and Mrs Whetnall was doing all she could to help. Armchairs were on order but had not yet come.

10/3/47 Armchairs were still needed badly and the Ministry of Works would have to be reminded again. Two small tables were also required for the sitting room; the bathroom door handles were not working; and the dormitory needed attention. Curtain rods and fixtures were required for the dormitory windows too, and the bunks wanted repairs. New ones had been requested and iron beds would be preferred.

There was not enough money in the hostel funds to pay £3 for the repair of the wireless. Could it be paid out of the WLA Welfare Fund and be repaid when the hostel had more funds, Miss Jacob-Smith asked?

11/3/47 One of the girls had not come back to the hostel and the others said she was not returning. There were orders for socks, towels, socks, gum boots etc. A wash basin had been broken.

19/3/47 Six armchairs had been delivered, but they still required the other six ordered.

26/3/47 Were there any thrifty cooking books left, Miss Jacob-Smith asked, as Mrs Whetnall would like a copy of one?

28/3/47 Mrs Whetnall was delighted that the hostel was to be painted and she ordered the paint from York, which Miss Jacob-Smith would collect and deliver. Miss Jacob-Smith stressed that the recreation room must be painted first and the ablution block distempered, then the quarters upstairs. The woodwork would receive only one coat. The hostel required twelve new mats.

1/4/47 One of the Land Girl had an operation for spots and warts on her shoulders. The hostel needed twelve coconut mats. The chimney also needed sweeping, so Mrs Whetnall was told to get a local sweep.

14/4/47 The same Land Girl had further spots on her arms and legs. A specialist was suggested but she did not want to go. Orders were made for some more slipper socks.

15/4/47 The Land Girl who had been sent home for being dirty had not yet returned and Mrs Whetnall intended to give her one last warning to keep herself clean. When Miss Jacob-Smith called Mr Whetnall was feeling ill and it was the Cook's half-day.

17/4/47 One of the girls hoped to learn to ride a bike in a week to ten days, but Mrs Whetnall was doubtful. Another girl was going to the hospital that week. Miss Jacob-Smith collected some paint and took it to the hostel. Another pair of dungarees for milking was required.

24/4/47 Gum boots and slipper socks were required. The girl mentioned in the 15/4 entry had returned to the hostel perfectly clean. Mrs Whetnall had received a letter from her mother and thought she would be all right. Her mother wanted her to go home each week so she could keep an eye on her.

Sandwich tins had been ordered but had not yet arrived. The Doctor advised that the girl suffering from spots must have medicine and ointment before she saw the specialist. Mrs Whetnall said the girl was very worried about her spots, as they had got worse in the last few days. The girl refused to eat, she could not sleep, had no interest in anything and was very depressed. Mrs Whetnall suggested that she went home. Miss Jacob-Smith wanted to see her but she was too ill and in bed. If she went home there would only be Mrs Whetnall and the

Cook to serve breakfast and the evening meal. The other two members of staff were daily women, so a replacement was necessary.

24/4/47 Miss Jacob-Smith thought the dormitory looked untidy and she said so. Mrs Whetnall said the dormitory had been tidy until the girls came in and as they were changing at the time, her story could have been true.

Mrs Whetnall had been worried about the butcher's bills recently. She thought the butcher put down the wrong weights and then charged too much. Miss Jacob-Smith looked at the April invoices and the last week's bill and Mrs Whetnall said she had not had all of it. She told them they must keep a strict check on all future meat and weigh it and she promised to get a price list from the Ministry of Food, so they could double-check it.

Miss Jacob-Smith asked Mr Whetnall about the possibility of his leaving and he said the couple had applied to the YWCA hostels, as the girls at Dishforth expected too much of the staff. They were cheeky to him and used bad language, but he had been instructed by Miss Jacob-Smith not to answer back. They would be willing to go to another WLA hostel anywhere and they would let her know when they planned to leave so she could look for a replacement.

29/4/47 The cook was anxious to become Assistant Warden as well as Cook. The WLA had received an application from a Miss Nicholson a week ago for the position of Warden. She was ex-NAAFI. The Cook had worked under her and said she was excellent.

The Cook wanted a holiday before Mr and Mrs Whetnall left. The Domestic would take her place for a week, if she could manage to get on with Mrs Whetnall. Evelyn said Mr and Mrs Whetnall were to take so much holiday that they will be leaving early. The Whetnalls' child was thought to have measles. When the doctor saw him he had already had it ten days and they were keeping him in their room so he did not mix with the Land Girls. Miss Jacob-Smith saw the child on Thursday. He had a streaming cold and a very red face.

1/5/47 A girl had been sent a bill for her glasses and asked if some help could be given towards the cost, as she came from a poor home with several small children. Miss Jacob-Smith also received a long list of clothing wanted. One girl badly needed stockings, dungarees, gum boots, and slipper socks. A second wanted stockings, shoes, breeches and dungarees. A third required dungarees, stockings, shoes and breeches. Girl number four had lost her oilskins and she wanted a replacement. Yet another said her mac was stolen when she was at Crayke Hostel.

Mr Whetnall rang and asked if Miss Jacob-Smith would come to the hostel, as there had been 'a minor revolution'. She went but could find no evidence of a revolution. The girls had been very noisy according to the forewoman. Before or after the lights had been put out, there had been a good deal of noise but the girls were apparently just teasing each other. There had been no revolution!

Mr Whetnall said he fully intended to have certain girls removed from the hostel before he left. The Forewoman knew he was lying, as he had blamed six girls for the noise but these six were no worse than the others! She said the girls were just tired of Mr Whetnall. Apparently, another girl had been cheeky when he turned the wireless down, saying it was too loud. The girl said they were expected not to make any noise when the Whetnalls' child had gone to bed.

The impression Miss Jacob-Smith received was that Mr and Mrs Whetnall were not going to do much before they left. Miss Jacob-Smith then brought up the matter of their child suffering from German measles. She told Mr Whetnall that he should have notified the WLA Office. Miss Jacob-Smith was of the opinion that Mr and Mrs Whetnall were going to make it difficult for anyone to follow them. Mrs Whetnall had tried to make a success of the hostel but Mr Whetnall had not been satisfactory. He was distempering and painting part of the hostel, however, which improved the look of it. The mats supplied by the Ministry of Works seemed very small.

4/5/47 The Land Girl affected by spots had been in hospital. Her ailment had been caused by animals, so she was entitled to compensation and her wages were also sent to her. She was recovering at home in bed.

6/5/47 Miss Jacob-Smith saw the possible relief Warden Mrs Shaw getting off the Thirsk bus and she told Miss Jacob-Smith that if ever the hostel was short of staff then she would be willing to go back to Dishforth for a short period, such as when the Warden wanted a holiday, or if there was any gap between the Whetnall family leaving and a new Warden arriving. Miss Jacob-Smith questioned whether this would be for the best.

7/5/47 When Miss Jacob-Smith arrived at the hostel she found all the Whetnall family about to go shopping to Boroughbridge with the hostel Forewoman. She asked if the child was still infectious and found it was. She said they should not go in the van with the Forewoman.

A girl from the hostel had German measles and she was infectious for ten days. It was unlikely that she had caught the infection from the child. The Cook said she wanted to go home to do the cleaning but Mrs Whetnall did want to be left with all the cooking. Had the office any idea about anyone to help, Miss Jacob-Smith enquired?

The hostel had no firewood, could it be ordered, Miss Jacob-Smith asked? A girl had gone home with scabies, but she had not had it before and no other girl in the hostel had it. Miss Jacob-Smith promised that all the blankets should be fumigated.

Orders were made for a mac and gum boots.

13/5/47 The girl who had suffered from scabies returned fully recovered. More orders were made for stockings, gum boots and shoes.

21/5/47 Mr and Mrs Shaw, the temporary Wardens, were prepared to remain at the hostel until the harvest. They intended go to the hostel to collect the keys, rather than sleep in the Whetnall child's room. Mr and Mrs Shaw were drawing the old age pension and so had only one insurance card. Their pension would be reduced to 10s.

Mrs Whetnall was having a week's holiday and then she was going to a job at a workhouse with Poles.

The Dishforth Hostel needed a three burner oil stove with an oven attached, as the present stove was worn out.

27/5/47 Mr and Mrs Shaw had settled in. They told Miss Jacob-Smith that the girls had been allowed to come to breakfast in their curlers and the Forewoman was allowed a key and could come in late. Miss Jacob-Smith was of the opinion that this must stop immediately! Mrs Shaw also said there was little crockery and would like to send in a requisition. Mr Whetnall had apparently been in a temper before he left, as there were cups on the kitchen floor. Pan and kettles were also needed.

The Domestic would not be needed at the hostel after 4 June and they would prefer that she left then. Mr Whetnall had not brought in the coke and Mrs Shaw felt it was rather a big job, as it would entail putting it in a wheelbarrow and throwing it in a shed. Miss Jacob-Smith said the office would be willing to pay a girl's wages for doing the job.

A girl needed two pairs of dungarees, two long-sleeved shirts and one short-sleeved shirt, plus stockings. Another girl was badly in need of slipper socks.

10/6/47 Mrs Shaw would like to know who was the contractor for the hostel. It was Westwicks of Thirsk, but they thought to change to Waddingtons of Kirby Hill as Westwicks were so slow. There were three outstanding requisitions from Westwicks sent from the Ministry of Works: 23 April 'Block for Bread machine'; 24 April 'Repairs to broken wash basin'; 18 March Curtain rails. Wicks for oil lamps were needed urgently so she had bought them.

Mrs Shaw said the hostel towels were in a muddle. The Whetnalls had allowed the girls to use hostel towels, so Miss Jacob-Smith asked for a list of the girls who appeared to have lost a towel. Two alarm clocks were needed. Some of the girls had asked for fires in the evening, as they were cold. Mrs Shaw agreed to allow them to go in the kitchen and warm themselves by the stove.

18/6/47 Could someone from the WLA Welfare Office visit the girl with a bad shoulder, Miss Jacob-Smith asked?

23/6/47 Mr and Mrs Shaw were out when Miss Jacob-Smith called, but she saw the Cook. The new beds were allocated as follows: staff room one iron; Cook one iron; Wardens two iron; sick bay two camp. According to the Cook, there had been three beds originally but one had disappeared at Christmas, whilst she was away. A camp bed was folded up in the Warden's room and another in the Cook's room but this only accounted for two beds.

A new oil stove was needed for heating and cooking. It was doubtful if the Ministry of Works would be able to supply what Mrs Shaw wanted. Could it be bought out of hostel amenities, Miss Jacob-Smith enquired? The Ministry of Works had arranged to bring a new kitchen stove from a hostel that had closed down.

Mrs Shaw had never liked one of the girls and she was now complaining about her rudeness. Miss Jacob-Smith thought the girl loved her bed but she worked well, so she did not think she was as bad as Mrs Shaw made out. The girl's mother was known to be in a mental hospital.

23/6/47 Miss Jacob-Smith looked at the walls of the hostel and she thought it would be difficult to fix brackets on the wall so that the girls could read in bed. She thought a hanging lamp would be a better idea, but that might not solve the problem of light for the bottom bunks.

3/7/47 The girls and staff were upset about the news that the hostel would be closing and several of them wept when they heard. Several of them thought they would go to farms near Dishforth. Miss Jacob-Smith promised to go to the hostel the next week and to see their respective farmers or find out which hostels they would like to go to.

Mrs Shaw said that Mrs Hardy had told her that the quilts at the hostel were YWCA property and wanted to know if this was correct. Mrs Shaw wanted to know the procedure about the disposal of food, fuel and outstanding requisitions.

7/7/47 Everyone continued to be upset about the closure of the hostel. A petition had been sent by the local farmers requesting that the hostel would remain open until after the harvest. The girls had made their request to go to new hostels at Ripon, Easingwold and Thirsk.

15/7/47 Mrs Shaw was upset because she had not yet received an official letter from the WLA office about the closure of the hostel.

There were thirty-two quilts at the hostel, some were worn, the others not so bad. Thirsk hostel wanted the sewing machine if possible. Miss Jacob-Smith did not think anyone from Stockton Hostel would want to sew any more for a bit after Miss Rabjohn had left. (Miss Rabjohn, the tyrant of a Warden at Stockton had made the girls do handicrafts. See the section on Stockton Hostel for more details.)

Mrs Shaw was upset again about the change of date of the closure, as she had made arrangements about going home and the farewell party etc. She said Mr Barker, a WEAC official, was a nuisance. Arrangements needed to be made to ask Mr Barker if the WAEC could take the girls' luggage from Dishforth to Thirsk, as well as the sewing machine?

The hostel closed after the harvest in 1947.

CHAPTER SEVEN

Easingwold Hostel

(This record has been compiled from eighty of the duplicate books written by Miss Jacob-Smith. To protect personal information about individual Land Girls their names have been omitted. The notes have been transferred into the past tense for the ease of reading and, where appropriate, to clarify a statement the author has added an explanation in brackets. Each entry was punctuated with notes about Miss Jacob-Smith's visits to individual farms and other hostels. Some of the more mundane comments about ordering uniform, travel warrants and other miscellaneous details have not been included.

Where there is a gap in the chronology, Miss Jacob-Smith has probably used another representative to make the visits.)

EASINGWOLD HOSTEL WAS ONE OF THE EARLIEST HUTMENT HOSTELS to open in December 1941. It was also the first WLA hostel to appear in the North Riding.

A joke was made that the walls of the hostel must have been made of expanding material, as over 400 people managed to get into the recreation room in the hutment for the first birthday party of the hostel, on 26 December 1942. It was combined with a whist drive and a dance in aid of the Red Cross 'Penny a Week' Fund.

Messages of congratulation were read from the Minister of Agriculture, Katherine, Lady Graham and the pupils of Bingley Grammar School, who were attached to the hostel during the summer holidays. The prizes for the whist drive were presented by Mrs Cliffe, the WLA District representative. The total funds handed over to the Red Cross amounted to £55.

Not many people managed to have two parties for their birthday, especially during wartime, but the Easingwold Land Girls did! On the following day, a Sunday, Lady Coates gave a party for the hostel girls and those billeted on farms in the neighbourhood. At this party, a birthday cake with one candle was cut by Miss Nora Dowkes, who had been at the hostel for the longest time. Diamonds (badges given for length of service) were presented by Lady Coates and then the girls gave Mrs Grace, the Warden, an ornament for her sitting room, in appreciation of all that she had done for them. Both parties must have provided extra work for the staff, especially for Mrs Grace and her daughter.

Easingwold won the Inter-Hostel Competition for the best working hours record in August 1943, which was organised by the North Riding WAEC. The hostel also set a new record for the number of points won in the competition. This was the fourth time that Easingwold had been at the top of the list since the competition started in 1941. The hostel sent the prize money to the Chancellor of the Exchequer, as a gift to the nation.

November 1943 The YWCA, which managed many WLA hostels, organised a collection in the hostels in aid of its funds. There was a promise that a Land Girl from whichever hostel raised the most money should present the funds raised at a special ceremony at the Mansion House in London, on 2 November. There was great excitement when Mrs Grace received a telegram stating that the Easingwold Hostel had collected the most money. A Land Girl named Ada Senior was chosen as the representative of the hostel, and to Ada's surprise she was to present the purse to Her Majesty the Queen. Other important figures at the ceremony were Mrs Churchill and the Lord Mayor and the Lady Mayoress of London.

December 1943 Some Easingwold girls went carol singing for the WLA Benevolent Fund (the fund grew slowly and it was suggested that girls should be invited to give one day's pay per year to the fund. With the new rates of pay from 1943 this meant donating 7s 6d.)

One of the Easingwold girls appeared before Knaresborough Juvenile Court, accused of stealing some shoes from other Land Girls. As she was only sixteen, she was sentenced to be bound over for twelve months, or to pay a £5 fine or 30s costs within fourteen days. The magistrate said that girl should remain in the WLA and work nearer her home, so that she would be free to go daily to her work. This would be her last chance with the WLA.

April 1944 Miss Grace was very upset that her cook was leaving and there was no one to replace her. She felt that hostel staff should be a reserved occupation and they should not be allowed to leave. Mrs and Miss Grace, the Warden and Assistant Warden, were also due to leave on 10 April. They had been at this hostel since December 1941, and the hostel would miss them very much indeed, noted Miss Jacob-Smith. A farewell party was held on 14 April for them.

Miss Lloyd, the new Warden, had apparently settled in well. She reported that girls had been coming in late but she had satisfactorily settled the matter. Miss Jacob-Smith did not think this would happen again.

Some girls were not with the local doctor's panel and so the doctor called to see the nineteen girls not presently on his list. Miss Reddam said she much preferred to collect the medical cards as part of the Warden's duty, and she would have them ready within a week to ten days.

One girl's clothing had been burned by spraying and Miss Jacob-Smith enquired of the WLA office whether the girl was eligible for replacement uniform and whether she should be given more protective clothing.

May 1944 Miss Jacob-Smith took supplies of cosmetics to the hostel. Miss McLeod, the new Warden arrived. She had formerly been the Warden at Ripon Hostel. She appeared most disgruntled and said she intended walking out, as the hostel was so awful! There were no members of staff, as the Cook and Cleaner had both walked out since she had arrived. They were both local women, the Cleaner having been there since the hostel had opened. A new Cook had been found. The girls were behaving very well, however. Miss Reddam was staying on as Miss McLeod was so short-staffed. Miss Jacob-Smith wrote to the WLA Office: 'Miss McLeod does not seem to be a suitable warden. Can this matter be taken up?'

June 1944 Miss Bullard had been at the hostel for the previous week and was due to return to Leeming Bar Hostel. A new Assistant Warden, aged just eighteen, was coming. She was due to take up nursing in January but would be the Assistant Warden until then. All the girls were happy and the Forewoman said that Miss McLeod was improving. She thought Miss McLeod would settle, if she was left on her own, without other wardens coming to help. She was anxious to be friendly with the girls and was interested in them.

23/8/44 The girls were rebelling against the collection of clothing coupons. They had given up thirty-six coupons for first year, twenty-four during the last year and now the WLA Office wanted twenty-four coupons for the year ahead, although they had not been given any replacement clothing.

September 1944 Mrs McLeod telephoned the WLA Office because some girls had been rude to her when she had refused to give them a third late night pass in a week. She asked for six girls to be removed but Miss Jacob-Smith told her to control the girls, as they had not done anything really bad.

October 1944 Miss Jacob-Smith discussed plans for raising funds for the WLA Benevolent Fund with the Forewoman. The Forewoman suggested a dance, whist drive and possibly a concert given by the girls. The dance was held later in the month.

A Land Girl had been ill all week with acute pains and was being cared for by the Forewoman. The Warden wanted her to settle at Easingwold as she thought her a sweet girl and everyone liked her.

24/8/45 A new Land Girl had arrived at the hostel without the second half of her coupons for the ration period. All her coupons had been used up. She did not bring her identity card and ration book and, after repeated requests from the Warden, they were to be replaced.

[Here there is a gap in Miss Jacob-Smith's records, possibly where another WLA inspector took over visiting the hostel.]

3/10/46 Miss Jacob-Smith saw Mrs McLeod, who was very pleased to hear that Miss Wilson, the former Assistant Warden at Stockton Hostel, was coming to Easingwold. She was leaving Easingwold for the weekend and Miss Wilson was to stay until she returned.

One of the Land Girls had two brothers, who were about to be demobbed and she had asked to be transferred to Stokesley Hostel, as she could then go home every weekend to help with the washing and cleaning. Miss Jacob-Smith thought that this transfer should be given if possible.

The cosmetic order from the hostel included Drene shampoo (not Amami), four dozen combs, lipsticks and Ponds Vanishing Cream.

A Land Girl had gone home with a strain after an accident. She had not returned the form requesting compensation and Miss Jacob-Smith asked someone from the WLA Welfare Office to visit her at home. Other sick girls had also gone home. One had fallen off her bicycle and damaged her forehead; one had a carbuncle; and another an inflamed ear.

9/10/46 Miss Jacob-Smith brought Mrs Browne to give the lecture on 'Health and Happiness. There had been some trouble at the hostel that evening, however. The Forewoman had been trying to help whilst Mrs McLeod was ill and she had decided that the dormitory needed tidying up. Miss Jacob-Smith had agreed, as Mrs McLeod was not very strict about placing suitcases on top of wardrobes. The Forewoman had been in hostels where wardens refused to allow anything on wardrobe tops, so she took all the suitcases and put them in the suitcase room. The result was intense annoyance when the girls came in. One girl was particularly annoyed, as her suitcase contained her best clothes and she swore at the Forewoman. When the Forewoman asked if the girl could be transferred, Miss Jacob-Smith saw the girl and decided that the Forewoman was in the wrong. Miss Jacob-Smith had no intention of transferring the girl, as she was an excellent worker.

Miss Jacob-Smith went to the Royal Bath Hospital to see about another Land Girl. She got the girl admitted and filled in the necessary forms, saying she should be in for a fortnight. The cost of this was £5 5s. As she would be paid for the time, she should be able to afford to pay it herself, Miss Jacob-Smith concluded.

The Forewoman thought that one of the other Land Girls could also be due for an accident case. The Doctor had said that she should take four days off work but she has been away for ten days. If she was away for fourteen days, then she would have to give a better account of the accident for any claim to be paid.

Temporary Warden Miss Spiers had settled down all right but there were doubts about her rate of pay. Miss Jacob-Smith told her to telephone Mrs Wright if there was any difficulty. A new domestic had arrived, but there were still two vacancies. There was a request that if the East Riding orderlies at Howden were given their notice, then perhaps they could fill the Easingwold vacancies. All the hostels had more work than they could cope with.

One Land Girl has been married for three years and had not seen her husband for over a year. They now wished to be together as he had found a flat. Miss Jacob-Smith thought the girl should give in her notice and get a release.

4/11/46 Miss Wilson (an Assistant Warden sometimes loaned out to other hostels as a Relief Warden) had arrived safely but she had found Mrs McLeod in bed! Mrs McLeod said she had arranged for a friend of hers, a Mrs Woodhouse, to come to the hostel from Monday to Saturday of the next week. Mrs Woodhouse wanted to be a WLA warden and Mrs McLeod thought she would prove excellent. Miss Jacob-Smith did not see how Mrs McLeod could engage her friend for a week without any references being sent to the WLA Office, as she had never been in a WLA hostel before. She might 'do' for Dishforth, Miss Jacob-Smith noted, if the advertisements were showing no recruits.

Mrs McLeod was also considering engaging another domestic. Miss Jacob-Smith wanted confirmation from the Office whether Mrs McLeod could do that. Her theory was to have a larger staff and pay them less than the WLA Office rates, but let them work on a shift basis and do much shorter hours. This would mean that expenditure on staff was no more than in other hostels. Miss Jacob-Smith asked the WLA Office what should be done.

Mrs McLeod was agitating to know if she would be refunded 5s for a lock which she had paid for months ago, in anticipation of getting the money back. Mrs McLeod was at her most difficult, Miss Jacob-Smith complained. Perhaps she had been in bed too long and had had time to think about all her troubles.

Miss Jacob-Smith had been to the hostel on two afternoons that week. Both times the kitchen staff had been cutting sandwiches and making tea for the WASC men. When Mrs McLeod was better, Miss Jacob-Smith intended to investigate this matter further. She did not see why Miss McLeod should complain about the shortage of staff, yet allow the staff to spend so long each day making food ready for the WASC. It was probably done using the hostel's rations, too. Miss Jacob-Smith thought she had better let Mrs McLeod's mood improve before mentioning this, though.

5/11/46 Twenty dozen Christmas cards were ordered for the hostel.

8/11/46 While the Warden had been on holiday Miss Spiers had done relief duty for her. As usual, everyone was charmed by her, Miss Jacob-Smith noted, and the girls had given her a scarf as a present, to show their appreciation for the way she had looked after them. This was unusual at Easingwold, as the hostel was regarded as 'tough'. There had been two more recent domestic changes.

One Land Girl's father had been a miner but, after becoming unfit for this work, he had gone into an ammunition works during the war. When this had ceased, he became unemployed and had now been out of work for eleven months. She was worried about her father and Miss Jacob-Smith promised someone would visit and assess the situation.

Mrs McLeod was very annoyed, as she had seen an advertisement for the new Guisborough Hostel Warden at £3 per week. She had worked in hostels for three years, and now at a forty-bed hostel she only got a little more than this. Miss Jacob-Smith pointed out to Mrs McLeod that her salary was the province of the YWCA not the WLA Offices.

A prisoner of war interpreter came to complain about the girls fraternising with the POWs working near the hostel. Mrs McLeod ought to tell the girls of the consequences, Miss Jacob-Smith remarked.

The girls had also complained about not being able to use the telephone. As usual there were various orders for clothing. Mrs McLeod had engaged another resident domestic at a salary of £2 a week.

11/11/46 Mrs McLeod suggested that wardens should be told when a Land Girl was to be released from a hostel, so the warden could check things. This would prevent letters being sent from the WLA Office asking for uniforms long after girls had left.

Mrs McLeod was in very much better health and would go away on 15 November for a fortnight. The hostel was very short of toilet rolls and Mrs McLeod did not want to leave Miss Spiers short when she went away. Miss Jacob-Smith told her that she would bring a small supply in the car on her next visit.

15/11/46 There were various orders for slipper socks from the hostel. One Land Girl said she had never had leggings when she was enrolled in Durham. The Forewoman was anxious to know when she could have some more girls, as she was short of hands for work.

22/11/46 A girl had been away from the hostel for three weeks and Miss Jacob-Smith requested that someone from the Welfare Office should visit her to see if she would be returning? Another girl had asked to be transferred to a hostel in the South of England, as she said she could not settle.

26/11/46 Can anything be done about speeding up the requisition for chairs, Miss Jacob-Smith asked? More cosmetics were requested, as well as Gala and

Tattoo lipsticks, combs, Miners face make-up, Ponds face cream, face powder and Evan Williams hair wave set.

30/11/46 Mrs McLeod was full of complaints about the slackness of other members of staff. They took too long over their dinner and they wasted time, she said. Miss Jacob-Smith thought this was due to the lack of discipline exercised by Mrs McLeod. Linoleum for the dormitory was required and bath and chair repairs were needed urgently. Apart from this, the hostel was well kept and the food was excellent. A whist drive had been organised on 22 November and £7 had been raised for the Benevolent Fund.

11/12/46 Miss Jacob-Smith saw Mrs McLeod to talk about the Cook leaving and she told her that she definitely could not have the cook from Dishforth, as cooks were very hard to get. Mrs McLeod had got arthritis in her knee and one of the domestics had to go to hospital to have her tonsils out, so she would be off for four weeks. Mrs McLeod had employed a WLA girl for the week to do the cooking.

Two other Land Girls were off work: one had fallen in the recreation room and bruised her knees. Yet, Miss Jacob-Smith did not think they were all that short-staffed.

Mrs McLeod was staying in the hostel over Christmas with her two sons. Her husband was returning from India.

16/12/46 Miss Jacob-Smith took orders for stockings (at 2s 2d a pair). The stockings ordered some time ago had not yet arrived and they were needed urgently.

Mrs McLeod was not at all anxious that Miss Jacob-Smith should visit the hostel Cook, who had just left. She was deliberately very vague about the directions to where she lived. The Forewoman had praised her cooking and Miss Jacob-Smith found that the Cook was sorry she had walked out. She had been tired lately and looked very white. She liked hostel life though, and said she would go back to Dishforth or Easingwold, but would like a holiday first. Miss Jacob-Smith was sure Mrs McLeod would make a fuss about having her back. The Cook said Mrs McLeod was very difficult at times, as sometimes she liked to do the cooking herself and then grumbled because the Cook did not do it!

3/1/47 Mrs McLeod was lunching in her sitting room, with her son aged about twelve, when Miss Jacob-Smith arrived. The Cook was with her sister in the kitchen and they were looking after the smaller boy. Mrs McLeod's husband was also there, as he had arrived from India that Sunday, but since then he had been feeling ill. Miss Jacob-Smith asked if any payment had been made by him for the younger boy's keep.

Mr McLeod had been at the hostel Christmas party and Miss Jacob-Smith thought he must have been in the hostel ever since. There has been some trouble between Mrs McLeod and the Cook, who had now returned to the hostel, but Miss Jacob-Smith hoped they would both settle down. She judged the hostel satisfactory.

8/1/47 New bunks were to be ordered. Various socks had also been ordered, three at 2s 2d and three at 1s. One girl wanted the remainder of her order for second-hand socks.

15/1/47 Distemper was used for decorating the sick bay and the Warden's bathroom. The bricks needed replacing around the kitchen stove, but Miss Jacob-Smith told Mrs McLeod that no more should be bought without permission from the WLA Office.

Mrs McLeod thought that some new drains were also needed, as there was a permanent pool of water at the side of the hostel and she noted that there was some water near the fence near the machinery yard. An open drain needed cleaning out too. Miss Jacob-Smith said that when the Ministry of Works man came next to the area he would see what was needed, and she pointed out to Mrs McLeod that it had been an exceptional year for rain.

Mrs McLeod was now agitating for new type of bunks and asked if they had been ordered. The linoleum had arrived, which Mrs McLeod had previously agitated for, but she now thought it should not be put down until the weather improved. An extra bath was being installed as well.

Hard work shifting snow (*Eden Camp Collection*)

Miss Jacob-Smith did not consider the recent pantomime outing a great success, as several girls had been unable to go owing to the flu. Mrs McLeod thought it would cost £8 for two buses but it was in fact £8 for each bus!

The youngest McLeod son was now in Filey and the eldest boy was going to join his father in India next week. It was thought that they would stay in the hostel until then.

Eight of the Land Girls had the flu and Mrs McLeod insisted that Miss Jacob-Smith visited them in the dormitory.

24/1/47 There was an order for twenty mattresses to be requisitioned. A Ministry of Works man had been to see the floods around the hostel and another man would accompany him the next week. There were various requests for items of uniform.

31/1/47 Mrs McLeod wanted to know who would pay for the wireless licence for the hostel. The Forewoman had not received a letter asking her to sign on for another year.

3/2/47 The kitchen had been distempered and the new linoleum supplied. The water had also been de-limed. Mrs McLeod had returned and settled down again. A pantomime trip was organised and enjoyed by the girls. Ten girls were attending the shorthand classes held weekly in the hostel and several were making things for the local WLA handicrafts exhibition.

3/3/47 The winter was particularly harsh in 1947 and the Land Girls were employed to move the snow in the surrounding streets and in the centre of Easingwold. This continued for weeks and the girls became heartily sick of the job, feeling that they were doing work that some of the locals could have tackled. After all, they were employed to do farm work!

A group of girls rebelled against the snow shifting and said they would not do any more. However, only one entirely refused to return to work. Her version of the story was that several girls had said they would not move snow any more and would rather forfeit a day's pay, then the others had changed their minds. She still thought she would just lose a day's pay, but she was wrong! Miss Jacob-Smith thought that she might be dismissed.

The girl in question was not keen to live on a farm or have her release, however. She could not work at milking and had done two years' excavation tractor driving. She was a big strong girl and would not mind going to another county but her mother was not too well and so she wanted to stay in Easingwold. Her case would be discussed at the next meeting of the WLA. The girls felt strongly about her dismissal, as they believed they should not be asked to move snow. They felt the Easingwold residents should do their own bits of pavement.

One girl said she had asked a magistrate about the matter and he had told her that the WASC was in the wrong. He advised the girl to write to her MP. Miss Jacob-Smith told them about the WLA Conciliation Committee. The girls thought their friend might go before the committee but she was not so keen. Miss Jacob-Smith suggested that they discuss it amongst themselves, for if she did not appeal she would probably be dismissed. The result was that no action was taken against the girl, however.

A girl had been off ill for several weeks and on returning to the hostel she found her gum boots missing. Could she be issued with another pair, Miss Jacob-Smith asked? Various orders were made for aertex shirts, gum boots, stockings, slipper socks and socks.

Another girl had to go to York to see an eye specialist and it was suggested that Miss Wilson should take her as she was going that way. Miss Wilson refused at first because of her dog. Then arrangements were made and she took the girl.

6/3/47 Mrs McLeod had been off ill but was recovered. Miss Wilson had acted as the Warden in the meantime. The girls were still clearing a good deal of snow.

7/3/47 A girl had paid 3s 3d for her hospital contribution. Orders were made for socks, gum boots, headscarf, gloves and a new hat, also one girl had leaking boots. The Land Girls wanted a supply of milk of olives, as they could not buy it anywhere. A hot water bottle had been bought using hostel funds by Mrs McLeod and she intended to buy another.

When sending ration books Miss Jacob-Smith told Mrs McLeod to register them, as one sent out to a girl seemed to have been lost in the post. The linoleum was not down, as the Warden was still waiting for better weather and the new decorations. Miss Jacob-Smith told her it must go down straight away.

Mrs McLeod had not been impressed by Miss Wilson and had a poor opinion of her as a potential Assistant Warden. She complained that the sitting room had dog hairs over it from Miss Wilson's dog and that the mats in the hostel were not as clean as when Mrs McLeod had left. The cause, Mrs McLeod said, was that Miss Wilson was inclined to stay in the sitting room rather than get down to working herself and the staff tended to slack off because of this.

Miss Wilson liked to go out and about around Easingwold, but Mrs McLeod thought that these journeys were unnecessary. The store cupboard had also gone down, as Miss Wilson had only bought what was needed immediately. This meant that the February bills were lower than normal. To catch up, Mrs McLeod would have to buy more that month. How did Mrs McLeod know about Miss Wilson staying in the sitting room and going out for walks? Miss Jacob-Smith thought that this must have been due to gossip from the staff!

One of the hostel staff was to have a pay rise and Mrs McLeod thought that two others should have the same amount. One was an excellent girl and always working, but the other was inclined to be cheeky. Mrs McLeod had the chance of a new daily women and had engaged her to start on 14/3/47, at 1s 6d an hour, subject to the WLA office's approval.

Mrs McLeod thought that the boiler man was stealing coke, as he has been seen with bags on his back when leaving the hostel. She called the police to investigate but there was no proof. She told the kitchen staff not to mention it to him. He had also used bad language in front of the girls when they complained about the water being cold.

Proficiency tests were not to be held until May, as the WASC felt they needed to be postponed in view of the work done after the thaw. More orders were made for gum boots etc. and travel warrants.

3/4/47 Miss Jacob-Smith was late arriving at the hostel, as her car had a puncture. She spoke to the boiler man. He said he had asked Mrs McLeod to provide a lock for the boiler house door, as the kitchen girls were in the habit of going into the boiler room to get shovel loads of burning coke to light the dormitory stoves. They often left the boiler door open and then complained that the water was cold. Five tons of fuel had been delivered some time ago and Mrs McLeod had told him there was another five tons if he needed it.

Yet, just before Mrs McLeod went away, she told him no more was due and he would have to manage, then she had made some remark about him taking coal and coke home. He said that he had sufficient at home and that this suggestion was not true. Later, he found that the boiler room had been broken into and he asked Miss Wilson who had done it. She said that she had but would not give him a reason why. The boiler man said he was quite willing to return to the hostel, provided no one interfered with his work. In any case, Miss Jacob-Smith concluded, a duplicate key to the boiler room should always be available in the hostel in case of emergency.

However, Mrs McLeod had just given the boiler man a raise. According to Miss Wilson, he would take large lumps of coal into the boiler room and then take them home in a sock. On one occasion, a member of the kitchen staff (a girl Miss Jacob-Smith did not like) had shouted to him, 'I hope it burns well,' at which the boiler man looked very annoyed. On Friday morning, he had been seen taking large lumps of coal to the boiler room. When he had gone, a Land Girl and Miss Wilson had broken into the boiler room and found the coal missing. Miss Wilson then rang up the police and they said they could not help if Miss Wilson did not help them. Miss Wilson told them the boiler man was suspected and that she understood they had interviewed him. She was uncertain of what had happened, as the police had not been in contact with her.

In the meantime, the kitchen girls were stoking the boiler and Miss Wilson said they kept the water boiling hot. Miss Jacob-Smith suggested that this was because of the excessive use of fuel. She could not see that Miss Wilson had helped matters by breaking down the boiler door, as no one could say whether or not the coal had been used on the boiler or taken home.

Mrs McLeod said that sun tan lotion had been sent instead of Ponds Excel and new chairs were badly needed. The new bunks had arrived and, in general, the hostel was running smoothly.

10/4/47 Mrs McLeod was feeling better after spending time in hospital. She had also spent Easter in bed at the hostel. Mrs McLeod thought one of the domestics was an odd shape and she felt that she may have to leave soon. Nine days later Nellie had fallen off her bike and was in hospital with stitch in her head. The doctor had confirmed Mrs McLeod's suspicions and told her that the girl was seven months pregnant. She was unlikely to return. Another girl had a rash and was not be allowed to mix with the others.

Mrs McLeod was very short staffed and asked if anyone was available, then the WLA should please send them to Easingwold.

24/4/47 Miss Jacob-Smith had exchanged oilskins for macs. Mrs McLeod was anxious to get the decorating of the hostel done. If she supplied the distemper herself, she asked would the Ministry of Works do the work? She had done so while Warden at Crayke. Mrs McLeod was also asking about a rise, as she had been working in the hostels for three years but got little more than someone who was starting out.

Several girls were ill. Orders were made for stockings, a pullover and shoes.

1/5/47 Mrs McLeod phoned to ask for a girl at the hostel to be moved. She had come in at 1.00 am the previous night and she had always had a reputation for fraternising with soldiers as there was a camp next door. Mrs McLeod has had no trouble for some time and does not want the girls unsettled by this, but she said they were always objecting to that girl's goings on. Can she be transferred, she asked? However, her farm boss gave the girl a good report.

The hostel seemed satisfactory to Miss Jacob-Smith. Two of the staff had left that week but had now been replaced. The Ministry of Works had been to see the drainage. A whist drive was organised in aid of the National Farmers' Union Food Relief Fund.

4/5/47 New chairs had arrived at the hostel, but the linoleum had not yet been laid. The Ministry of Works needed to be reminded of this.

9/5/47 Mrs McLeod was very upset about the 30s wages to be paid to the new girl, who was only sixteen. Another girl, aged sixteen and a half, who had been at the hostel for eighteen months and was excellent, was getting only 29s. Could her wage be increased, she asked?

Mrs McLeod requested to take her holiday on the week commencing 2 June. She hoped the WLA would send Miss Wilson from Stockton, but Miss Jacob-Smith decided not to, as she felt Miss Wilson might upset the boiler man again! Miss Spiers might go to Easingwold instead, she thought.

Repairs were needed to the outbuilding door, chairs and the top of the kitchen stove. Grids were required for the drains and the gate and fence needed mending. Mrs McLeod was upset about the removal of a girl from the hostel. She felt that the Forewoman had been hard on the girl, who had not been in any bother except for the suitcase episode some months ago.

Mrs McLeod was perturbed to find that Miss Jacob-Smith and the WLA Office had been worried when she was away from the hostel on two successive days. On Thursday, she had been at the chiropodist in York and on the Wednesday she had needed to attend to some family business. Miss Jacob-Smith did not find out any more about what that might have been.

15/6/47 A girl came to the WLA Office and bought some second-hand stockings. This had caused antagonism, since there was a long waiting list for stockings.

16/5/47 A girl returned dungarees on 9/5/47 and had not received the replacement.

2/6/47 An Easingwold girl who had been working before she joined the WLA had her card stamped with a greater value than it should have been, and Miss Jacob-Smith asked the WLA Office to please investigate this?

Miss Spiers was to come on Saturday, 31 June, so Mrs McLeod could hand over to her before leaving on 2 June. Mrs McLeod wanted to see Miss Spiers on her return and suggested that she stayed until the following week. The Forewoman had not been well and so she had gone home. It was believed that she might benefit from 'Restbreak', a WLA holiday hotel/hostel usually at Torquay or Llandudno for Land Girls who had been ill.

26/6/47 Mrs McLeod thought that the food situation at the hostel could deteriorate during the next winter. She was therefore buying in food that was not rationed and tins of soup. These would appear in the bills over the next two to three months, she warned.

Two girls had both been at Easingwold for some time, five years at least. They were both tractor drivers and both would claim their release that autumn. Both of them said they would like to do the harvest, when they would be driving tractors, not doing contractors' work. They would be working many hours extra overtime and Miss Jacob-Smith asked them if they would like to go to Restbreak after the harvest, but they felt a break before the six weeks of really hard work would be better.

Mrs McLeod wanted to claim for her holiday fare, totalling £2 12s 6d from York to Glasgow.

7/7/47 Mrs McLeod had been away on holiday and in her absence Mrs Spiers had acted as a relief warden. All the girls were pleased to have Mrs Spiers back again, as she was certainly a popular warden. A whist drive was to be held the next week for the Flood Disaster Fund and another was to be held in aid of the local Children's Hospital.

28/8/47 The Orderly nearly cut off her finger in the bread machine and had hysterics. Miss Wilson fainted at the sight of blood, but Mrs Spiers coped well.

The Assistant Warden had given in her notice. The Warden could do more for the recreation, Miss Jacob-Smith felt, however the girls were invited to the camp for dances and the cinema.

11/9/47 An ill Land Girl was no better. She had suffered two hysterical attacks that week, as well as acute pains in the head and an attack of dizziness. When she felt an attack coming on, she could not bear to hear anyone speaking and wanted to pull her hair round her throat. A bad shoulder had apparently started it. She was recommended to see a psychologist at York Hospital.

11/11/47 Mrs McLeod and the girls wanted to keep a pig and they wanted to know if the Ministry of Works would provide a building that could be used to house one.

29/11/47 There were complaints about one of the girls, who had been swearing continuously.

31/1/48 Miss Spiers was to act as a relief warden again. The new Assistant Warden seemed to be the most promising for some time.

31/2/48 Miss Mitchinson settled in, with the help of Miss Ackroyd. The hostel was running smoothly.

All the hostels were short of cups and if a new girl came to Easingwold there would be no cup for her, Miss Jacob-Smith warned the WLA Office! A uniform policy on cups in all hostels was needed, she noted.

2/4/48 One of the Easingwold Land Girls had appeared in court, where she was fined 10s and 10s 6d costs and told not to do such a silly thing again. There were six railwaymen in court, a detective from Walsall, a policeman from Easingwold, the ticket inspector and the man who issued the railway ticket.

The hostel was running smoothly, nevertheless. One Land Girl's head was dirty but Miss Mitchinson took steps to clean it up. A girl had signed out but she had not been at the dance with the other girls. Miss Mitchinson had counted in eighteen that night but there were nineteen on Sunday. The girl had entered by the window, as she had been with her boyfriend, who was at the Police Training School. The hostel was charged £4 10d for lost library books from July to September.

25/4/48 A dance at the hostel had been a great success.

6/5/48 Miss Jacob-Smith took a supply of Ryvita to the hostel. Miss Mitchinson felt she had been hard on Miss Wilson and admitted she was not lazy. She told Miss Jacob-Smith that the Forewoman was unpopular with the girls. Miss Jacob-Smith spoke to the Forewoman, who said she was thinking of asking for a transfer. She could not get on with Miss Mitchinson, as she was always bad tempered with her. She said the girls disliked Miss Mitchinson, as she did not give any reasons for making rules. For example, the late nights were just put on the noticeboard, with no indication as to why there had been changes. They complained to her, rather than Miss Mitchinson, as she was so bad-tempered. Everyone appeared to be cross with each other.

20/5/48 The trip to the Speedway at Middlesbrough had gone well. There was to be a dance in the hostel the next week.

30/6/48 Miss Mitchinson was proving to be a very good Warden, Miss Jacob-Smith decided, and Miss Wilson, the Assistant Warden, also appeared to be settling in. The boiler man had left but as yet he had not been replaced.

22/7/48 Miss Mitchinson told Miss Jacob-Smith that the girls had too many late nights.

31/7/48 The hostel's Ryvita supply was delivered. Miss Spiers took Miss Mitchinson's place, whilst she was on holiday.

28/8/48 The hostel was well-kept and clean on Miss Jacob-Smith's visit, especially the kitchen. The domestic staff seemed good too. The Assistant Warden had given in her notice. The Warden could do more for the recreation of the girls, but the girls were invited to the RAF camp dances.

5/9/48 Miss Jacob-Smith told Miss Mitchinson about the prospective closure of the hostel. She wanted some cloth to cover the quilts sent from Canada. She also thought an electric kettle was needed for the kitchens of all the hostels. If there was a case of illness, then hot water would be required. It took twenty minutes to boil a kettle on top of the current electric stove.

1/10/48 Miss Mitchinson wanted extra wardrobes, as there were thirty-five girls and they nearly all shared a wardrobe. She needed extra help to give the dormitory a really good clean and wanted to know how much should she pay for this. The hostel staff seemed very happy. Mrs Mitchinson was by herself a lot and seemed a little unsettled, though. The hostel was in a good state. A successful dance had been held at the beginning of the month. Nothing else had been arranged, as the girls were working most nights.

14/10/48 The piano needed tuning. One of the hostel domestics was being investigated by Mrs Bottomley of the Welfare Office. Miss Spiers thought the domestic had been behaving badly, as she had difficulty in getting her to come in at night. Miss Spiers had had to go out and tell the woman's boyfriend that if he did not let her come in at night, then she would be locked out. On another evening, she had borrowed 3s 6d from Miss Spiers, so that she might go to York by bus. Miss Spiers thought she only went as far as the local pub, however! Miss Spiers thought the woman would be better kept apart from her boyfriend and perhaps she should go to Stockton House, if the Cook agreed.

10/11/48 Miss Spiers was acting as Relief Warden at the hostel. A successful dance was held. Some of the girls also attended the Symphony Concert with funds from the Welfare Grant.

13/11/48 Miss Spiers would like another daily at the hostel, Miss Jacob-Smith noted. The library books had not been changed for three months. The water in the fire buckets was dirty.

21/11/48 On the night of the dance, on 14 November, a girl went to the pub and had too much to drink. Miss Spiers spoke to her the next day and told her that she was horrified by her behaviour and if it occurred again she would be transferred.

11/12/48 A girl was sent home with a cracked elbow after falling from a horse.
The hostel was in a good state and the staff was satisfactory. The Cook was to leave the next week. Mrs Robinson had come to the hostel to take over from Miss Mitchinson, who would be leaving at Christmas. Miss Mitchinson had looked after the hostel well and succeeded with the catering but she had been poor in arranging social activities, Miss Jacob-Smith judged. A Christmas party and a trip to the pantomime were arranged.
Mrs Robinson said the hostel was very nice but she seemed surprised by the rumours that the hostel might be closing soon. Miss Mitchinson and Mrs Robinson were to do the cooking. The girls did not know Miss Mitchinson was leaving yet.

14/12/48 Mrs Robinson and Miss Mitchinson were cleaning the recreation room themselves, owing to staff shortage. Miss Mitchinson was more cheerful with company. She had not got another job but said she would like to stay with the WLA, though not at Easingwold. Miss Mitchinson felt she had had a bad start by being an Assistant Warden under Miss Spiers and Miss Holroyd. It would have been better to be in charge from the outset, she thought. Miss Jacob-Smith suggested that she should apply to Northumberland.

31/12/48 The mats at the hostel were worn. An orderly had been off ill for a week and this had made the remaining staff tired. Miss Michinson had left. A

Christmas dinner was held on 20 December and it was much appreciated by the girls, who also had many social events at the camps.

Mrs Robinson had settled in but said she found the hostel a bit lonely. She had been changing wardrobes and chests of drawers to make decorating easier. She had also done an inventory.

Miss Jacob-Smith announced that Easingwold must close and the girls had to be away by 24 January. The men from the former WLA hostel Alne Hall were to go to Easingwold.

15/1/49 Most of the girls were to go to the new hostel at Croft. One girl went to Leeming Bar Hostel for two weeks and another to Stockton House.

One Land Girl, who had been six years at Easingwold and was older and sensible, not going out much, was to be put in charge of a hut at Croft.

21/1/49 The hostel Cook and Orderly were to go to Croft with most of the Land Girls. The WAEC needed to take the girls' luggage to Croft. They could not get all their luggage into suitcases and so needed some kit boxes.

25/1/49 The hostel was to hold a farewell dance and there was a request that the WLA Welfare Fund should help towards the cost of the band.

Twenty-six girls were now to go Croft and three to Stockton House.

29/1/49 As regards the girls going to Croft, Miss Jacob-Smith wondered if the hostel would be ready for them. Mr Roberts had requested that two painters should live in the hut, as the painting was not completed, nor the electrics, and they still had to paint the concrete huts. Small kit bags were needed for the girls' belongings.

3/2/49 The hostel was unsettled owing to change of Warden and the uncertainty surrounding the closure. There was still a Christmas Dance, though. A domestic who had worked at the hostel for years left to go into private domestic work. Miss Jacob-Smith also wrote about some of the girls being transferred.

One of the girls at Easingwold had previously lived in the West Riding and she was admitted to WLA after spending six months as an orderly at Stockton House. She was reportedly quite good for six months but then asked for a transfer to Retford, where her boyfriend was stationed. She only stayed for a week and eventually she came back to Easingwold saying she had been married and wanted her release. Miss Jacob-Smith told her this was not possible, unless she had a house and was looking after her husband. The girl claimed her husband was going abroad and her sister, aged fifteen, was to live with her.

Miss Jacob-Smith insisted on getting an address from her, so the WLA Office might investigate. An address was given and, before the Welfare Department could investigate, she had gone missing again. She eventually came into the Office and confessed she had made it all up. The WLA agreed to give her another chance and since then she had been no bother.

Miss Jacob-Smith gave her verdict on some of the other Land Girls. 'Girl no 1' she said was 'a bit rough' but honest and willing and she had been four years at Easingwold. 'Girl no 2' was said to be untidy and dirty (mice had been found in her kit box, living on old bread she had left in the box). She had been a poor worker. 'Girl no 3' was supposed to be a good type when she enrolled, but had started to come back into the hostel through the window late at night in her first week. However, she had not been much better since and had proved a poor worker and disgruntled some of the time.

'Girl no 4' was described as very glamorous. 'Girl no 5' was also thought to be very glamorous but inclined to grumble. She had got drunk at the party given for Miss Spiers, but it was her twenty-first birthday. 'Girl no 6' could be relied upon to be on the hostel committee. 'Girl no 7' always looked pale and had been off sick but was always grateful for anything done for her. She came from a poor home and her father had Parkinson's disease and so she only worked for short periods. She had an illegitimate child, which her mother cared for. The father was an Italian prisoner of war. The WLA had been told about the child when she was interviewed.

Easingwold closed on 4 February 1949 and the girls were transferred to Croft.

CHAPTER EIGHT

Thirsk Hostel

Many of the following details were recalled by Edna Dancy, a former Land Girl at Thirsk Hostel:

THIRSK HOSTEL OPENED IN OCTOBER 1942 and was probably attached to a mid-Victorian villa called Stoneybrough, situated on the Stockton Road. It was used for several enterprises after the Women's Land Army left and was once an egg factory.

According to Edna Dancy, who was stationed at Thirsk, the hostel was situated some distance from huts in which soldiers were stationed. Edna commented that they were a 'blooming nuisance', as they were always pestering the young Land Girls. (Moore, 2004.) The Warden at the hostel was Mrs Keep, who had a 'daft' boxer dog as a pet.

Girls outside the Thirsk Hostel. (*Murton Farming Museum*)

The hostel consisted of one large room, which was the dormitory, with two further rooms and the Warden's rooms. There were also bathrooms and a dining room. The hut was heated by coke stoves but it always seemed cold! The girls were expected to help in the kitchen and do their own laundry. A mangle was provided and one day a girl decided to dry her hair in it. Her hair became entangled in the machine and had to be cut.

Edna was issued with two pairs of overalls: one to wear and one to put in the wash. Reveille was at 6.00 am. In the beginning an agricultural van would pick them up and take them to the outlying farms, but later they were issued with bicycles with a lunch box strapped on the back. At one farm Edna was invited to sit with the men and the farmer and his wife, but when they took out their false teeth and laid them on the table she fled in disgust. On another occasion, a farm worker put a litter of mice in her pocket and she screamed.

Normally, they worked five and a half days a week and finished at 5.00 pm. In their spare time, when not too tired, they went to the YWCA in Castlegate, where chocolate could be purchased and magazines and comics could be read. Sometimes she would go home to Middlesbrough or work at the farm. As money was short, there was only an occasional visit to the cinema. Edna spent her money on mending materials, soap and the odd treat. One of her pleasures was attending the local church, All Saints, and participating in all the church had to offer. The girls also visited the White Horse Pub, on the corner of Stammergate and Long Street. The girls had a game of darts there and put a notice on the door 'No men allowed'. The landlady was not pleased.

(The following record has been compiled from eighty of the duplicate books written by Miss Jacob-Smith. To protect personal information about individual Land Girls their names have been omitted. The notes have been transferred into the past tense for the ease of reading and, where appropriate, to clarify a statement the author has added an explanation in brackets. Each entry was punctuated with notes about Miss Jacob-Smith's visits to individual farms and other hostels. Some of the more mundane comments about ordering uniform, travel warrants and other miscellaneous details have not been included.

Where there is a gap in the chronology, Miss Jacob-Smith has probably used another representative to make the visits.

An account of Thirsk Hostel, given by Joan Lund, appears in Chapter Nine. There is also some information on this hostel in Chapter Three.)

October 1943 Thirsk Hostel celebrated its first birthday with a social. The programme consisted of a concert by Joan and Joy Davies and members of the

Forces, followed by a delicious supper and then dancing. The whole evening was organised by Mr and Mrs Davies the Wardens. Everyone realised how hard they had worked to make such a success.

1944 The Thirsk Land Girls took part in two parades and the first was a particular success, as the girls from the hostel were congratulated by the Colonel who took the salute on their smartness at the 'Salute the Soldier Parade'. In view of the many criticisms made of the ways in which the WLA members sometimes wore their uniforms, those congratulations were most appreciated. The girls also organised a dance for 'Salute the Soldier' week, raising £16.

Miss Jacob-Smith started her account of Thirsk Hostel in August 1945.

12/8/45 One girl went home for the week but she was now ill in bed and expected to return to the hostel very shortly. Miss Jacob-Smith was asked to keep a constant eye on her. The girl's British boyfriend had returned from abroad after two years, but he had returned fourteen days later than she said he would. He had recently sent her £15, but this may have been before he knew she had had a baby. The day he arrived in England he telephoned her, but she had heard nothing since.

Before her boyfriend came home, the Land Girl had said the father of her baby was a Canadian and that he intended to get a divorce and would marry her. However, when her British boyfriend said he would marry her, the Canadian's divorce was not mentioned. The Canadian had been on leave and he returned at the end of that week, when perhaps the divorce question could be raised again.

October 1945 A farmer who employed Land Girls from this hostel was so impressed with the Thirsk Hostel girls' work that he offered prizes for the best performance over a period of six months. These awards caused much discussion as to which girls should get them, as so many deserved them. First prize went to Edna Goode, with the second prize going to Tilly Emms, and third prize was divided between Lily Dunn, Nan Broadhurst, Kay Davison, Mary Lee and Vera Taylor.

May 1946 Miss Jacob-Smith was glad that there had been so many entries to the WLA Handicrafts Exhibition held at the hostel, and that so many people had come to see the exhibition. Those who came had been pleasantly surprised by what they saw. When it was planned, no one had envisaged the quantity or the standard later received. Mrs Thompson of Escrick was the judge and she said how impressed she was with the exhibits. The Thirsk Warden Mrs Keep and her Assistant Mrs Boddy, had worked extremely hard to make the exhibition a success and all were indebted to them. The prizes were provided from the WLA Welfare Fund.

October 1946 The hostel girls went to Scarborough on an organised trip one fine Sunday.

3/10/46 Mrs Keep asked about the wages for the new Orderly. Miss Jacob-Smith said 37s 6d and the Warden also enquired whether anything could be done about getting six more quilts, now that numbers were increasing? An orderly had to go to Leeds for treatment on 8/10/46. Could accommodation be arranged in another hostel near Leeds, Miss Jacob-Smith asked the WLA Office?

A girl from Thirsk went home for the weekend. She has not returned and from remarks made by other girls it seemed that she did not intend to come back.

10/10/46 Mrs Keep telephoned Miss Jacob-Smith about one of the Land Girls at Thirsk. For the last two weeks she had taken time off work to go for treatment for an ear condition. There was no medical certificate or any other evidence, however, and Mrs Keep wondered if the treatment was really necessary. Miss Jacob-Smith visited the girl's mother, who said she had had the problem for a long time. She did not mention this when the WLA interviewed her. She took the girl to the local doctor, who said he could treat her and save her going to the hospital and having a day off work.

Judging at a handicraft competition. (*Eden Camp Collection*)

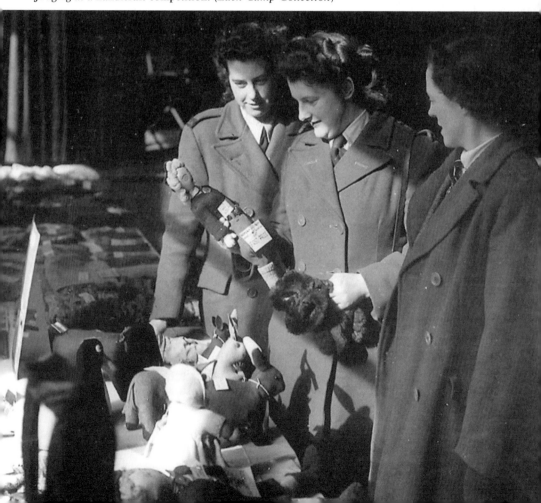

Mrs Keep (centre) with Joey and the cook (left). (*Joan Nicholson Collection*)

14/10/46 Mrs Keep agreed about using a Land Girl as an orderly and questioned how much to pay her. She still had to pay for her billet and would stay overnight at the hostel. Mrs Keep looked really ill and tired, Miss Jacob-Smith thought, although she did not complain. Miss Jacob-Smith hoped that the hostel would retain her until it closed.

17/10/46 Dorothy, a Relief Warden had gone home to look after her mother who was ill, so the arrangement for her to come to the hostel in Mrs Keep's absence would not materialise. Mrs Keep was to notify the WLA Office as soon as she heard anything from Dorothy.

22/10/46 A Thirsk Orderly was to be married on 8 December to a soldier she had met just three weeks earlier. If she left Mrs Keep would need a replacement. Three girls had been summoned for riding their bicycles the wrong way down a one-way street and they had to go to court on the Monday following.

5/11/46 The recently married Orderly was leaving and so Mrs Keep wanted to know if she could have a replacement? A Domestic at the hostel had been off ill for ten days and Mrs Keep thought she might be off for some time. The Cook had a boyfriend who lived in Scotland and she wanted her leave extended to seven days, from 30 December, and hoped it would be convenient.

Mrs Keep was feeling better for her holiday. Her husband would get his leave at Christmas for about for two weeks and she asked if there was any objection to him staying at the hostel? He would pay and Mrs Keep would continue her hostel duties. Various orders were made for Christmas cards combs, slipper socks and stockings.

8/11/46 Mrs Keep was delighted to hear about a new domestic. What wages should she be given, she asked, as the woman was not in the WLA Orderly Corps? She was to receive £2 a week, although Mrs Keep felt that other staff would be annoyed, as the other domestics and orderlies got £1 17s 6d. Mrs Keep wanted to increase the Assistant Cook's wage to £2, as she was excellent.

11/11/46 Mrs Keep was worried about the rations at the hostel, particularly meat. Miss Jacob-Smith told her she must take it up with the Ministry of Food and explain that they were entitled to more under Category A, because they were agricultural workers.

One of the orderlies did not like being in the kitchen. Miss Jacob-Smith told her she must stay but if they ever had a spare orderly, then the WLA Office might consider allowing her to go on the land instead. She was a strong girl and would be able to do farm work.

Miss Jacob-Smith found Mrs Keep in bed with a bad headache and she said she had suffered with them a lot recently. She had been to the Doctor and he was referring her to the oculist. She would like leave for 26 October to 1 November, as her child would have a holiday then and she had not been away for a long time. Mrs Spiers could not come to stand in, as she would be at Easingwold. The Cook could manage everything in the kitchen, as she had managed when Mrs Keep had time off before. It was suggested that Relief Warden Dorothy Morton might come and sleep at the hostel and have her evening meal there so that the Cook would have some support. At present all the girls were well behaved and there was no trouble about coming in.

Miss Spiers had thought the Thirsk staff very reliable when she was there, apart from the new Orderly, as they had all been there a considerable time. The other alternative temporary warden would be Miss Wilson, the Assistant Warden at Stockton. Miss Rabjohn, the Stockton Warden might be difficult about allowing her to go to Thirsk, Miss Jacob-Smith thought.

30/11/46 As usual, the hostel was well run and very clean. A hostel birthday party was held on the anniversary of the opening of the hostel.

16/12/46 Only eight girls would return for Boxing Day. Some of these had leave due but preferred not to take it. Mrs Keep would not get back in time and asked would it be all right if the Cook and Forewoman could sleep in the hostel for one night and be left in charge of eight girls. This was the only way Mrs Keep could spend Christmas at home, so Miss Jacob-Smith agreed. The Cook was quite reliable. The hostel Orderly who helped with the cooking, anticipated being married in February and the Cook also planned to marry in July. Miss Jacob-Smith wondered if it would be a good idea to send a girl from Dishforth, who wanted to cook, over to Thirsk. She could take the Orderly's place and subsequently the Cook's, if sufficient food was available.

1/1/47 A woman had called at hostel and asked if there was a vacancy at Thirsk for hostel staff and, if so, could she be considered. Mrs Keep would like to have her when there is a vacancy. Would this be possible if the girl signed on for a year?

136

9/1/47 Please could someone send a price list for second-hand uniform to the hostel for the notice board, Miss Jacob-Smith asked? The previous list had disappeared.

13/1/47 This girl who did the dairy work never went off at weekends. She had only just had her 1945 Christmas leave and cannot see how she could have her state paid holiday for some time yet. Was there any limit as to when she must take this holiday, Miss Jacob-Smith asked? Could she be paid her holiday money and be paid to work at the same time?

A girl said she had returned some dungarees as they were too large and she had requested some taller and narrower but these were never sent. She required some waterproof trousers also. Miss Jacob-Smith took an order for shampoos, forty-eight combs and twelve tooth brushes. A member of staff wanted to buy two pairs of dungarees if she was allowed to do so.

One of the Thirsk Land Girls said she could not live with the other hostel girls. She obviously considered herself to be superior to them and would not work with the others. Instead of attending the Christmas dance last week, she had gone to bed. Miss Jacob-Smith suggested to her that she should live on a farm, but the girl thought that would be worse and she wanted to return to the WAAF. Miss Jacob-Smith told her it was impossible and that she must stay in the WLA. She agreed that a smaller billet of girls might be better, say at Scarborough, if the girl would do her best to settle down. The Forewoman said she was a good worker, provided she was sent to a better kind of farmer. She would never settle in Thirsk Hostel, Miss Jacob-Smith concluded.

2/2/47 The hostel continued to run satisfactorily. This was largely to do with the Warden Mrs Keep, who looked after the staff and girls very well. There had been a little pilfering lately but it was hoped that the girl responsible had now left the hostel.

4/2/47 A girl had left the hostel when she received a medical certificate to see a specialist about her eyesight. She had previously had trouble with her eyes but she had never mentioned it to Mrs Keep and did not mention an operation when leaving. Mrs Keep had been thinking of asking for her to be moved, as she was thought to be too friendly with another girl. Mrs Browne also noticed this and agreed with Mrs Keep. She thought it might be a good opportunity to move her to another hostel when she came back. The daily woman had returned, so another orderly was not required. Orders were made for slipper socks and stockings.

21/2/47 A girl was to see a psychologist about bed-wetting. It was suggested to her that she was going to see a doctor and no more. Miss Jacob-Smith thought it right that the girl remained in the hostel, where the girls knew her and where she was happy.

24/2/47 An orderly required green boots for going to the boiler room and outbuildings at the hostel.

25/2/47 The girls complained about the poor quality of towels compared with those from Southalls, a manufacturer of linen.

The Prisoner of War Concert Party was supposed to be very good, and they had recently toured the men's hostels. The girls would like to see the concert so if they invited the POW Concert Party would the WLA Office approve?

1/3/47 A girl wanted to use an auto cycle for her milk recording job and wanted some help to purchase it.

6/3/47 Things appeared satisfactory at the hostel. Mrs Browne gave her third lecture, which proved to be the most popular yet and the girls really enjoyed it.

8/3/47 The drains were badly blocked and Mrs Keep had asked the contractors to do something about it. The job took three days. The bed-wetting girl was no better and Miss Jacob-Smith asked the WLA Office to please hurry to arrange an appointment with the psychologist. There was a complaint about the quality of pullovers, which were being sent with frayed cuffs.

Gum boots were returned, as size five was sent instead of seven. There was a query about some dungarees and some leggings which had been ordered but never arrived. Two girls had received hospital treatment but had not been sent a bill.

11/3/47 One of the girls was still waiting for her dungarees and a milking coat which she had ordered. The Cook was to receive a pay rise of 2s 6d per week. All the other staff had had a rise except her and it was feared that if a pay rise had not been given she may have sought another job.

There were twenty-six girls now at the hostel and more were coming. It might be a good idea, Miss Jacob-Smith thought, to put any new girls into this hostel rather than other hostels. However, there was a problem about a girl becoming too 'friendly' with another girl whose best friend was away.

18/3/47 Another girl had been ill for some time and so was to receive her formal notice from the WASC. A Land Girl's boyfriend had returned from abroad and she had asked for leave, but had been given six days when only due one and a half days. She said she would take fourteen days at least! A hostel orderly was thinking of asking for her release, so Mrs Keep would need another orderly.

26/3/47 Mrs Keep was still anxious that something should be done for the girl who was wetting the bed. Another girl was also in hospital with a septic foot. The doctor had told her to rest but instead she wanted to work on Saturdays and Sundays. She was an excellent worker.

28/3/47 Everything was satisfactory. There was some back-up with the drains but they had now been cleared out. More hostel orderlies were required to replace the two claiming release.

1/4/47 Miss Jacob-Smith collected a girl from hospital after a week at home. A new orderly has settled in. Twenty-four coconut mats and a mat for Warden's room were delivered.

19/4/47 Mrs Keep was planning holiday dates but not before August, probably in October. The Land Girls would like a new alarm clock as the present one was impossible to repair.

16/4/47 Mrs Keep rang to say that one of the girls has had an attack, the first since coming to the hostel and she was taking her to see the doctor.

21/4/47 The Cook was to have a week's holiday in August. A girl had been off with fibrosis. Could she be visited by the WLA, Miss Jacob-Smith asked?

22/4/47 Mrs Keep said one of the girls had been released two weeks ago, as she was pregnant. The father was not married but he was said to have fathered a baby somewhere in Germany. Could Mrs Bottomley call to see her in Middlesbrough, Miss Jacob-Smith requested?

1/5/47 Everything seemed satisfactory. There was some damage but the Ministry of Works would repair it.

6/5/47 The Forewoman would like a more clerical job and might consider being an assistant warden. Miss Jacob-Smith saw four girls who all complained about the Forewoman, saying that she was determined to get them transferred. If the office had received any requests to the WAEC for transfers could they be investigated to see if the complaint was justified, Miss Jacob-Smith asked? Mrs Keep was not in when she visited, so Miss Jacob-Smith could not discuss the girls' complaints. A married Land Girl wanted to work in Swansea, as her husband had been demobbed and they needed the money. She did mostly field work.

9/5/47 Mrs Keep wanted her holiday from 20 June. The Forewoman would be willing to look after the hostel while Mrs Keep was away.

A girl was away with scarlet fever and she was not due any money, but Miss Jacob-Smith felt the Benefit Fund might help her. Another girl had had a temperature and a sore throat but she was better by the next morning.

13/5/47 Two girls had asked if they could have holiday pay rather than take their holiday. One of them was not sure whether she had received money from the WLA or the WAEC. Orders were made for gum boots and slipper socks. Miss Jacob-Smith collected some blankets belonging to a girl infected with scabies.

27/5/47 Mrs Lumb was liked by Mrs Keep and she should prove useful. When she arrived she did not pay the 3s taxi fare from the station. Mrs Keep had paid for it out of her own money. An external Land Girl (the author is unsure of the status of this girl) was living at the hostel this week and Mrs Keep wanted to know if she should put her name down as amongst the girls (i.e. paid for by the WAEC) or should the girl be asked to pay as a visitor? She gathered from the other wardens that they do not ask her to pay for her meals at the hostels. The Warden always asked her to pay, although she obviously objects to this.

A hostel Orderly would be seventeen in July and was determined to go on the land and leave the kitchen. Mrs Keep wondered what her position was. Some time ago, a girl from Northants had expressed the desire to work at the hostel. Should she apply to the Ministry of Labour?

27/5/47 A girl had apologised for apparently asking for two travel warrants for the same day. She had posted the first letter without a stamp and then someone told her it would not be allowed and so she wrote another. She had had no intention of using two warrants to Blackpool and apologised for the trouble.

Mrs Keep thought that the work was too much for Mrs Lumb. She got quite tired and had a rest in the afternoons, as she could not stand all day. She was very willing but was just not up to it and loved to sit down and mend. She also found the hostel noisy but she got on well with everyone. She had got a job as a housekeeper at Polam School, preparing the lunches etc. but she was prepared to stay until Mrs Keep returned from her holiday. If Mrs Keep did not go on holiday, then she would like to go as soon as possible and said she did not need paying if she was no use to the WLA.

10/6/47 Mrs Keep's husband was moving to another area from 24 June, so Mrs Keep did not know what to do about her leave, as she did not know where he would be going. His job involved staying in one place for a few days and in another for a month at a time. If he went to some impossible place, then Mrs Keep may not want her leave.

Miss Jacob-Smith explained to one of the girls thought to have been 'too friendly' with each other, that they could no longer keep her in the hostel and that she could be sent to a farm or billet instead. She suggested that the girl should approach her present farmer and that she should behave properly in future! She said she had no intention of doing anything else.

10/6/47 Miss Jacob-Smith also spoke to the other girl involved and told her unless she improved she too would have to go. She promised to do her best. Another girl was leaving her farm on 21 June and wanted to go to the WLA Restbreak at Torquay from 28 July, as a great friend of hers was going then. She deserved to go, Miss Jacob-Smith thought, as she had worked really hard at the

Girls displaying craft work in the East Riding. (*Eden Camp Collection*)

dairy farm. She would like her release too, as she wished to return to her previous job with the *Yorkshire Post*. Miss Jacob-Smith thought that she should be allowed to go, as she needed a break before returning to an office job. She had done more than any girl for the WLA and the North Riding, as she had helped with everything and had raised a great deal of cash for the Benevolent Fund. She had never had any time off for sickness in five years.

10/6/47 A girl who worked in the kitchen at the hostel wanted to join the WLA when she was seventeen on 12 July. She said she would like to be in place immediately after that date. She did not mind being posted to a farm or a hostel but would prefer it not to be Thirsk.

13/6/47 Mrs Keep wanted to know if she could claim for her railway fare to her home last year. Mrs Keep would like her salary cheque before going away.

13/6/47 Mrs Keep told Miss Jacob-Smith that the bed-wetting girl was still suffering from her complaint. Miss Jacob-Smith spoke to the girl and told her she would have to leave on 28/6/47 or be released if this could be arranged. She admitted that before joining the WLA she had received hospital treatment and had appeared to be cured. She thought she would go back to her own doctor. If she was cured again, Miss Jacob-Smith promised that if she could produce the medical certificate to that effect, in about six months' time, the WLA Office might consider reinstating her.

The Forewoman would like to sign up for another year; she said she had not received anything from the WLA Office.

3/7/47 The Assistant Cook was to be married on 9 August. The Cook had several boyfriends and Mrs Keep thought she should decide which one she was going on holiday with!

4/7/47 Mrs Keep said she would like to take her leave on 16-23 July and wanted Miss Spiers to be asked to go to Thirsk on 14 July. She wanted to claim a small amount of white paint and dark green so that it could be mixed.

7/7/47 Mrs Keep wanted to know if she could employ a relief cook for one week, as she had done last year, and pay her the same amount. Three thermos flasks were required.

Mrs Keep had been away on holiday and in her absence Mrs Lumb had managed very well indeed. Both staff and girls were very sorry that Mrs Lumb decided not to remain in the hostel, as they all liked her immensely. The hostel was still well kept, especially the dormitory.

15/7/47 The small sister of a hostel girl had taken her clothes away. Another girl had been sent home with a suspected gastric ulcer. A girl was questioned by police about a theft at Guisborough, but the police could not find any evidence. Mrs Keep had no intention of leaving until the hostel closed, but she would like more than a month's notice if it does. Mrs Keep would like twelve quilts from Dishforth.

18/7/47 The roof was still leaking in parts, but there was a friendly and excellent atmosphere in the hostel. Recreational facilities were ample and the Warden was always organising socials and dances.

8/9/47 Mrs Keep was worried as a sheet had disappeared from the dormitory and also a blanket in the last four to five weeks. She was threatening the girls with a police search if anything else went missing. She had no suspicions about who might be taking them. The new Cook was poor, but she would keep her until after the fumigation. The fumigation had caused considerable dust around the Warden's end of the hostel and there was insufficient sleeping accommodation for all the resident staff. They also needed to buy another wireless.

11/11/47 A girl had not come in until 11.40 pm, when she should have been in at 10.00 pm one night. She had been out with a German prisoner of war. She said that they had both heard the clock strike at what they thought was 10.00 pm, not 11.00 pm!

Mrs Keep is bored of J Rigby, a WLA inspector, using the hostel telephone as she stayed in the office to use it and Mrs Keep could not get on with her office work. The telephone was constantly ringing with messages for her!

29/11/47 All seemed well at the hostel.

31/1/48 Mrs Robinson was the new Warden for Driffield and she would stay for a few days to learn from Mrs Keep. When will the clock be repaired, Mrs Keep asked?

31/2/48 The boiler man was so old that it was decided he must be given notice. Could they have an orderly instead of a boiler man, Miss Jacob-Smith asked? He was so vulnerable and not entirely satisfactory. The hostel had not been decorated for two years.

13/3/48 The WLA Handicrafts Exhibition was held at Market Weighton.

31/3/48 Mrs Keep had called in the police because the whole of the Land Girls' wages had been stolen last week. Mrs Keep suspects one of the Land Girls, as a farmer has also complained about the same girl. He did not make an official complaint, as after he had asked her to do the spring cleaning in the house when she had left several things were missing from the farm house.

23/4/48 What was the rule about travelling time to hostel, Mrs Keep asked? Thirsk girls left at 7.15 am and returned at 6.00 pm. Could they get overtime?

9/6/48 Ministry of Works officials Mr Bean and Mr Roberts had been to see Mrs Keep about removing the coke heap, as it was too much for the coke house. They thought it looked untidy. Mrs Keep had received a circular from the Ministry of Works, saying that she should get a store of coke in summer. The Ministry of Works should therefore build fuel sheds, she thought.

The Cook wanted to leave at the end of August, as she now had a house. One of the orderlies should have a rise of 3s. The roof was still leaking. Mrs Keep wanted to give her own beds to the two orderlies, as they used wooden folding beds and wooden mattresses. Could she requisition a warden's bed, that is, a bed with wooden ends?

23/6/48 The Forewoman came in at 11.15 pm on Saturday night. Mrs Keep was very cross but the girl did apologise. Miss Jacob-Smith said she would be moved if she did this again. Mrs Keep was very strict about the girls arriving back at the hostel punctually. The Thirsk staff queried closing at weekends, as Leeming Bar and Stokesley Hostels had been closed at the weekends. Originally, Leeming Bar closed every fourth weekend because the Warden Mrs Bullock was away ill. Mrs Bullock was now back but the girls still had to go home for the weekends and the hostel continued to close. They wanted to know why Thirsk could not close at weekends.

30/6/48 Thirsk was very well kept but needed decoration, which the Ministry of Works had promised to do. A film show was held and was judged most enjoyable. A Handicrafts exhibition for the North Riding was also held at the hostel. The atmosphere among the staff was good and the boiler man had been better since the threat of notice.

1/7/48 The Cook had been at the hostel for years and was anxious to move to her own home, but she would stay until end of December. She was also quite willing to train another cook. Mrs Keep continued to be excellent, but her son had failed to pass his scholarship exam and if a place near Thirsk could not be found for him, then Mrs Keep would have to leave Thirsk.

The roof had leaked badly during recent rain. The dormitory portion had been repaired but the passage between the dormitory and the ablution block was still bad and got very wet during heavy rain. A successful trip was arranged on Friday to Whitley Bay. The girls paid for the mini bus. Three of the ten girls chosen to go to the Royal Show were from Thirsk.

15/7/48 Mrs Keep telephoned Miss Jacob-Smith to say that there was friction between the girls and the Forewoman, who had admitted to Mrs Keep that she could not control the girls. She was not a good example, as she did not help in the garden and went off in the hostel van. The girls also said she locked herself in the shed with her boyfriend, so no one could use it. The Forewoman was going to see Mr Barker to ask if he could transfer some of the girls, but Miss Jacob-Smith did not think the girls were at fault.

The Forewoman was an attractive girl who lived in York and when she was at Stockton House she could not agree with the Warden, Miss Rabjohn. She had had various love affairs and told Mrs Browne about them. Mrs Browne thought she should be transferred away from her current boyfriend.

30/7/48 Mrs Robinson was in charge whilst Mrs Keep was away. She would not remain after September, when Bubwith Hostel was reopening. She told the staff that the girls at Howden Hostel were not allowed to stop in the hostel at weekends unless they had nowhere else to go. There may be some repercussions among the staff at Thirsk, Miss Jacob-Smith thought. Could something be said to Mrs Robinson about not mentioning this to the girls, especially when she went on to Stockton Hostel.

3/8/48 Mrs Robinson had settled in. The Cook thought she was getting tonsillitis again as she had had it badly before. Mrs Robinson wanted to run a hostel. The hostel garden was a disgrace and was full of weeds. Two girls were in the hostel doing nothing and the Forewoman was going to Sutton Bank. Another girl was not working, because the man who stoked the boiler could not take her to work, as his motorbike had broken down.

10/8/48 The girls had complained of being bitten at night and of things crawling on the walls but they did not know what species of bug.

13/9/48 Mrs Keep rang to say that several of the girls had returned feeling unwell and several had been violently sick but refused to stay in the dormitory and insisted on moving to the ablution block. Mrs Keep admitted that the smell in the dormitory was bad. The turnips outside the hostel had turned black. Miss Jacob-Smith thought if the hostel was fumigated then the girls should not return as soon as the day after fumigation in future.

The Orderly was now eighteen and paid National Insurance, but her wage was less than anyone else's. She had not had a rise for some time. Could her wage be made up to £2 6d? She was an excellent worker and she was always polite, Miss Jacob-Smith pointed out.

16/9/48 The Cook wanted to leave in about a month's time, possibly at the end of November. Her replacement would come from 29 September and, provided she showed promise, she could go on the WLA Cooks' course if this could be arranged. Mrs Keep needed to know her wage.

24/9/48 In the past when the van was available, the girls had been taken to the doctor and Mrs Keep went with them. Now, the journey was to be entered on a till, for the cost of the bill to be paid by the WLA Welfare Office. There seemed to be no information about this and Mrs Keep wanted to know if she could have back-dated repayments for this. The Forewoman appeared to use the van for many unnecessary journeys and Mrs Keep did not see why she should be made to pay for these if they were put down as trips to the doctor.

1/10/48 The staff appear contented. The Cook was to leave the next week and the new girl showed promise. The hostel state was good and now free from bugs. The smell of the fumigation had made several girls sick and one was in hospital for two days. A birthday party was being planned, but there had been no social activities because the girls were working overtime. A girl had had her mac stolen.

21/11/48 Mrs Keep was finding a girl difficult and thought she was a bad influence on the hostel. She was very awkward at times but she was a good worker. The cookery course would be of no use to the new Cook but Mrs Keep would like her to go for a fortnight under a good hostel cook so she could get new ideas. Miss Jacob-Smith suggested that she had tuition in November at another hostel. The Cook did not like the idea of going to elsewhere but she was told that she must! So far she was doing very well indeed.

The hostel needed 150 toilet rolls. An orderly said that when she was at the Market Weighton Hostel she had been allowed to send a pair of dungarees to the laundry each week and the WLA had paid for them. Why cannot she do this at Thirsk, she asked? The boiler man was ill with rheumatism and Mrs Keep wondered if he should still be working.

10/11/48 The Cook had finally left, having been at the hostel for four years. The roof repairs had not been done and the Warden was worried about them in view of the coming winter.

11/11/48 The WLA had flatly refused to alter the date of the closure of the hostel.

27/11/48 Mrs Keep had no money for the papers and had spent, as agreed, from the WLA Welfare money 10s, but she was owed 5s and 2s 6d for five weeks. Mrs Keep also had no flower money for the forthcoming party.

30/11/48 The hostel needed curtain repairs and, if material was provided, then the girls would make it up. A hostel birthday was held with a dance. A birthday cake was made by a Cook from a local camp.

11/12/48 Miss Jacob-Smith queried as to what had happened to the hostel's large clock which was being repaired. Could they have a loud speaker extension from the wireless to the kitchen, as indicated at the Ministry of Works conference in London? Mrs Keep needed some more notebooks. What had happened about the hostel wringer, Miss Jacob-Smith asked? Only twelve cups had been delivered and more plates were urgently needed.

14/12/48 Five girls had lost their hats. Can they use berets instead, Miss Jacob-Smith asked?

31/12/48 The hostel looked well-polished. The new Cook was satisfactory but she had found the Christmas dinner beyond her and the Warden had to do a large proportion of it. Despite this there had been an exceptional Christmas lunch on 23 December. The girls had bought presents and they were distributed by the boiler man dressed as Father Christmas. The hostel was well decorated and the Warden had arranged for a party of carol singers to come to the hostel.

3/1/49 Mrs Keep had seen the contractors about the roof repairs.

3/2/49 The roof repairs were in hand and the garden was much improved. The Cook had been on compassionate leave and the previous Cook had come to help out for a while. The Christmas dance had been a success, but the hostel was unsettled due to the impending transfer of Mrs Keep to Croft.

26/2/49 During the last month, the hostel had had three wardens. The girls and staff were unhappy about the changes. Repairs had been carried out and the girls had made great improvements in the garden.

4/3/49 One of the girls had a bad cough and her father had died of TB. A married girl needed three pairs of stockings. She was fairly fat and had split both pairs of breeches around the knees and her legs had got even bigger since she joined. Another girl had got black lead on her dungarees after cleaning the hostel stoves and she needed another pair.

Was it possible to have the pillows cleaned as the covers were stained, Miss Jacob-Smith asked? Mrs Shaw wanted the bedding that had been taken to the Croft returned, as she was short. The WEAC was to arrange transport for this. The new Cook was doing the cooking well and it was considered quite amazing that she was so good, but she did not like being on her own. The staff worked well but Mrs Shaw thought one of the orderlies was moody!

11/3/49 Mrs Shaw was still agitating about the return of the quilts from Croft. The pigswill had not been collected for ten days. The collection was erratic and all the fumes were becoming unpleasant. Mrs Shaw thought she was paying too much for potatoes and asked if the WAEC could supply them instead? It had been Mrs Shaw's birthday yesterday and the staff had given her some flowers and a birthday cake.

23/3/49 A girl had returned from compassionate leave and she now had no money and had contracted ringworm. The date had been arranged for the Harvest Festival on 2 October, at 2.30 pm or 3.00 pm.

1/4/49 A pair of gum boots had been stolen. A girl had had trouble with her feet and needed support in her shoes. The hostel was not so well kept as under Mrs Keep's care and it needed decoration. The staff worked well together and the Cook was proving most capable, in spite of being so young. No social events had been arranged but parties of girls went regularly to the dances at local camps.

Mrs Shaw seemed to have settled down well and she was very strict about the girls' appearances at meal times. She would not allow any girl to come into the dining room wearing curlers, even if covered by a scarf, and hands and faces must be washed. The girls did not seem to mind being sent back to tidy themselves before they came into meals. They were keen to talk to Mrs Shaw about their families and boyfriends.

11/4/49 It was stock-taking time at Thirsk. A small fire had occurred at the hostel and two blankets had holes burned in the middle of them. The fire was caused by a piece of cloth being picked up off the floor and put on the bed to be cleaned. The cloth had been near the dormitory stove and it must have been smouldering. Library books amounting to £1 were missing and Miss Curtis was endeavouring to find these. If she failed, then she would collect 1s from all the girls on Friday night, unless this could be paid out of hostel funds.

13/9/49 Some annoyance had been caused because Miss Robinson had left her puppy at the hostel. It was only a few weeks old and was apt to chew things up, but it was not house-trained so it took time to supervise it.

Miss Curtis had arrived safely, although she had been on the point of sending a telegraph to say that she might not come, as her dog had been killed. Could anything be done to take away surplus equipment which was getting dusty? The hostel girls were having a trip to Blackpool illuminations, costing 12s 6d a head. Seventeen girls out the twenty-one were going. The thirty-two seater bus was to be filled up with their boyfriends etc. Could anything be given towards the trip from the hostel funds? None had asked for this, so they would not be disappointed if the WLA Office refused.

8/10/49 The girls were annoyed that Miss Curtis had refused to give them supper after 10.30 pm. Miss Jacob-Smith made the comment that they were lucky to have it as late as 9.30 pm!

Surplus equipment in the hostel comprised: one hundred blankets, thirty mattresses, fifty sheets, thirty pillows.

26/11/49 The auctioneers were willing to take the hostel piano in a month's time.

* * *

Of all the hostels visited by Miss Jacob-Smith, according to her comments, Thirsk had been managed the best. It had always been clean, tidy and well-polished. The food was always of a good standard because of the continuity of the cooking staff. The Cook had been in place for over four years and she had trained her replacement, who although very young had become an excellent cook. There had been few changes in support staff, and Mrs Keep, the Warden often referred to as 'Matron', was the steady influence in the hostel. She was firm but, according to many girls, she was homely, friendly and interested in them and their friends.

It was this type of warden that the WLA sought for the hostels and many of the advertisements for future wardens cited some of these characteristics. However, many of the wardens in other hostels fell short of this ideal. Mrs Keep was chosen to run the new hostel at Croft.

CHAPTER NINE

Tales From Women's Land Army
Hostels Across Yorkshire

Alne Hall, North Yorkshire

ALNE HALL WAS ONCE A MANOR HOUSE and the present red brick building was erected in the nineteenth century, with a rear look of the seventeenth century. The staircase is eighteenth century. It is situated in the village of Alne, four miles from Easingwold and twelve miles from York. During the Second World War, twelve Land Girls supervised working holiday makers here, in what was termed 'Harvest Home'. They had to show them how to do the various farm tasks and sometimes they set such a back-breaking pace that there was little time for 'cheek' from the city folk, which was apparently not uncommon. These girls remember packed lunches of grated carrot sandwiches, baked beans in slabs of bread and the dreaded beetroot sandwiches which became soggy by lunchtime. There are no records of any visits to this hostel by Miss Jacob-Smith.

Alne Hall as it is today.

About a hundred people came for a week at a time, usually arriving by train. They were met at Alne Station by lorry. Each day, they were taken to local farms to help with jobs, which might include potato picking, harvest work or pulling flax. Armed with 'doorstep' sized sandwiches of cheese or marmite, they worked really hard and returned hungry for the basic, no frills evening meal. They ate with the Land Girls in the large dining room and socialised with each other in the lounge. They retired early to the bedrooms, each with four or five bunks. The Land Girls at Alne remembered with affection the Saturday night dances in the ballroom of the Hall, when members of the local Bomber Squadrons came to socialise. (Bradley, 2013.)

When Alne was closed by the Women's Land Army, the girls were transferred to Easingwold Hostel. The present Hall is now a Leonard Cheshire Home for the disabled.

Arkendale Hostel, North Yorkshire

Arkendale Hostel, which was open from 1944-1948, was a mile away from the village of Arkendale, near the town of Knaresborough. When Moat Hall, the WLA hostel in Ouseburn, had to be evacuated because of bomb damage the Moat Hall girls were sent for six weeks to Kirk Deighton. Then, the girls came to the isolated old mansion at Arkendale. (Beer, 1978.) On arrival, the assorted group of ex-typists, mill girls and knowledgeable town girls – twenty-six in number –

inspected the two very large bunk lined bedrooms. There were two very spacious bathrooms, where they often had a spit and polish wash, rather than the luxury of private bathing. There was a public telephone in the corridor upstairs and the noise from the girls often made the reception difficult. The floors of the entire Hall were always beautifully polished and well cared for. The Warden's bedroom was over the porch area and this was strictly private, as was the kitchen.

On wet days the kitchen, hall and back room next to the stables were used for sewing bags, just like prisoners. At these times they

Arkendale Hostel in 1947 (*Murton Farming Museum Collection*)

150

exchanged stories and frightened each other with tales about the old Hall! The garden was a private leisure place, where even their vegetable patch was overtaken by weeds and couch grass. Here the girls could write their letters home or to their boyfriends. Films were often shown in the dining area and the younger element enjoyed pounding the floor with rock and roll and jiving. Friday was the weekly night out, when the WLA driver would take them to Knaresborough, York or Harrogate. The roads were virtually empty, except for the occasional military vehicle.

The work was long and hard, however. Those working locally walked or used one of the many bicycles in the stables. The ladies' bikes soon developed punctures but those left behind by the military were great, provided they were mounted with a run and a jump to get over the crossbar. Girls who worked further away assembled in the courtyard. The old Ford V8 was cranked up by the WLA driver, who was paid one shilling a day extra. She was always the last in to the evening meal. During journeys, she demanded that the girls sit level, on both sides, so that the vehicle would not swing on the road. The girls spent their time on farms near Green Hammerton or Minskip. Some were involved with market gardening near Poppleton. (Beer, 1978.)

Postcard written by Aline Richard to her Grandmother. (*Sue Rodrigues Collection*)

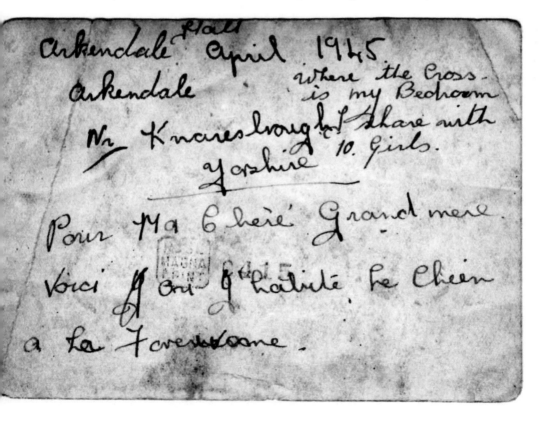

One of the Land Girls at Arkendale, Aline Richard, had been transferred from Moat Hall when it closed. She was known as 'Jersey', as she came from the island, and her story is told more fully under the Moat Hall section. Aline wrote a card to her grandmother in Jersey from Arkendale Hall, which showed a picture of the Hall. She added a cross on the photo to show which room she occupied. The postcard was never sent and is now retained by her daughter, Sue Rodrigues.

Another former Land Girl at the Hall, Peggy Bailey (née Barraclough), still lives in Arkendale. Her father, who was a policeman, was very strict and insisted that if she went to a dance she was back home by 9.00 pm. She would no sooner get to a dance than she would have to go home. She decided that she wanted more freedom, so she joined the WLA – much to her father's horror! She was first posted to Wrangle in Lincolnshire. In December 1945, she asked to be moved nearer to her home in Leeds, as her young brother was very ill. Her travel permit was given once a year and she was earning little money, so Arkendale was more convenient than Wrangle to get back to Leeds.

Peggy can still remember her journey to the hostel. On her way to Arkendale, she had met girls from Rotherham and Sheffield at the railway station in Leeds. The trains had stopped running because of 6ft snow drifts, so she took all the girls home and they slept on the settee and on the floor of her parents' sitting room.

Arkendale Hall was half a mile from the village and up a narrow lane, which in the deep snow was accessed only by the milkman and the postman. The girls had to dig through the snow to keep the lane open. One of Peggy's colleagues, Nellie Tingle, can remember walking through the snow to Boroughbridge to get supplies. Peggy recalled that they did not have any work for nearly two months because of the weather conditions. Eventually, they were sent to Acomb near York, to a market garden where they picked sprouts in the finger-biting cold. They were joined by Poles and German prisoners of war, who were 'very polite and well-mannered boys', she said.

Peggy had vivid memories of life at Arkendale, and said that her time in the Land Army was the most enjoyable period of her life. They had two baths for some thirty girls and there was not enough hot water for individual baths, so the girls would scramble for the baths and share the water with each other. There were some very shy girls who would not get undressed in front of the others. One such girl, a Jewess, was extremely shy, so the girls laughingly stripped her and put her in the bath. Afterwards, Peggy says, she was fine about bath times.

The girls loved dancing and as the Hall had polished floors they danced in their socks which, in consequence, were always wearing out. It helped keep the floors fully polished, though! Peggy was the only Land Girl who sewed, so she mended everyone's socks. The girls would go to the dances at Dishforth and Tockwith airfields. A lorry would pick the girls up at the hostel and return them afterwards. Peggy never went to these social affairs, as she had started going out with the local milkman in her first week at the hostel and he did not want her to mix with the servicemen. She married him in 1948.

The first Warden Peggy encountered at Arkendale said she did not like girls. She carried a small dog under her arm and was often heard to say, 'The more I see the girls, the more I love my dog!' One Saturday, the girls came home from work to find that there was no dinner ready. The Warden and the Assistant Warden never agreed on anything and they were having a terrible argument. One of them had a knife and they were about to fight, when one of them cut the other. Peggy was uncertain which of the two, but one of them was taken away to a mental hospital. The girls were taken to Boroughbridge to the Crown Inn for their dinner that night!

The meals at the hostel were generally good. The Cook had a sister who was in the Land Army at Arkendale and this was an added incentive for her to provide good meals. Peggy remembers making cheese and beetroot sandwiches for the packed lunches. She made her own clothes and many of the girls used to borrow them. She left the Land Army three months before her wedding, so she could get her trousseau made.

One of the wardens at Arkendale, Miss Kennedy used to trim and cut the girls' hair. She herself had the Eton Crop, a very short, fashionable cut and Peggy's boyfriend, the milkman, used to cut Miss Kennedy's hair! Peggy was once invited to tea in the Warden's room, which she says was very nice and deluxe. Peggy still organises reunions at her farmhouse near the former hostel, which is now a private house. (There was no record of a visit to this hostel by Miss Jacob-Smith.)

Askham Bryan Hostel, near York

As mentioned earlier, Askham Bryan Hostel was built in 1936, financed by the three Ridings but was not used by the Women's Land Army until 1939.

Aughton Hostel, East Yorkshire

Aughton village is seven miles north-west of Howden. The population is tiny and it has a lovely Norman church down a long country path, a little remote from the village. The church would often remain isolated when the fields around it were flooded. Aughton Hostel closed to fill vacancies in hutment extensions in other hostels. Most of the girls from Aughton went to Bubwith Hostel.

There are no records of a visit to the hostel by Miss Jacob-Smith and no one in the area today appears to know anything about the Land Army's occupation of the hostel. The present owners of the Old Hall at Aughton thought it was possible that it had been used as the hostel, but the author could find no other information, despite placing advertisements in local newspapers and visiting the village.

Balby Hostel, Doncaster, South Yorkshire

Balby was a YMCA hostel, situated in Oswin Avenue, Doncaster, and it opened in July 1942. In October 1942, there was an advertisement for an Assistant Warden for the hostel. Little information aside from this has been discovered about this hostel.

According to the news sheet sent to all WLA hostels in 1942: 'This hostel was very lucky in having Mrs Prior as its Welfare Officer. Through her, Mr Abercrombie, of Finningley offered to give lectures at the hostel, at a few hours' notice, on any day, when the weather was impossible for the girls to work. As a result of the bad weather this year, Mr Abercrombie had given three lectures. The first dealt with general matters, the second with soil and the third with clean milk. Following the last lecture twenty girls were taken to the Doncaster Cooperative Societies' Dairy and on the following day the remaining 20 girls made the tour. As a result of his talks, all the girls who will spend their time planting and picking potatoes will find their work much less uninteresting. Their backs will still ache. In addition to these lectures, Mrs Prior has given a lecture on Burma where she lived for several years. The girls were most interested in this especially now that so much is heard and read about the country in the war news.'

In *They Fought in the Fields*, Nicola Tyrer makes the point that sometimes the WLA Wardens were as unworldly as the girls and they were unable to cope with the sexual advances and teasing of the local servicemen. She relates a story told to her by Dorothy Brant, who was an official for the Northern Division of the WLA. The Warden of Balby Hostel had approached Miss Jacob-Smith about the girls' use of condoms, which she referred to as 'French letters'. She was an elderly lady who had led a sheltered life and ran the hostel on strict Christian YWCA lines. She had found all the shrubs around the hostel scattered with condoms and she was distressed about the girls. When Miss Jacob-Smith arrived at the hostel she noticed the army camps nearby and pointed out to the Warden that some of the 4,000 servicemen were taking delight in alarming her and just teasing the girls!

Beacon Garth Hostel, Hessle, East Yorkshire

Beacon Garth stands at the corner of Cliff Road and Redcliff Road in Hessle. It was mentioned by Pevsner, who said it was an impressive early twentieth century Tudor style house. It was built in the Edwardian Arts and Crafts style, of red brick with stone details, half timbering, a large mullion window and battlements.

In May 1943, Beacon Garth was requisitioned for use by the Armed Services. It was the second WLA hostel to open in a requisitioned building. The owners had a choice between the building being occupied by the army or the Women's Land Army. The management of the hostel was a co-operation between the

Beacon Garth. (*David Wright*)

YWCA and the WLA. The opening was by Lieutenant-Colonel Dunnington-Jefferson, Chairman of the East Riding Agricultural Committee. As it was in the East Riding, there was no record of Miss Jacob-Smith visiting this hostel.

The hostel accommodated about thirty girls. Gwen Marsh (née Burkitt) had been at Sherburn before she was billeted at Beacon Garth, where she was extremely happy. Her shared bedroom overlooked the River Humber. She worked at farms near South Cave and found her time in the Land Army a memorable experience. She watched the Bombers going over the Humber.

Beacon Garth was closed in 1944, to fill up existing vacancies in the hutment expansions of other hostels. Gwen then moved to Rolston Hall outside Hornsea. Rolston Hall was old but was in excellent condition and needed little doing to it, although it had been empty for three years. It could easily accommodate forty to fifty girls. It had central heating and even a swimming pool, but whether this was ever used by the girls was doubtful.

Beckwithshaw Hostel, near Harrogate, North Yorkshire

(See Moor Park.)

Blois Hall, Ripon, North Yorkshire

Blois Hall sits on an ancient site with henge monuments and ancient barrows. The house was built by John Aislabie, in about 1760, as part of the Studley estate and was associated with Fountains Abbey. John Aisabie made a tour of Europe and visited Blois Castle in the Loire Valley in France, hence the name of the Hall. The house was built at the same height as Ripon Cathedral and it is in a direct line with Ripon Cathedral and the church spire in Studley Park near Fountains Abbey. There are wonderful views from the house towards Studley, but the house is remote from the nearest villages and is approached from the road by a long drive. It would have seemed isolated to the Land Girls.

Members of the Chapman family still occupy the house at present. The family lived in the house at the beginning of the war, and then moved out about 1941. The Land Army probably occupied the house from about 1943-1945, as Miss Jacob-Smith's records for this hostel start in September 1943. Like many of the requisitioned houses, Blois Hall had numerous problems. In April 1944, Miss Jacob-Smith wrote about the lack of water in the ablution block and the upstairs water supply being out of use also. She warned that unless the Ministry of Works did something immediately, the hostel would have to close because the girls might contract scabies. In July, the roof was leaking and the Ministry of Works made plans to repair it and clean the gutters. There was a problem with mice and traps had to set around the hostel.

There were also teething troubles with the organisation of the hostel. In August, the girls complained bitterly about their packed lunches and said that the meat in them was bad. The Warden was doing the cooking, as there was no cook. Problems occurred about having milk delivered, due to Mr Chapman's labour difficulties. Milk had to be collected from the garage at Copt Hewick by the girls on their way home from work. There was a good deal of jealousy between the Warden and the Forewoman, which also had an adverse effect on the girls.

In August, there was extremely hot weather and they could not open the front windows because of the smell from the drains. Five days later the drains were inspected and repair work started.

In September, Bridget (a Cook or Orderly) came down to the kitchen and put on the oil stove and then went back to her room. When she came down again the kitchen was full of smoke and the cooker was burnt out. The wall behind the cooker was blackened and so was the ceiling. The Hall now needed a new cooker.

In October 1944, there were further problems with the water supply. The contractor from Burton Leonard said there was an overflow of water, at six gallons per minute, and that the pipes cold not stand the pressure. A permanent engine could be fitted at a cost of £100, with maintenance costs of 15s a week.

This was a considerable amount at the time. Mr Chapman, the owner of the Hall, agreed to pay the cost of installing the engine but the WLA would have to pay the 15s weekly maintenance. The work could not be started for six months though, because of the shortage of pipes.

There were complaints from the girls, because the water supply was switched off sometimes. The girls were not allowed to use the upstairs bathroom, because

Blois Hall.

the Warden said that it meant pumping water and they left it untidy. Miss Jacob-Smith insisted that the girls should use the upstairs bathroom if they so wished.

In June 1945, the girls complained that the blankets at the hostel had not been washed for two years. Miss Marshall, the Warden, assured Miss Jacob-Smith that the blankets had been washed. A month later, all water at the hostel needed to be boiled but there was no sufficiently large container to store the boiled water in. The girls refused to drink it and said it tasted queer and that it caused spots on their faces. Mr Brocklehurst, who came to investigate this complaint, said he could not see any sign of spots on their faces.

There was a sense of hopelessness amongst the girls at Blois Hall. In August 1945, the Forewoman said that six girls had refused to work, they had no interest in their work and they had many complaints. Their wireless did not always work and this was the only immediate source of entertainment in this remote hostel. They complained that the Warden did not always keep the accumulators charged up and Miss Jacob-Smith suggested a rota, so that the girls could take responsibility for the charging of their own wireless. Further complaints were made that the wireless was being used during the day by hostel staff, but this could hardly be stopped. There were additional moans about their butter rations and the lateness of some breakfasts. The farmers worked them too hard, they said, but admitted that they had not been asked to do overtime all the year. Many complained that they were not provided with drinkage (tea at breaks in the working day), and the matter was taken up with farmers by the Forewoman.

The girls at Blois just felt fed up with the WLA and did not want to work any more. On the day she visited, Miss Jacob-Smith tried to get them to turn in for work for the afternoon, so they would at least get half a day's pay, but they refused saying they would prefer to rest.

There was also a lack of entertainment in the village. A film was shown in the village hall once a week to which they were invited, but they said the seats were too hard and there were no men to go with. A hostel social was suggested but the girls said it was no good without men and most of the troops had left the area.

All the girls remained tired and dispirited and the Warden was not inspiring. Miss Jacob-Smith thought she could have done more to motivate the girls.

It was no surprise when Blois Hall closed on 31 January 1946.

Boltby Camp, near Thirsk, North Yorkshire

Boltby Camp was disbanded in 1945. It was one of the camps used by the Lumber Jills, members of the Women's Timber Corps (WTC), who worked in North Yorkshire in 1942 to 1945. The camp consisted of a series of Nissen huts in an extremely wet field. The girls slept in one hut, with a log burner in the middle. In freezing temperatures, even rain, sleet and snow, they carried out their tasks without the benefit of modern machinery. They felled trees, made pit props, measured the trees and logs, loaded the logs on to trucks and drove them. Edna Holland became a tree measurer at Boltby. She was seventeen when she went to the hostel in 1942.

The girls were picked up at 7.30 am and travelled in the back of a lorry, returning at 5.00 pm with the evening meal served at 6.30 pm. Lunch consisted of a meat or cheese sandwich and the evening meal was often stew, accompanied by lots of vegetables. Their main entertainment at the weekends was going to the dances at Thirsk. The war did not really affect the Land Girls at Boltby, except when someone they knew was injured or died. Such was the case with Edna, when she heard the sad news of her brother's death during the invasion of Italy in 1943. (*Yorkshire Post*, 8 June 2012)

Brompton Hostel, Northallerton

Brompton opened in Little Lane, Northallerton in July 1943 and closed in 1946. The first girls at this hostel were from Leeds and Selby and all were new to farming but keen to learn. The hostel accommodated twenty-five girls and five staff. There was a dining room and recreation room, kitchen, shower and slipper baths and dormitories. Although it was fifteen miles from the nearest town, the hostel provided all the facilities of a modern dwelling and had a flower and kitchen garden.

The unit ran its own dances and boyfriends were welcome. The girls had to be in by 10.20 pm and two late passes until 11.00 pm were allowed each week. Miss Audrey Barnard was the Forewoman in charge of recruitment and the girls' work. In 1944 the hostel celebrated its first birthday with a cake made and iced by hostel cook.

At Brompton Hostel the girls worked on local farms. Sometimes they would put on parties for the local schoolchildren and hold fancy dress competitions. As there was not much going on in the village, the children looked forward to these events. The children's freedom was curtailed after the soldiers were brought back from Dunkirk and billeted in the empty houses and the halls nearby. A curfew was imposed and soldiers were posted everywhere. They would challenge the locals with a "Who goes there?"

A field bakery was set up in the recreation ground, near the church hall. Lorries were parked there and on the local village greens, covered in camouflage netting. The soldiers also put on concerts in the village hall. The local children used to sit on their bunks and listen to them singing 'Please don't send away the Border Boys, we'll need them by and by', referring to the Border Regiment then billeted in the village. They must have written the song themselves.

There was also a prisoner of war camp at Stone Cross, which housed German, Italian and Ukrainian POWs. Some former prisoners married local girls and many stayed on after the war. The farmers were glad of the extra help on the farms, as most of the local young men had been called up into the forces or to serve as Bevin Boys in the mines. (Newcombe, 2013.)

During the May 1944 'Salute the Soldier week', the hostel was very busy and ran activities which included: a Beetle Drive; entertainments by the girls; an ENSA Show, a bring and buy sale, which raised £12; and a children's fancy dress party to which twenty children came and had a wonderful time. They had to be persuaded to go home at the end of the party!

In 1944 Brompton held its most ambitious event so far for the WLA Benefit Fund: a 'Harvest Home Ball', organised by a committee of WLA representatives and the girls of Brompton Hostel. It was held at Allertonshire School in Northallerton. Land Girls, farmers and members of the forces came and the figure raised was thought to be about £130. (*The Land Girl*, November 1944.)

In 1946 the hostel closed down. On 24 September 1948 Miss Jacob-Smith took Mrs Keep to see the former hostel at Brompton. The recreation room was enormous and a great improvement on the original premises. Brompton had a brick shed and a recreation room had been built in the garden. There was no indication as to why they visited, perhaps they were looking for new hostel accommodation. Subsequently, a new hostel was opened near Northallerton at Croft Airfield.

Brooklands, Selby, East Yorkshire

This hostel was open between 1943 and 1950. It was visited by Miss Jowett and has already been discussed. Further information about the hostel was given by Joyce Jenkinson (née Clarkson), who resided in the hostel from 1946 to 1950. She said that the hostel had five bedrooms with five bunks in each, sleeping ten girls to a room and there were about fifty girls in the hostel in total. Twenty girls shared each bath and toilet. The temperature in the hostel was cool, the food was

Joyce Jenkinson née Clarkson on left with friend. (*Joyce Jenkinson Collection*)

A gang of girls at Brooklands, Selby. (*Joyce Jenkinson Collection*)

Brooklands, Selby.

adequate and at night they had little time for recreation. Most of the girls went home at the weekend.

In 1947, Joyce remembers water coming down the walls and the hostel being so badly flooded that the girls were evacuated for six weeks to Pollington Hostel, fifteen miles away. Here she remembers that Wilfred Pickles, the great radio celebrity, came to entertain them. Pollington was the largest Women's Land Army hostel in the area and was located on an airfield.

Bubwith Hostel, East Yorkshire

Like many of the Land Army girls from Hull, Ivy Taylor was stationed at Bubwith, one of East Yorkshire's largest hostels. Others nearby were at Market Weighton and Muston near Filey. Ivy joined the WLA in 1944, aged eighteen. She had previously worked at the John C Mallory Hardware Store in Hull and said that the reason she left home was because she was 'always being told off'.

The girls slept in dormitories, with top and bottom bunks and four girls in each stall. The dormitories had concrete floors and an iron stove in the middle and there were ablution blocks outside. The girls in Bubwith rose at 6.20 am, ate breakfast and made sandwiches, usually of potted meat or beetroot. They were in the fields by 7.00 am and left at 5.00 pm. Their work consisted of ditching, chopping hedges and pulling sugar beet, turnips and kale.

The hostel was just down the road from the RAF base at Breighton. The girls could see the ground staff load the trailers with bombs and they watched the Lancaster and Halifax bombers going out. The girls used to count the planes back in, listening for the alphabetical call sign being called over the airfield tannoy. The airmen at Breighton provided much of the entertainment for the Land Girls by hosting dances, unless operations prevented it. The girls were out for a good time, Ivy recalls, kissing servicemen on the buses but 'doing nothing wrong'.

Breighton was a small village with little more than a pub, a shop and water pump, so the girls had to travel for entertainment. The closest large village was Howden twelve miles away, a regular venue for dances. The main attraction was York and buses were laid on to the city, where the girls were entertained by airmen at Betty's Bar and the Half Moon. They also enjoyed dances at the Guildhall.

During her time in the Land Army, Ivy started courting a Canadian serviceman called Eddie, who was based at Bubwith. Some of the Bubwith Land Girls used to sneak out of the dormitory at night and others would let them back in through the window after hours. Ivy recalled going into a plane and climbing out of the window when she had spent time with Eddie. Yet, one day Eddie never came home.

Ivy left the Land Army in 1945 with suspected heart disease. (From Archive Comment Thursday, 24 July 2008, entitled 'Honouring my Nana'.)

The hostel was closed in May 1944 and reopened in September 1948.

(There are some short notes about this hostel by Miss Jacob-Smith, as she seems to have taken over the monitoring of some additional hostels in 1950.)

3/3/50 A girl went away from the hostel at least six weeks ago and had previously been in hospital with yellow jaundice and tetanus, although the hostel doctor did suggest she might be pregnant. There was a rumour that she was to be married in June. She had ceased receiving sick pay and Miss Jacob-Smith suggested that she should be written to.

4/3/50 Miss Jacob-Smith spoke to all the girls on her visit. Feelings were running high and they were definitely annoyed at the charge of 31s board, as they were all members of the Farm Workers Union. They had written to ask the Union Secretary to come to see them. The girls admitted they did not want to leave the WLA, but they could get more money working in Hull, where there were plenty of jobs to be had, and they would only have to pay their mothers a pound for their board. Miss Jacob-Smith explained they would miss their travel warrants, WLA uniform and would also have to pay PAYE in civilian jobs. She pointed out the advantages of hostel life. If they had an offer of a good job, then she said they should go but only one girl had done anything about it.

24/4/50 It appeared that the cost of transport worked out at £1 per trip, when the large van was used. A smaller van had been used on occasions, and the cost was only 6½d per mile, but this van was no longer available. The journey to York was twenty-seven miles and was not done every week. Because of reduced numbers of girls, it was difficult to run the van for ten girls even for a good social life.

6/6/50 The decorators were busy doing up the kitchen and recreation room. It would be a great improvement but made it difficult to cook the meals. Miss Robinson thought it very hard that she had to suffer the inconvenience. They were to be turned out soon and would not have the benefit of the improvements, she complained. Miss Robinson had ample supplies of sardines and pilchards.

15/8/50 Land Girls at the hostel wanted transfers to Market Weighton and Howden and Kirk Deighton.

The hostel was used by the National Health Service until the 1990s, when it was demolished.

Cappleside Hostel, Rathmell, West Yorkshire

Cappleside was open between 1943 and 1944. One Land Girl who worked there said that it was a lovely old house. Another said that the part of the house where she slept was cold and had a scarcity of water. She had to go home to have a bath. (Bullock, 2002.)

Cappleside accommodated forty girls, but former inhabitants have said that the capacity was sixteen to twenty only. It had two dormitories, each holding between eight and ten girls, three baths, ten or twelve wash basins, six toilets and a large kitchen and recreation room. (Bullock, 2002.) The hostel was managed by the YWCA. It was a machinery hostel for WLA tractor drivers and machinery personnel, who were housed separately from general farm workers. The hostel was shut down for the winter months, as it was too remote for recruits to travel to outlying farms. It closed completely in 1944, with the nineteen girls being sent to Settle, Skipton and Holden Clough hostels.

Catterick Hostel, North Yorkshire

This hostel has been discussed earlier in Mary Tetlow's account of her time there. Mary's account mostly consists of letters written to her parents in Heaton, Bradford. Some of her first comments were that she could not believe that there was so little cupboard space in the hostel. They wore dungarees in the day and changed to frocks at night and she demanded more nice clothes from home. She noted that aeroplanes were flying overhead all the time. Her first tea at the hostel was 'lovely pieces of fish', especially saved for the Land Army, with lots of butter and jam for the bread.

For entertainment, Mary wrote, the girls often visited local houses and especially one whose residents, the Hunts, had sons in the forces and so made the Land Girls welcome. One evening's entertainment on the nearby base was a Hungarian band, with two singers. That same evening they had three slices of spam, two tablespoon of peas, two tablespoons of carrots, some beetroot and a great slice of cake for tea. There was enough left over for their suppers.

Mary was pulling cabbages one day when she was told to report to 'Rabbits'. Everyone had to do 'Rabbits' once a week. She gave thistles to the rabbits. On another occasion, she had put tea leaves and breadcrumbs into a mash for the rabbits. She threw some of it into the trough and some fell on to a rabbit and the others rushed on it and nearly smothered it. She worked from 7.45 am to 5.30 pm, with an hour for lunch. Most of the toil was simple, she thought, picking peas, lettuce and cabbage or sowing potatoes, weeding or raking stones, whilst others excelled in pushing and carrying.

In July 1943, Mary borrowed a bike and it was accidentally run over! She was uninjured and no word was said about the bike, nor was she presented with a bill. In comments to her parents, she said that only on wash night did she get her hands clean and they were permanently grey.

Mary once went to a concert given by the ATS but thought it was a dreadful failure, except for the pianist, so she went to a beginners' ballroom dancing class

164

instead. This was held in a small room at the back of the YWCA. An airman demonstrated the steps and the men stood in a row and then the girls followed suit. A batman, Harry, whom she described as 'clean as a new pin', with a rosy face, kept laughing at his mistakes and persevered.

Her immediate neighbours in the hostel were Kathleen who liked reading, Doreen who was the manager of a town shop and appreciated clothes and Dorothy who was fond of horse riding. They all appeared keen on music and listened on the wireless to the Symphony on Saturday afternoons. When they visited the Hunts, one evening, Mrs Hunt was listening to a concert. Doreen often tried to get the Forces Programme on the wireless, as she wanted to listen to an orchestra. The set seemed strange, for if anyone passed by, the music faded and they could hear voices apparently speaking German and French.

Mary and her friend Amy often walked to Richmond along the river and later bought steak and chips at the NAAFI canteen. The canteen sold everything, papers, soap, toothpaste, and lots of necessary items. It was just like a family shop at home, she thought. The next day they celebrated a birthday with a 'Poor Man's Bun', which was a plain bun sandwiching a piece of chocolate. The evening was spent by Mary doing needlework and Doreen using long strands of red wool and a bobbin to decorate some slippers.

In June, Doreen returned from her break at home and she said the train was so crowded that people were passing children in through the windows! They often went to the pictures and saw films like *Me and My Girl* or *We'll Meet Again,* during which a cat appeared under Mary's feet. Mary once received a parcel from home containing an orange.

Another Land Girl, Christine had decided to move rooms, as she thought Mary was too untidy, but Mary said the stand where Christine kept her cosmetics was nicknamed the 'Jug and Bottle Shop'.

Mary's letters are preserved at the Imperial War Museum Archives. They reveal the better aspect of WLA accommodation and indicated a loving, intelligent and bright girl.

Crayke Castle, North Yorkshire

This hostel was used, like Alne Hall, as a holiday home for people volunteering to work on a farm during their annual holidays. It was an old castle with an interesting history. Mrs McLeod who had been the Warden at Ripon and Easingwold hostels worked at Crayke also. No other details are known about Crayke Castle, except that the WLA again trained and supervised the public volunteers.

Crockey Hill, near York, East Yorkshire

Frances Forth (née Cooper) stayed at Crockley Hill, which she described as an old house, with two beds in each room. The Land Girls had to get up on time and then do physical exercises to 'wake the brain', placing their hands above their heads and running on the spot. In the mornings, before the lorry picked them up, they would leave the blackout curtains open to show the daylight. Alarm clocks were rare at the time and it was not easy to buy one.

They went to RAF dances at Pocklington, Rufforth and Linton. An RAF lorry would be sent for them and later brought them back. Tea was provided at dances. The girls wore their uniforms, gingham dresses or gym slips, which would be dressed up with scarves around the waist. Soot was used in lieu of mascara for the eyelashes and often blue bag as eye-shadow. Salt and toothbrushes were used to clean the teeth. They got nylons from the American servicemen. (Murton Farming Museum Archives)

Unfortunately, there are no further records of this hostel and Miss Jacob-Smith did not inspect it.

Croft Hostel, near North Allerton, North Yorkshire

Croft Hostel was located on the airfield near Northallerton. Mr Barton hoped to open Croft in January 1949 and transfer the girls from Easingwold Hostel to

Girls from Easingwold who transferred to Croft. (*Eden Camp Collection*)

it, followed by Stokesley. It was also suggested that some Middleborough girls at Stockton might like to go to Croft and their places could be taken by the girls at Easingwold.

It was decided to appoint the WLA's most successful Warden, Mrs Keep, who was then at Thirsk Hostel, to the post of Warden at the new hostel at Croft.

Miss Jacob-Smith made the following records about Croft Hostel:

10/12/49 Mrs Keep was not anxious to use her kitchen as the hostel kitchen. She felt that her sitting room would be very small, unless the hostel numbers were very much reduced. A suggestion was that the present dining room kitchen block should be closed and the kitchen in the recreation block be opened. The present sitting room was to be a dining room and the quiet room was to become the sitting room. Staff would sleep in the bedrooms in the Warden's block and also in the spare bedroom in the recreation block.

The chief problem was with the electric points, as there were no plugs in the recreation block kitchen. In Mrs Keep's kitchen, plugs would be needed for the refrigerator and the electric cooker and water boiler. This had only just been connected in the present kitchen. There was some difficulty in getting the Ministry of Works to do the work. The recreation block kitchen was used when they first moved in. Mrs Keep was quite willing to cut down staff to seven and a half and she would try to see if she can manage with this number.

4/3/50 Eight Land Girls had been employed by Mr McFarlane in planting trees. It was a very wet morning and the girls had got wet through. Someone suggested going home at midday. He said he did not mind if they did and signed their time sheets. He then telephoned to say they had gone home and that five of them had worked badly, but he did not know which ones. Subsequently, eight girls had their 7s 8d stopped for half a day. The Land Girl who was in charge had been in the WLA for six years and she said she would not have thought of going home if Mr McFarlane had objected, but he had said they could go and made no complaint.

20/1/50 The Forewoman received a note from Agricultural Executive Committee about the afternoon when the girls were not paid. Their pay had not yet been included in their wages.

Three men had entered the hostel kitchen block by breaking a window in the Warden's lavatory. Food was taken from the larder and refrigerator. Members of staff were in the sitting room at the time, at the other side of the kitchen. Mats, a chair and a curtain were also taken from the concrete hut. Two unoccupied Nissen huts were also entered by breaking open the locks on the doors and they also took mirrors, chairs and one table. The burglars finally entered the linen hut and items were removed.

The Warden was an ex-policewoman and she took all precautions against further theft. The police were most co-operative but they said that the remaining sites at the airport were occupied by squatters and this was a bad area for stealing. The huts were scattered and after dark it was difficult to watch all parts of it. The Warden had formerly kept a bulldog for protection but, owing to old age, she had had him destroyed. On the Saturday after this the burglary had occurred.

The following items were thought to have been taken: meat worth 30s approx; a few pounds of lard and margarine; ½lb butter; biscuits in a large tin; home-made crunch; nine coconut mats; nine folding chairs; four mirrors; two curtains; six white blankets. Mr Saunders wanted the WLA Office to write to the Ministry of Works, informing them of the theft and asking for details of the cost of mats etc. Once the cost had been worked out, they needed to write to the WLA Headquarters and get the amount written off, with permission to be obtained from the Treasury. Mrs Keep had asked for the police report.

13/3/50 At the meeting of the Labour Sub-Committee, after some discussion, it was agreed that the WLA should be asked to keep Croft Hostel open until the end of the harvest. All the Land Girls were fully employed and it would not be fair to farmers to take away the labour at the busy time. There was a possibility that the Croft may be retained as a voluntary hostel for agricultural workers. It was pointed out that if it was to remain open, the existing kitchen and the small kitchen would have to close, as it had no power points. Whilst the decisions were awaited, should Mrs Keep be moved into the small kitchen, Miss Jacob-Smith asked? This would mean that two or possibly three dailies could be given notice, to save a little money.

9/5/50 A large amount of kit bags were needed to pack up the bedding at the hostel. The remaining Croft girls were to go to Leeming Bar Hostel.

11/5/50 A friend of the farmer's wife, for whom one of the Croft girls was working, telephoned to the hostel whilst Mrs Keep was out. She said £11 was missing from a child's money box in the farmhouse and the girl was the only person to have been in the house besides the family. She had not notified the policeman, as he was away for the week and she wondered if Mrs Keep could deal with the matter. Mrs Keep and Miss Jacob-Smith felt that if the farmer wanted to accuse the girl, then he must go to the police. They had no idea when the money had gone. Miss Jacob-Smith thought it just as possible that anyone passing the farm could have taken, as the girl.

Dishforth North Hill, near Thirsk, North Yorkshire

(This hostel was visited by Miss Jacob-Smith and extracts from her notes are included in a separate chapter.)

Dishforth was opened in November 1943 within an old farmhouse situated opposite Dishforth Airfield. There was an American crew based there, but they were less popular with the girls than the Canadians. Dishforth originally had two spinster ladies for Wardens, who were very laid back in their approach to the girls. They could bring their boyfriends into the hostel if they did not go home at the weekends.

Edna Braithwaite (née Partington) remembers a particular soldier who knew all the dances. As her home was in Lancashire, Edna rarely went home so she enjoyed the dances. When girls went to a dance, the outside door was left open by the last girl entering, so the times for coming home were variable! She also remembers the lack of electricity (see the chapter on Dishforth for more information). The bathroom was located next to the dormitory and it had an open top. Someone opening or closing the bathroom door would invariably extinguish the girls' candles in the dormitory.

Driffield Hostel, East Yorkshire

This WLA hostel, open from 1943-49, was in Queen Street, Driffield, and it was formerly the East Riding Nurses' Hostel, established by the late Lady Margaret Bickersteth. Owing to the war, its original purpose could not continue and the hostel was closed. It was reopened in January 1943 as a Women's Land Army hostel. The opening ceremony was performed by Mrs Dunnington-Jefferson, the Chairman of the East Riding WLA.

The hostel Warden was Mrs Scott. Mrs Dunnington-Jefferson said it was the first hostel to be opened in the East Riding in the shape of a house and it was the first venture of its kind. The hostel would accommodate twenty-five girls who would do all kinds of farm work. The girls would be in the charge of a foreman, Mr J Burton, and a Mr Gregg would visit the hostel and give advice. The girls would be able to leave work at midday on Saturdays and would be free to go home at weekends.

Lynne Mullenger (née Wales) worked on private farms for four years during the war and spent two and a half years at Driffield Hostel. She often went to the pictures in Driffield, where the programme changed twice a week. The girls went to the town hall for dances and the Hull Fair. She used to go to Bridlington for the weekend. She once went with a friend to London and, as they travelled overnight they were exhausted all day. They went to hear Lou Beiger and they stayed at a hostel in London.

In December 1948 Driffield Hostel closed and the Land Girls were transferred to Bubwith, which had reopened. Mrs Robinson, Miss Bertram and the rest of the hostel staff accompanied them. The hostel building is believed to have been demolished in the 1990s.

Easingwold Hostel, North Yorkshire

Easingwold was one of the first WLA hutment hostels to open in December 1941 and it was the first hostel to appear in the North Riding. (See the chapter on Easingwold Hostel for full details.) Once a fire was caused at the hostel by a regiment of Royal Engineers. Sparks from something they were working on caught on the hostel roof in the spring of 1947 or 1948.

Kathleen Kay (née Fawell) was born in 1913 at Sand Hutton, near Thirsk, and had been brought up on a farm. She had been a physical training teacher at Baldersby School before she joined the Land Army in 1939, as she wanted to teach girls to drive tractors. She was first sent to a general farm in the South of England, with horses and dairy. There was little machinery on the farm and she sowed seed by hand. She moved from farm to farm, staying in bed and breakfast houses. She was involved with potato handling and storage.

After six months, she was recalled to Yorkshire, where she spent six weeks at Strensall Hostel, where she selected six of the most suitable girls for tractor work. They then went to Easingwold Hostel, where she became the Forewoman.

Easingwold Hostel was purpose-built for the Land Army and there were thirty-three girls there, with a married couple and their daughter as wardens. They were responsible for the catering in the hostel. The sleeping quarters consisted of individual cubicles, with one bed and chair and dressing table and drawers, and each had a tiny window high up and a curtain acting as the door. The dining room also served as the common room and recreation room. There was no garden for growing vegetables. The Wardens were miserable and were unreasonable about rations, Kathleen recalled. They were given sandwiches with raspberry jam and she was ready to eat hers on one very hot day when she noticed half a wasp sticking out!

Lady Celia Coates invited the Easingwold Hostel girls to afternoon tea at her home, Helperby Hall. She spent considerable time with Land Girls, despite having a terrible stutter. She usually visited girls on farms while on horseback, riding side saddle. Later on, Kathleen Kay had to plough up the Coates' beautiful park land! It was particularly difficult to plough round the wonderful trees because of their roots.

Kathleen was particularly involved with the flax industry during the war. In the past, flax had been grown in Southern Ireland where the land was wet and the conditions ideal. About a fifth of the flax plant was used for cattle feed but the major part was used in the hessian industry. Unfortunately, there were no specialist machines available for pulling flax during the war. The major problem workers had was getting the plant out of the ground, as its roots curled round itself, making it almost impossible to pull by hand.

The Agricultural War Committee adapted a machine with large cement discs which grabbed the flax plant and pulled it out of the soil. It was pulled and operated by tractor, but the machine was highly dangerous. If the machine pulled up a scotch thistle it caused the rubber belt to fly off and this would mean putting these rubbers belts back by hand. Accidents occurred because the tractor clutch had to be kept pressed down to disengage the machine. Kathleen almost had her hand amputated in such an incident. Fortunately, her reactions were very quick and she escaped with a very severe cut across her palm. It required hospital treatment because flax was poisonous.

Kathleen travelled to see each of the Land Girls she supervised by motorbike and she found that the farmers respected the girls, because they were supervised and cared for by herself and she was very experienced in farming.

When asked about the girls' behaviour in the hostel, Kathleen commented that the girls were too tired to get up to mischief. She did speak of one girl who had been courting a lad from her own town and always spoke fondly of him. Like most of the girls, she went to the local dances and met an officer and soon afterwards she announced she was getting married. The girls all thought she meant that she was marrying her long term boyfriend. She assured them that it was the officer, but Kathleen thought she was unsuitable to become an officer's wife! As she was concerned about the girl, she made a few enquiries and found that the officer was married already. Although she informed the girl of this, the bigamous wedding apparently went ahead.

One Easingwold Land Girl named Doris recalled spending her spare time in sewing, knitting and making her own dresses. She was also keen on cross stitch. On one occasion, when she was at an auction mart, she took a bull into the ring. Someone called out 'Who are you selling – the land girl or the bull?'

On one occasion, Doris went to London to parade in front of the Queen. She was given £3 50d expenses, with all her fares and accommodation provided. There were about 500 Land Girls in the parade. They learnt how to march on the parade ground; they had to march too close, so they kept knocking each others' shoes off. On her return, Doris stayed in the York YWCA hostel, which she thought a dreadful place, with other people's unwashed sheets on the bed.

Edna Braithwaite (née Partington) was a Forewoman at Easingwold. She had enrolled in the WLA when she was sixteen and officially under-age. She lived in Lancashire and she feared going to work with munitions, as the workers' skins turned yellow. She quickly joined the WLA and she lied about her age in order to be accepted.

Edna's papers had been destroyed in a bombing raid at Preston and when she arrived in Yorkshire, Miss Jacob-Smith knew nothing about her. She worked in many hostels and later, like Miss Jacob-Smith, she visited and reported on other hostels. She met regularly with Miss Jacob-Smith, Lady Celia Coates, and Mrs

Bottomley the Welfare Officer, and Kay Keep, the Warden at Thirsk and later Warden at Croft.

As the Forewoman at Easingwold, she was responsible for the payment of staff. Every Friday, she went by bicycle to the bank to fetch the money for the wages, which involved carrying lots of coins. The money was put into a bag and she hung it on the handle bars of her bike. Cycling back, she once came off her bike and the bag, with all its contents spilled all over the road. Many local residents came to her aid. Every coin and note was collected!

Gisburn Hostel, West Yorkshire

This hostel was opened from 1943-1944. It had previously been the Corner House Café and probably accommodated around forty girls. The girls were issued with bikes for work but they also used them to go to dances at Clitheroe. There appear to be no surviving records of this hostel. Gisburn Hostel closed in 1944 and it was taken over as accommodation for prisoners of war.

Guisborough Hostel, North Yorkshire

There are few records of this hostel, which was of the hutment variety and open between 1946-1950. The hostel was situated just off Bolkiv Street, next to the Territorial Army Club. The site is now covered by flats and houses.

Joyce Cameron (née Ashton), formerly lived at the hostel and she was interviewed by Ian Peace for the People's War Website in 2004. Joyce had been working in the drapery department at the Leeds Co-operative and the most energetic work she had done so far was to measure women for corsets. When she was eighteen she had a horror of being sent to a munitions factory, so she joined the Land Army, as she said she 'quite fancied being in the fresh air', like her friends who had previously joined. She got a rude awakening, she said, as life in the WLA was 'hard work, really hard work'.

Having received her uniform by the post in March 1943, Joyce went to Leeds Station with a group of twenty-six girls, most of whom were from South and West Yorkshire. They travelled to Guisborough, which was a dead-end of the railway track. At the YWCA hutment hostel, they inspected their sleeping arrangements, which consisted of a dormitory with four bunks in each partition. The washing facilities consisted of four washbasins, two bathrooms and four toilets. The dining room was huge. The Warden and the Assistant Warden had their quarters at the other side of the dining room.

They were always woken by a girl with red hair, who used to shout, 'Wakey, Wakey.' She ensured everyone got up at 6.00 am, after which they stripped their beds and folded their blankets neatly on the top of their bunks. (Unlike most hostels, the beds were made up for them when they arrived back in the evening.)

There was a decent breakfast, often bacon and eggs and maybe some porridge. Two rounds of sandwiches were given to them, which might be jam and cheese or jam and beetroot.

Joyce travelled with another girl on the hostel van, getting to the farm by 8.00 am. They went to the cow byres to eat their lunch and the farmer brought them a chipped mug of tea. By 6.00 pm they were ravenous and enjoyed an evening meal of vegetables, roast potatoes and meat. Although meat was rationed, they always had decent food. (Ian Pearce supplied the following information for The BBC People's War Website.)

Another Land Girl at Guisborough, Ivy Hynes, remembers making her own sandwiches. As soon as the light went on in the dormitory, she knew she had to get up first to make her sandwiches. If she was late, all that would be left was plain bread, no butter and just beetroot. By lunchtime, the sandwiches were so soggy that they needed a spoon and the bread was all red. It was awful, she said!

Ivy still remembers the torture of picking the tiny sprouts off the top of the stick for the Christmas Market. By 12.00 pm their hands were frozen, but they were cheered when the farmer came and said, "Oh! The wife's made you a bit to eat." The hot meal of gravy and mounds of carrots and parsnips was greatly appreciated.

Joyce Cameron remembered that in Guisborough there were no air raids, but there had been an incendiary bomb at a farm where Joyce had worked. Middlesbrough Station was badly hit, but it was quiet during 1943-1946.

Joyce's parents were a little bothered to hear about her doing the heavy work in the Land Army, so they came to stay nearby for the weekend. Her father was a Methodist, so whilst they were staying at Lazenby, her parents went to the chapel and she joined them. The farmer was there and he wanted to be introduced to her parents. Now that he knew she was a Methodist she was treated as 'one of them'. After that, there were no chipped mugs served to her and no more eating in the cow byre!

On the next farm she worked with cows and the farmer's son was also working there. The family used to invite her in for dinner, so no more sandwiches were needed. When she went back to Leeds, the farmer gave Joyce eggs and produce. It turned out that they were trying to match-make her with their son. When she acquired a boyfriend in the village the farmer and his wife were furious, so she asked for a move. Her boyfriend, whom she later married, was in a reserved occupation and a member of the Home Guard.

The thing Joyce hated most during her WLA work was the earth closets. At home she was used to water closets, but in many parts of Yorkshire earth closets seemed to be the norm and they were often emptied at night. Fortunately, she did not have to empty them, though. On the second farm where she worked, the farmer had a brother who was too old to join the army. One day, she was sitting on the plank on the earth closet and she thought there was a bit of a draught behind her. She turned and noted that the door at the back, where they emptied the waste, was slightly open. Joyce was furious to find that the farmer's brother was peering in at her. She went out and grabbed a pitch fork and intended using it on him but was stopped by the farmer. Back at the hostel, she warned all the girls about working on that farm.

Another task she hated was plucking hens and geese, because she had lice running up her arms. She tried tickling and trying to catch them but they did not bite like fleas. Back at the hostel she dived into the bath and rubbed her arms and legs to get rid of the sensation.

For entertainment, the Guisborough girls would go to Middlesbrough or to the pictures. The first time they went to the pictures, there was a big cheer, because in Guisborough they had not seen Land Girls before. On Sundays, the vicar came and they had a service in the hostel. On most nights at the hostel they had to be in by 10.00 pm, with lights out at 11.00 pm.

The girls often went to dances at the two nearby camps of Dunsdale and Hutton Gate. Trucks would arrive to pick them up. A late pass was issued until midnight and the hostel wardens were quite strict about this. On reflection, the rule was really appreciated by the girls. Occasionally, according to Ivy Hynes, some girls who arrived later than 10.00 pm used to climb in through a downstairs window. Ivy also recalled making friends with prisoners of war. The Italians were 'lovely blokes', she said.

One day Ivy was chatting with one of her friends when two POWs came along. Ivy had worked with them and knew that they were allowed out at night. They stayed to talk to them, but some chaps passing heard the different accents and tore them off a strip for 'fraternising with the enemy'. Ivy pointed out to them that if her brother was captured, then she hoped he would be treated in a civilised manner. Many Land Army girls had to work with Italian and German prisoners of war and they found them courteous and well behaved, so how could they shun them?

Another Land Girl from Guisborough worked in the NAAFI in Hutton Gate. This was a big British Army Camp, where they transferred from one brigade to another. At the camp there were no POWs. She recalled that there had been a spy going around the camps and he was caught and shot on the railway at Hutton Gate.

At harvest time, Ivy Hynes worked as late as 10.00 pm, often getting back to the hostel wet through. She would wash her clothes in the sinks and dry them in an airing cupboard. One winter Joyce Cameron had been snagging turnips and on returning to the hostel, she found she had big blisters on her hands. She was taken to the doctor in Guisborough to have the blisters lanced. Her hands were bandaged for a long time. She believed these hardships gave her strength in later life, though. Whereas some of the girls got out of the Land Army within a year with sciatica and various other complaints, Joyce stuck it out to the end, when she was demobbed in 1946. She got nothing when released but a card with 'willing release' and later a letter from the Queen thanking her for her service. When she had joined the Land Army she had weighed 8st and when she left her weight was just 7st.

Many years later, Joyce went to see a fictional film about the Women's Land Army. At first, when the girls arrived on the train and found they had arrived at a dead end, Joyce thought it might be authentic but, she said, the stories of girls hopping into bed with the farmers' sons was not realistic and she, like many former Land Girls, felt that the film was false and degrading to the real lives of these hard-working girls.

In February 1947, Guisborough raised £10 by holding beetle drives, whist drives and a dance for the Benevolent Fund. 'Tina' Dickinson (née Goss) was at Guisborough from 28 November 1947. She said one of the girls used to get 'plastered' every pay day and she would become quite uninhibited and take her clothes off. She became a spectacle for all the villagers! Tina's most vivid memories were of collecting the chaff. They all donned head scarves to cover their curlers, as the job was excessively dusty. They were paid 6d extra for this task.

In May 1948 Guisborough won the silver cup, presented by the WLA Welfare Officer Mrs Bottomley, for sending in the most handicrafts for the WLA exhibition.

The hostel closed in 1950. On 6/1/50 Miss Jacob-Smith noted that all the food from Guisborough which was transferred had to be thrown away, as it was unfit to eat. Ten bottles of custard flavouring appeared OK, but Miss Nolan at Leeming Bar did not use it.

Holden Clough, near Slaidburn, West Yorkshire

Holden Clough was open from 1943-1947. It had been a private nursing home and accommodated forty girls. It was a machinery hostel for tractor drivers and machinery workers. In order to keep the hostel open, because of lower numbers, it was agreed to allow recruits employed on forestry work to also use the hostel. In May 1947 the hostel was closed and the girls went to hostels at Settle or Skipton.

Howden Hall, Silsden West Yorkshire

Howden Hall was opened in May 1942 for about 200 people, ranging from teachers to refugees, and it was passed as suitable accommodation for WLA recruits. There were more social facilities there than most hostels, such as a games room where darts and table tennis were played; a busy room, where one night a week an instructor taught craft and leather craft; a branch library with over 400 books and a large concert hall with a dance floor. Hostel sales were often held for the Red Cross and Great Ormond Street Hospital. A local newspaper made the comment that hostels had turned out to be valuable experiments in communal living. (Bullock, 2002.) Howden Hall closed in 1947.

Howden Hostel, Howden, East Yorkshire

This hostel was located on Thorpe Road, (near where the tyre and battery shop are sited today).

In March 1943 a Land Girl at Howden wished to thank Mrs Saltmarsh and Mr Brandon and many others of the Howden residents, who had helped make the dance held in the Shire Hall such a success. It had raised £20 16s.

Muriel Bezins (née French) narrated the following account when visiting the Farming Museum in Murton, York. During the war, Muriel French lived in Kingston upon Hull, which had been badly bombed. At nineteen, she was working in a grocer's shop and was very bored and expecting to be called up. Some of her friends persuaded her to join the WLA.

Muriel was sent to Howden, about twenty miles from Hull. There were around twenty girls at the hostel there and not enough room, so some of them also slept in a cottage nearby, two to a bed. One of the girls she met there became her dear friend Beatty, whose parents were bargees. Her friend, unlike herself, was excessively strong and able to pick up potatoes and sand bags with ease. Beatty was very popular as a farm worker! Muriel was a tiny and petite girl. There was much opposition to Muriel's size and height, as she was less than 5ft tall and she caused much amusement with her oversized uniform.

Muriel Berzins with her friend at Howden Hostel. (*Muriel Berzins Collection*)

Yet, one of her first jobs on a farm was with shire horses. The farmer asked her to put a collar on an extremely large shire horse. Gamely, she stared up towards his head and said to the farmer that she would have to be helped. He grunted and came back with a couple of boxes for her to stand on to reach the horse's head. Like most of her friends, Muriel wore curlers under a headscarf so that her hair was good for the local dance on an evening. Being so short, she had problems trying to empty the potato basket. She climbed on to the wheel to empty hers, and for sport, many times the horse was encouraged to move forwards, making her fall backwards!

When she went home at the weekends it took her two hours by bus! However, on Saturdays, when she had finished work at midday she would join other girls to thumb a lift to Queens Hall in Hull. On one occasion, seven of them hitched a lift on a potato lorry. Sadly one girl fell off and broke her leg!

Certain jobs on the farm guaranteed a bath back at the hostel, Muriel recalled. When stoking barley, for example, it clung to the jumpers and socks and the clouds of dust and thistles made the face black! Often the mice and rats ran all over the place. One girl in the hostel was a trained rat catcher and she went around in a little van.

Of the hostel, Muriel remembered concrete floors, two bunk beds per partition, a shared wardrobe and a tin roof which rattled in the rain. There were about sixty girls employed by the War Agricultural Executive Committee. In the dining room they queued patiently for their meals. However, she can remember strikes by girls who refused to work in protest against the loss of rations which they believed had been taken by the Wardens and sold. Food went mouldy and the Wardens were accused of making Christmas cakes using the girls' rations, and selling them in the local pub. Lady Dunnington Jefferson came from York to see what was going on.

Another Warden, Miss Curtis was fine, very strict and stern but good to the girls, Muriel recalled. When a new dormitory was built Miss Curtis selected the 'nice' girls to sleep there, so this was called the 'Fifth Avenue'! The Land Girls were like sisters, Muriel said, they knew everything about each other. So hungry were they at times, they were often reduced to eating beetroot sandwiches. Yet, girls were still willing to give a 1d a week to the Red Cross.

The hostel girls would save up and go for the weekend to London or Blackpool. At Blackpool, two of the girls entered a beauty contest and they even went into a night club. On one visit to London they went to the opera, sitting in a box which was cheaper than separate seats. During their evenings in the hostel, they would play cards, use an Ouija board, darn socks, do embroidery and cross stitch. Muriel embroidered linen and pillowcases for her bottom drawer. She made moccasins from braid, using cross stitch. By unpicking a floor cloth she could use the strands to knit jumpers and create patterns in the knit.

Howden girls. (*Eden Camp Collection*)

They often counted the Lancaster Bombers going out, so they knew when to expect the cancellation of the local dances – if the bombers had left there would be no partners until the planes returned. They particularly enjoyed the dances in the Shire Hall, but often sadly someone's RAF boyfriend would never be seen again. She went to lots of dances at RAF camps, including Breton RAF camp. Her friend Joan was waiting for her sweetheart Bill, who was in Burma and some of her colleagues had loved ones who were in Japanese prisoner of war camps. The girls all celebrated, dancing and singing in Hull City Square on VE day.

In 1947 Muriel married a handsome Latvian, who had worked on the farms with her. He gave her presents he had crafted himself. One was a bracelet made and refashioned out of silver sixpences. He was a displaced person and was still trying to claim back two farms in Latvia. Now in her nineties Muriel still participates in meetings or visits associated with the WLA.

During the very hard winter of 1947, the Howden girls were still expected to work in the fields. They had been riddling potatoes for the Hull markets and had to use pick axes to get the soil off the potatoes. Others had been threshing every day in the snowstorms. They ate their sandwiches in barns or cowsheds. Particular praise was given to the girls and the market gardeners who had supplied Hull with potatoes and fresh vegetables in such terrible weather.

Jean and Betty (now Jean Haigh and Betty Bond) lived at Howden Hostel for about eighteen months. Their most vivid memories were of spam and piccalilli sandwiches and the same for supper, as a special treat, when they returned home at the weekend. They have not been able to eat either of these things since!

Keyingham Hostel, East Yorkshire

Keyingham opened in November 1943, according to the *Land Girl*. It was a hutment hostel. Mrs Beadle, a resident of Keyingham, although not a Land Girl, remembered the hostel and her account of it follows. The hostel building was erected at the corner of Saltaugh Road, for the accommodation of fifty Land Girls. It was known locally as the Agricultural Hostel and it was on the site of the present Horrox Court, a home for the mentally handicapped, opposite the Ship Inn. The Land Girls came mostly from Hull.

The Land Girls sometimes worked as long as fourteen hours a day, milking, ploughing, harvesting and potato picking. There was a fatal accident in October 1944, involving a Land Girl named Winifred Galloway, who was well-liked in the village. Her husband was abroad fighting with the army at the time. Whilst working near Saltaugh Grange in the potato field, she fell off a tractor and was run over. Two Italian prisoners of war witnessed the tragic accident.

Mrs Beadle remembered that the Land Girls used to help at farms on threshing days, either forking sheaves or carrying the chaff. For recreation, film shows were put on in the hostel. The villagers were invited to go to watch the films. They also organised dances which the locals attended too. Partners were plentiful, as there were many army camps guarding the coastline. There were two pubs in the

Girls outside Keyingham Hostel. (*Linsey Blenkhorn Collection*)

village, the Bluebell and the Ship, opposite the hostel. Sometimes the girls would cycle to Withernsea and dance at the glorious ballroom in the Grand Pavilion.

Mrs Beadle was a teenager at the time and because of the clothing shortages she had just two dresses. These had been made out of old coats and she decorated them with ribbons and stones to make them look different.

The war was always present in Keyingham. The downstairs storeys of local houses always had blackout boards at the windows, including the hostel. Mrs Beadle's father was an air-raid warden and everyday casualties were reported from the nearby dock area in Hull. When the bombs were dropped, all the windows in her family's farm house shook. Two land mines exploded in the village and there were timber blazes all over. Mrs Beadle can remember seeing bombed-out houses with beds and furniture suspended out of the top of buildings.

Lindsey Blenkhorn's grandmother, Jessie Hugens, served at Keyingham Hostel and Lindsey has inherited her uniform, minus the hat. She later asked some of her grandmother's Land Army colleagues about the missing hat. On the day the war ended, a group of Keyingham Land Girls had been working at Spurn Point. They were so pleased about the news that they threw their hats into the River Humber. Jessie was Dutch and her maiden name was Hugens. She lived in the back streets of Hull and had few prospects of ever doing anything exciting, until she joined the Land Army. Like so many girls, she later said it was the happiest time of her life! She was at Keyingham Hostel and later Bubwith, where she met and married a farmer at Willifost, near Howden, East Yorkshire. Keyingham Hostel closed in 1946, as the *Land Girl* reported in March 1946.

Kirk Deighton Hostel, near Wetherby, West Yorkshire

This hostel opened in 1941. Kathleen Robinson, from Brighouse near Leeds, came to the hostel in 1942 and she related the following information about it. Kirk Deighton was a purpose-built hutment hostel, a little remote from other buildings. It was a single storey building for use by forty Land Girls and staff. It was situated in a field, about a mile and a half from Wetherby and five miles from Knaresborough.

The YWCA was responsible for the organisation, accommodation, staffing etc at the hostel. The Warden was Mrs Whitehead and the Cook was Miss White. Other staff included the boiler man and various locals who assisted with the cleaning. Miss White, who was elderly, was crippled with arthritis in both her hands and feet but she contrived to make some really lovely meals. Mrs Whitehead was a good Warden and kept the girls in order. However, the girls did feel some resentment towards her husband who was a Conscientious Objector. The Land Girls had fathers, brothers, husbands and sweethearts fighting abroad and risking their lives, so many of them were disparaging about Mr Whitehead.

Kirk Deighton Hostel. (*Courtesy Mrs Rawkins*)

The hostel comprised a dormitory of twenty double bunks down each side for the forty girls. Each bay had two small slim wardrobes, one on each side of the tiny dressing table. The floor was concrete, with a small mat for each bay to pay lip service to comfort! The sleeping area was heated in winter by three combustion stoves at intervals down the length of the dormitory. The fuel was fed through an opening at the top of the stove. The small windows in each room were built to take blackout cover. At one end was the ablution block with lavatories, three baths and a row of six hand basins. There was a small room, a sick bay, at the other end of the dormitory.

The large dining room doubled up as a common room. There were three trestle tables down each side of the room, where the girls sat for their breakfast and the evening meal. The main meal of the day was served from the hatch and fast eaters were able to get 'seconds'. Any scraps left from the meal, together with peelings, were put in a large canister and later collected by the local pig farmer. Staff had their own rooms and there was a large kitchen. The boiler house was at the entrance, where there was a coke fired boiler. This was used for heating the water and there were buckets of coke there to feed the stoves. A large bike shed housed enough bikes for the girls, so they could get to farms within a five mile radius of the hostel.

Each day began with the Warden knocking on each set of bunk beds at 6.30 am. One girl from Leeds always said in a loud voice, 'Good God, another bloody day!' She had the nickname 'Never Worry'. Another girl had her own chamber pot under the bed, even though she slept nearest to the bathroom. A rather genteel girl in a bunk above was fascinated by this. When the girl took her chamber pot to empty it she used to say, "Oh! Isn't she lovely!" The bunk above Kathleen was occupied by a girl from Guernsey, which was unusual since most of the girls came from the West Riding.

After breakfast they went off to work with a haversack containing three half-sandwiches of spam, cheese and beetroot. These had been prepared for them and also included were half a currant tea cake and a piece of fruit cake, which the girls called 'NAAFI cake'. A flask was also put in the haversack to 'see you through' until meal time at about 6.00 pm. The hostel had a jeep type van and Mr Dowell, an older man who organised the work on the farms in the Wetherby area, sometimes used to drive gangs of girls to farms further away. The hostel Forewoman learned to drive at the hostel and she used to take the girls to farms in her small covered jeep.

During the working week, lights out was at 10.00 pm and half an hour later was quiet time. The social life mostly consisted of a gang of girls, armed with bike lights, walking in the black out, down the Great North Road to the Fox. This was an unusually shaped pub, rather like a Swiss Chalet. Here the girls were joined by airmen from Rufforth, Tockwith and Marston Moor. The publican was pleased to welcome the girls and always said, 'Now girls, I don't mind if you only have half a shandy.' He realised that the lads would always come to his pub if there were these ladies present. One of the rooms had a polished wood floor and sparkling furniture and Victor Sylvester records were played for dancing. One of the girls met her future husband there. Some of the men imbibed too much and they spent the night in the ditch. On special nights the young men were invited to the hostel for socials.

Kathleen was at the hostel on VE Day and remembers marching in Wetherby on that day. There was no marked excitement in the hostel, as many of the girls still had friends and relatives fighting in the Far East. Kathleen said that there was no equivalent of the modern bombardment from the media and living a parochial life in the hostel meant they seemed remote from events outside the hostel.

Kathleen and her friend Vera decided to go to work on a farm in Dorset. After life at the hostel, they found the small cottage provided primitive and the locals hostile, so they went back to their homes in Leeds. A few days later, a brown envelope arrived with the news that they had to work either on the buses, in the munitions factory at Thorpe Arch or go into the ATS. Both Vera and Kathleen opted for the latter and they were sent to Pontefract Barracks for six weeks. It was a great shock after the homeliness and security of Kirk Deighton. The hours of physical training seemed so unproductive when compared with the useful job they had done in farming. They always had to wear uniform and could not go out in 'civvies'.

After the initial six weeks, Vera was sent to North Wales as a driver and Kathleen was sent to Catterick as a clerk. She sadly missed the Land Army and especially the warmth and friendliness of life at Kirk Deighton.

In 1942 Betty Farndale (née Webster) volunteered for the Land Army. Her parents had moved south and she resided with her grandmother, who was very worried about Betty going to a strange place. She went by taxi to Kirk Deighton

Hostel to inspect it, before she would allow her granddaughter to move there. (Information given by Betty's sister Joan Rawkins.)

In 1948, Barbara Whitehead came to Kirk Deighton from the WLA hostel at Arkendale when it closed down. Kirk Deighton was handy for visiting her home and she went back about once a month, when she had saved up the bus fare. Barbara remembered that they were punished if they were back late. Everyone was punished not just the culprit. Breakfast was jam and bread, lunch was rabbit and mashed potato, and tea was jam and bread.

Barbara worked at Simpson's farm, where she met her husband and they later married at Kirk Deighton Church. They used to go to dances at Linton on Ouse, where there was a lovely dance floor. They had a gramophone in the hostel and they would do the jitterbug. In the evenings they would sit round the stove and tell stories, sometimes about hauntings. Sometimes they would go to the Bluebell Inn and they would end up 'Singing in the Moonlight' and the lads would play the piano.

Barbara's first job was threshing and carrying the chaff, so she soon had a sore back. Some of the girls packed up and went home, but she stuck it out and knew the seasons would change. She then went to Hotley, a small farm where she had to wash the milking units. She got there early. At 10.00 am she had breakfast with the farmer and his wife, which was often a piece of bacon fat on a plate. You got to like it though, she said, as it had a really sweet taste with bread. She was the last drop off with the truck, so she decided to learn to drive and then she was always the last in for meals!

On 18/4/50 Miss Jacob-Smith visited Kirk Deighton hostel for the first time. Miss Jacob-Smith thought that Miss Luard the Warden's room, the larder, kitchen and recreation room were all well kept and there was an excellent atmosphere in the hostel. She did not see the dormitories, as the girls were getting changed. There were twenty-eight girls there at the time. There was a good deal of surplus bedding, which was kept in the small bedroom, as there was only one resident orderly.

Knaresborough Hostel, North Yorkshire (then West Riding)

Knaresborough Hostel was open between 1942 and 1950. Forty young women from shops, factories and offices volunteered for work with the Women's Land Army because they preferred it to any of the other women's services. They arrived in Knaresborough to take up their quarters in the new mobile labour hostel erected by the Ministry of Agriculture in Chain Lane. (The building has already been described under the section on hutments.)

The very first afternoon and evening was spent settling in. Mr Nigel FitzRoy, a member of the Executive Committee of the West Riding War Agricultural Committee, came over from Harewood to welcome the new arrivals.

A vase of golden chrysanthemums on a bookcase struck a homely note in the recreation room at the hostel. A bright fire burned in the stove, around which was a semi-circle of inviting fireside chairs. On arrival, the girls were fitted out with the familiar Land Army uniform of green jumpers, corduroy breeches, green oilskins and jaunty khaki felt hats. Refreshments were served. Soon, there was a cheery group round the fireside and letters and postcards home were being written. Early the next morning, ten of the girls went off to a hard day's work on the land.

The party at the hostel included two sisters, who were formerly tailoresses in Leeds and had joined the Land Army together. Some of the girls had already done land work, however. One, a former weaver, had been in the Land Army for some time and said she was delighted with the life. 'It's a bit stiff at first,' she said, 'but you soon get used to it, and it's grand to be in the open air after working in a mill.' Another girl, who had been employed at an electric lamp factory, was a farmer's daughter, and had a good knowledge of farm work. Others among them, a former insurance clerk and a shop manageress, had not had much experience, but all were enthusiastic about their new life and keen to get on with the job of helping with home food production.

Incidentally, the Land Army uniform was praised by all thirty of the girls for its combination of smartness and utility. The girls were from all parts of Yorkshire, their home towns being Leeds, Halifax, Whitby, Barnsley, Sowerby Bridge, York, Scarborough, Bridlington, Keighley, Hull, Todmorden, Dewsbury and Guiseley. (From an article published in the *Knaresborough Post*, November 1942.)

The hostel's second birthday was reported in the *Land Girl* in November 1943. It was celebrated with a dance at Knaresborough Town Hall on 25 November. Unfortunately, the Warden, Mrs Boddard, was not present as she was ill.

Betty Cocker, (née England) was at the hostel from 1947-1950. She married the farmer she worked for in 1951. Her home town was

Off to work by bicycle from Knaresborough Hostel.
(*Murton Farming Museum*)

Mirfield, near Leeds, and she travelled there by bus each weekend. Dances were held at Knaresborough Town Hall and in Ripon. Betty loved dancing and she remembers that the hostel had a nice dining room and good sitting room and her bedroom was above the sitting room, with five double bunks. One of the girls carved her name in the glass. It was evident for years but new windows have since been inserted.

Although Miss Jacob-Smith lived in Knaresborough she was not the visiting rep for the hostel, although she visited on a few occasions in 1950:

20/2/50 Miss Tullis appeared a little annoyed that an official had been to the hostel and had said the future of the hostel had not yet been decided. This had upset Miss Tullis. Miss Jacob-Smith told her that, as far as they were aware, the hostel would remain open after November and if the office heard anything to the contrary they would let her know.

22/3/50 There had never been a home book kept at the hostel. (This was the administrative diary kept by the wardens.) Eight girls were not working. A dance was being held that week.

21/6/50 Twenty girls were in the hostel and Miss Hodgson would like them to have single beds. The hostel closed in 1950.

Rat catchers from Knaresborough Hostel. (*Eden Camp Collection*)

Knowle House, Mirfield, near Leeds. (*Murton Farming Museum*)

Knowle House, Mirfield, West Yorkshire

This was an old requisitioned house in the small town of Mirfield, near Leeds. The hostel was described as a busy place on Sunday nights, as the Land Girls came back in all sorts of moods – some were glad to have seen their boyfriends, and others were homesick.

The building was L-shaped, one arm was a dormitory with forty beds, the other was the recreation and dining area, and each side was heated by a coke burning stove. The dormitory was partitioned and girls slept in bunks, two pairs to each partition, with a wardrobe, chest of drawers, and a mirror. The recreation area had some chairs around the stoves, and there were long tables and chairs in the dining room.

A young lady from the village was the Cook and their evening meals were plain but filling. Their lunch boxes were not so good, though. It was alright if they got cups of tea and something to eat from the farmers during the day, but otherwise, the few meagre sandwiches weren't enough to see them through.

Beyond the kitchen, lived the Warden. It occurred to some of the girls that the Warden was living in luxury with carpets, tasteful furnishings, and curtains! At the end of the dormitory was the ablution area, toilets, basins, baths, sink for washing clothes, and a large hand-wringer with wooden rollers. There was no hint of luxury within the building, but they were glad to gather round the stoves for warmth on winter evenings, whilst those who had the energy could play table tennis.

The hostel closed in December 1949.

186

Leeming Bar Hostel, North Yorkshire

The hostel was of the hutment variety. It was opened in 1943 and became the last hostel in the area to close in 1950.

The 14-15 October conference held by the YWCA, was at Leeming Bar Hostel, when three girls from each YWCA hostel in the North Riding were invited. Talks on the work of the YWCA were given by Miss Squires and Miss Hessel. Miss Sturgess Wells organised games, which left everyone breathless. The conference ended with a Green Forum in which many problems were discussed and many queries settled. (*The Land Girl*, November 1944.)

Miss Jacob-Smith rarely visited Leeming Bar Hostel. Edna Braithwaite (née Partington) became the visiting rep for this hostel. When she joined the Land Army in 1942 she was sent to Leeming Bar. Although she did not stay at the hostel, she became familiar with the area and later married into a family of horticulturists whom she had met on her first day.

Edna recalled that when her parents came to see her she had been working in a threshing team and her clothes were littered with straw and corn husks. She had tied her trousers tightly around the bottoms to stop mice running up and her face was exceedingly dirty. Her parents were horrified.

The Wedding at Leeming Bar of David and Edna Braithwaite née Partington.
(*Courtesy of the Braithwaite family*)

She had terrible billets on farms and remembered being told to wash in a hip bath. She had never used one before and she unfortunately got stuck in it. She had to knock on the floor to get help. When she lived in Leeming Bar Hostel, Miss Bullock was the Warden. Edna could remember being friendly with the Miss Nolan, who was the Cook at the hostel. Miss Nolan was a very large lady and she wore voluminous knickers. When she bent over to reach into the oven, the girls used to comment to her, 'Got your blue ones on today! Where are the red ones?'

Edna said many of the girls at Leeming Bar were very rough and down to earth, but they had hearts of gold when it really mattered. David Braithwaite, her future husband, courted Edna while she was living at the hostel. He lived in Leeming Bar and he used to come to the hostel on a tandem bicycle to meet her. The other girls used to tease him and demand rides on the tandem. When Edna and David married in 1950 the girls formed an arch of pitchforks. They had taken the trouble of cleaning and polishing the forks so that they gleamed.

There were a few comment notes about the hostel by Miss Jacob-Smith:

26/4/44 Miss Jacob-Smith collected the piano tuner and took him to the hostel but found it had already been tuned. The tuner was most annoyed, so she took him to Northallerton, where he went on to another job. Miss Mchera was to remain for a little longer to look after the Assistant Warden. Miss Game from Ripon was to come to help the Assistant Warden when Miss Mchera had gone.

22/1/47 There was a message from the Forewoman, asking if a girl could be moved, as she could not stop crying. A farmer had sent her home and the Forewoman wanted her marked absent, as she thought the girl was capable of working. Miss Jacob-Smith suggested that Mrs Bottomley from Welfare visit the hostel.

Feb 47 Weekly whist drives and beetle drives were being held at the hostel, and in addition to a dance in the Catholic Hall at Northallerton on 10 March during which the Royal Corp of Signals Band performed. All the Land Girls and their friends in the area were invited.

26/11/47 An Impressionist and a Celtic harp player visited the hostel.

4/1/50 Croft Land Girls were working at a factory at Leeming Bar on the day before Christmas and so the Leeming Bar hostel girls invited the Croft hostel girls to bring their pack ups and get a cup of tea at their hostel. Miss Bullock came into the sitting room and asked the Croft girls what they were doing. They explained that they came from the Croft, so she told them to get out of the hostel and that it was too late for tea in the canteen. The girls felt humiliated.

6/1/50 The hostel piano was to be sent to auction.

2/3/50 The following amenities were in this hostel: a sewing machine; gramophone and records ; a gramophone stand; a wireless; a dart board; a table tennis table; ; a cricket bat; two pianos; an electric iron.

12/7/50 Leeming Bar numbers were now down to seventeen, so the girls could all have single beds. Miss Bullock needed a new orderly.

18/9/50 The WLA Committee wanted the girls to stay until 27 October.

Leeming Bar became the last hostel to close after the Croft.

Market Weighton Hostel, East Yorkshire

Market Weighton Hostel closed in 1950. In his book *Memories of Different Happenings during World War II*, A.W Hodgkinson recalled an incident during which he met Land Girls from the Market Weighton hostel. He said that Market Weighton appeared to have a large group of WLA girls and commented that they were a great asset to putting food on the table. The girls had parked their bikes outside the Half Moon pub. He went in with his air force friends and noted the girls sitting around the tables. Smiles passed their way from the girls, which they returned. A chat started followed by a challenge to a game of darts in return for a kiss. The four girls each wearing breeches and a large green sweater did not seem to stand a chance against four non-commissioned officers in RAF battledress!

Yet, the men left the pub, with their tails between their legs. Bomber Commands' finest NCOs had been beaten by four ladies wearing green sweaters! The victors were a little tipsy at the men's expense but the ladies each kissed their lips as a consolation prize.

Miss Jacob-Smith seems to have been left with the role of supervising the last of the hostels, as the following notes are the only reference she made to this hostel. This particular hostel seemed run-down. There was no indication from Miss Jacob-Smith, however, that the WLA was going to be disbanded or that this hostel was soon to close.

6/6/50 The sewing machine was delivered. Miss Ravencroft was not interested in the sardines and pilchards offered from other hostels. The bread machine was not working. Miss Ravenscroft needed some autumn flowers for her bit of garden. Miss Ravenscroft wanted the potato machine and the bacon machine repaired. She needed twelve kit bags for uniforms. The girls had to surrender their uniforms when they left.

Some large earthenware pots were required, also more cushions and eighteen new or reconditioned arm chairs, the present being dirty and untidy. A sideboard was needed for the dining room to house sauce bottles and pepper pots, which were being kept on window sills. They wanted a large piece of coconut matting for the centre of the recreation room. One basin had come away from the brick wall and needed fixing, also the removal of a cracked basin. Rubber mats were needed for ironing in ablution block. At present, all ironing was done in the recreation room.

All the windows needed an overhaul, as the catches were not working. Heating was required in the back room. The curtain for the dormitory was dreadful and the blackout was faded. There was no curtain in the Warden's bedroom, though it had frosted glass and Miss Ravenscroft said people could see in when the light was on. Miss Jacob-Smith rather doubted it. An electric point in the small bedroom would be appreciated, so it could be used as an office. The wireless in the Warden's room was said to buzz.

The hostel badly needed to be improved and it would be useful if the Ministry of Works visited to assess the requests. Miss Ravenscroft did seem to be trying to make the hostel look nice but Miss Jacob-Smith acknowledged that it was difficult when the decorations, chairs and curtains were so dreadful.

Masham Hostel, North Yorkshire

This hostel opened in a house known as 'The Greens' in 1943 (as reported in the *Land Girl*). In addition to the earlier report the following notes were made about the hostel by Miss Jowett:

23/6/43 A rather attractive small house on the outskirts of Masham, with an attractive small garden and lovely views. The number of girls to be accommodated would be sixteen, with two staff. A small room would be required for the sick bay. The septic tank would need to be improved. The cooking range was inadequate and would have to be improved. It was thought to be a particularly nice, if small, hostel.

1944 Miss Jacob-Smith made a few comments about the hostel in 1944. The Masham girls had spent their £5 Hostel Competition Prize Money on giving a party for all the farmers who employed girls from the hostel. The party was held in Masham Town Hall and 150 guests were present.

24/8/45 There was a great deal of dissatisfaction in general amongst the Masham girls. Miss Jacob-Smith discussed the possibility of classes at the hostel but there was no real interest. A letter had been received by Mrs Jopling from the WLA Office, saying that Mrs Bolhoules would be taking over from Miss Rushworth. The Forewoman's hat was too big and her breeches were too small. They did not meet around the waist. Her mac also leaked.

In 1946, the National Farmers Union (NFU) gave a gratuity of 6d a week to twenty-one Land Girls who had been at the hostel for nine months. Five received the maximum amount in cheques given at the Christmas Party. (*The Land Girl*, February 1946.)

Moat Hall, Little Ouseburn, North Yorkshire

Moat Hall was opened in 1943-1944, within a Grade Two listed early eighteenth century mansion, incorporating part of seventeenth century or earlier house with later extensions and alterations. The front of the house does not show the full extent of the commodious building.

One of the local farmers, although only a boy at the time, could remember seeing the Land Girls working in the farms nearby. He said the girls used to bike down to The Green Tree pub about a mile away. They used to toss their bikes in a pile in a field nearby. This was a custom that the Canadian airmen had started. They, like the Land Girls, went everywhere by bike. On the night before troops returned to Canada, great celebrations would take place at the Ouseburn pubs and the Anchor at Dunsforth. After this, they would throw their bikes over Aldwark Bridge and on the following morning the incoming squadron would have to retrieve them. He also related another story about a Land Girl who could not start her tractor. A burly farm hand came to her rescue and swung the starting handle at the front of the tractor, but he was nearly run over, as she had left it in gear!

One of the Land Girls at Moat Hall was Aline Richard, known as 'Jersey', because she came from the island. Aline's parents had decided at the last minute to take their three children out of Jersey when the Germans were thought to be coming. They left on the last boat and were sent to Yorkshire. Her father had

Moat Hall as it is today.

been a coach driver in Jersey and could handle heavy vehicles, so he joined the Fire Service and went to fight fires caused by bombing raids in the Northern cities. The family suffered great hardships after leaving behind their home and relations to go to an unknown place where they knew no one.

Aline, who was born in 1926, must have lied about her age when she enlisted in the WLA in May 1943, because she was only sixteen. Yet on enrolling Land Girls did not have to produce a birth certificate. She served in WLA until July 1945.

Miss Jacob-Smith visited the hostel in 1944 and summaries of her records follow:

3/3/44 Mrs Allsop found life very lonely. One large steamer was needed. The bottom part had been ordered but was never delivered. The windows and clocks had not been mended.

A Moat Hall Land Girl had been accused of taking another girl's shoes. They had been found in her suitcase but she said she did not know how they got there. She was not yet seventeen and had been in the WLA two years. She was put on probation until 4 May 1944. She said she intended to commit suicide and, on the strength of this, the police were contacted. The girl admitted to taking two pairs of civilian shoes, one pair of gum boots and one towel from the hostel. The police said a responsible person should sit up all night with the girl, until they could remove her to a remand home. On Thursday, 9 March she came before the Juvenile Court at Knaresborough.

10/3/44 The Land Girl accused of stealing attended the Juvenile Court with Miss Allsop and Dorothy Allison. She was sentenced to be bound over for twelve months or pay a fine of £5 and she was to pay 30s costs. The Magistrate was sympathetic to her because of her young age and said she should be placed in work near her home. This was to be her last chance with WLA.

31/3/44 One Land Girl had fallen off her bike and cut her hand. Another was to leave and become forewoman at Crayke Castle. Two girls employed by Ouse Catchment Board had turned up unexpectedly at the hostel. A wireless had been obtained from the shop in Ripon. The girls appeared very happy.

November 1944 A Christmas party was held at the hostel, as reported in the *Land Girl*.

Moat Hall had suffered from the bombing of nearby Linton on Ouse. There were also many casualties at the airfield. On another occasion, in the next village of Dunsforth a chicken received a direct hit. In that village there were two telephones, one at the Anchor Pub, a favourite place for the girls. When the early warning of an enemy raid was telephoned to the pub, the ARP warden would run up and down the street blowing his whistle.

No doubt the girls were also aware of a dangerously realistic fire practice in Richard Turner's barn, when straw was set on fire. Local children were encouraged to crawl on the floor to demonstrate that there was more oxygen at ground level. The Home Guard was popular with the locals and their task was to look out for enemy parachutists. The Germans caused great excitement when they dropped dummy parachutists to frighten everyone. In the local area, all the fields were ploughed up, as the farmers were required to grow as much corn as possible. The Dutch barns were full. Every farmyard and drive was lined with stacks awaiting the threshing machines and the willing Land Army girls. There was an invasion of mice and rats and they had to cover the stacks with nets to help protect the corn. Many barn owls helped to control them.

The food shortages were not as acute at Moat Hall as in some hostels, and there was a plentiful supply of eggs, butter and milk. (*Dunsforth during the War.*)

Jean Minskip (née Broadbent) left her home in Morley, near Leeds, where she had worked in a paper factory and went to Moat Hall as a Land Girl in 1943. She said there were twenty girls there and they slept in bunk beds, sharing only two bathrooms. She remembers the Assistant Warden, Jean Chambers, who was related to the famous Mouseman furniture maker. Jean Broadhead met her future husband at one of the dances held at the village hall.

One evening, Jean remembered a terrible row seemed to be coming down the corridor from other bedrooms. The following morning the girls found two girls together in one bed. At this time, such relationships were not tolerated and both girls were dismissed from the WLA.

In 1944, an enemy bomb was dropped between the church and the hostel and parts of the hostel could not be used. The girls were sent to Kirk Deighton Hostel for two weeks, whilst Arkendale Hostel was made ready. Subsequently, a Canadian Bomber hit the roof of Moat Hall and the hostel closed January 1945 (as reported in the *Land Girl*).

Moor Park, Beckwithshaw, near Harrogate, North Yorkshire

This hostel was two and a half miles south-west of Harrogate. In December 1943, at the hostel Christmas Party Mr Swan, the Pests Officer, dressed as Father Christmas.

Miss Jacob-Smith visited this hostel and made the following records of it:

24/2/44 Four girls came into the WLA Office to complain about the conditions at Moor Park. Their complaints were:

1. Insufficient breakfasts, consisting of a very small helping of cereal, one sausage or beans without toast or one pilchard, and a very small ration of jam.

2. Inadequate packed lunches with just three kinds of sandwiches on offer: pilchard, fish paste and margarine. There was no variety except the occasional

Knowle House, Mirfield, near Leeds. (*Murton Farming Museum*)

meat pasties, which they complained about being inedible. They asked if they could not have meat pies and sausage rolls instead.

3. Potatoes and vegetables. There were not enough green vegetables and vegetables were not always served with every meal. The potatoes were never peeled. They were served baked, steamed and mashed with their skins on. When mashed they were very brown and unappetising. Miss Yate Lee said they could not have them peeled, as there was no one to peel them. Miss Jacob-Smith understood they had no potato peeling machine at the hostel, so she had asked the Ministry of Works to supply one immediately.

4. The Land Girls complained that they were treated like schoolchildren. Whilst they thought Moor Park could be a very nice hostel, they had never felt that they could make it their home, as they were so strictly supervised. They felt that Miss Yate Lee 'sneaked' in on them. They also said they felt very sorry for the twenty-year-old cook, as she was never allowed in the recreation room. As the other domestic was a WLA Orderly, she had to sit by herself in the staff sitting room.

5. Lack of recreational facilities at the hostel. Miss Jacob-Smith told them they could buy a piano and a sewing machine, to which the WLA Office would contribute £12 and £5 respectively. They had no dart board but the Ministry of

Works would supply that. The bus, which only ran once a week left about 9.05 pm, and they asked if they it could return a little later, so they could see a film show to the end. Miss Jacob-Smith told them that the matter rested with the bus company. Miss Jacob-Smith was to go to see Miss Yate Lee to discuss the matters with her.

Miss Jacob-Smith raised the criticisms made by girls of the breakfasts at the hostel with the Warden. Miss Yate Lee said that the WLA had no conscience. How could the WLA tell her to waste time using gas to make toast, in view of the fuel shortage? If she made toast it would be against her conscience. If WLA dealt with the complaints, then they would waste food. For lunch, a visiting WLA official Miss Lloyd said she had never tasted anything as delicious as the meat pasties made by the hostel. Dripping and cheese sandwiches were frequently provided. Meat pies and sausage rolls were impossible to get delivered and sausage meat was on allowance, as sausages were served for breakfast.

Potatoes were not peeled, as Miss Yate Lee felt this was a waste of time and as the skins were nutritious this would mean putting good food to waste! The girls always had large helpings and never leave anything. It was quite impossible to have a peeler in the kitchen as there was no room for one. She suggested that the Ministry of Works investigated the placement of a peeler before sending one. A second vegetable was always provided, not always greens, but maybe carrots or turnips and there was always some left over. The domestic staff did not mix with the girls. She did not want the Cook to sit with the girls, in case the new Irish domestic joined her, as she was very rough and was not considered suitable to mix with the girls.

When the girls came to the hostel they had bought a piano for £6 but it had proved to be no use, so Miss Jacob-Smith thought they should sell it and put the money towards another. There was a good amount in the hostel fund, so they would be able to buy anything they wanted. The later bus only ran on the late night when they had to be in by 11.00 pm. If the leaving time from Harrogate was altered it should not matter to Miss Yate Lee, she said.

The Warden was indignant that she had not been informed about the increase in numbers. The Ministry of Works had been to measure for installing more baths. She did not like to hear second-hand news about this. Miss Yate Lee also objected that the girls could go to the WLA Office with complaints and that the Office would listen to the girls without making it known to her. The correct procedure was for the hostel Committee to meet and suggest what complaints had been made and then take them to the Warden. Why weren't the girls sent back to the hostel, when the Warden had not been approached?

Miss Lloyd supported Miss Yate Lee in this matter and she thought the girls had not complained about anything to them. Miss Yate Lee was going to speak to the girls about this matter.

4/3/44 Miss Jacob-Smith returned articles of clothing to the friend of the girl who had gone to the Juvenile Court. Miss Jacob-Smith told Miss Yate Lee that there was no reason to suspect the friend of dishonesty.

30/3/44 Land Girls were waiting an hour or an hour and a half after work for transport, standing in the cold by the roadside. This also meant they were late in arriving for their evening meal, making more work for the hostel staff. This was caused by girls working in opposite directions, with only one van to pick them all up. Perhaps the WAEC could coordinate with the Staveley, Knaresborough and Moor Park hostels, Miss Jacob-Smith thought. This would prevent the girls from the Staveley Hostel going to farms near Knaresborough and the Staveley girls going to Starbeck.

Muston Lodge, near Filey, East Yorkshire

(This hostel has already been mentioned in the section on Miss Jowett's inspection of potential hostels.) During the war about a dozen land girls lived at Muston Lodge, with a Warden from Hunmanby in charge. The local farmers had made a request for help and the girls worked on different farms as needed. They did not receive any training for their farm work and learnt by experience. From the hostel they did general farm work, spending time with stock, poultry and sheep. They worked alongside the men in the fields at hay time and harvest. In the winter months they worked with the threshing set and were involved with carrying the chaff away or worked on the stacks forking sheaves onto the machine. It was rare for them to work with horses, as the male workers liked to work with and care for their own horses. The Land Girls from this hostel usually went to work by bicycle, which was something of an achievement as many had never ridden one before!

A WLA girl living in the hostel was accused of stealing meat from the kitchen and taking it to her family in Hull at weekends. The evidence was the blood stains on her baggage. On further investigation, it turned out that the stains came from the rabbits she had bought from a local rabbit-catcher and it was these she was taking home to supplement her family's rations. Later, it was found that a dog had been helping himself to the meat from the hostel and the girl from Hull received a full apology! (Clegg, 1996.)

In 1942, a German plane crashed on the hill top in a field in Muston. It landed on a small flock of sheep, killing seven of them.

Social life at the hostel seems to have been limited to attending the Young Farmers' Club, the Women's Institute, meeting Free Poles and later the Free French, who were based at Butlins, and attending concerts or going to the pictures at Filey.

Winifred Eade lived in Muston Lodge in 1941. She remembers being in the back of a truck going down Garrowby Hill, one of the steepest hills in East Yorkshire. The brakes had failed and the truck crashed in a farmer's fence, careering across the field and straight into his barn. The chickens were flying everywhere! Fortunately, no one was hurt and the girls got a day off!

Pollington, near Snaith, East Yorkshire

This hostel was officially opened in December 1946 by Lady Bingley. Accommodation was so scarce in the district that about one hundred Land Girls had moved in before it was officially opened. Most of the girls were from Yorkshire and about half of them were newcomers to the WLA. The rest had several years' experience of farming. They worked on farms near the Goole area and were mainly occupied in gathering in the root crops.

This was the largest WLA hostel in the country, usually accommodating between ninety and a hundred girls, with space for up to one hundred and thirty girls. It consisted of numerous extremely large huts, which had previously accommodated the WAAF. The site and many of the huts still stand today.

Pollington's huge recreation room as it is today.

The Warden, Mrs Kenden, lived with the Forewoman at the approach to the site. They both had their own quarters, together with the four other members of staff who slept in two small rooms on camp-type beds. The windows were large and in 1946 they no longer required blackout curtains. Olive Elcock (née Rowley), an Orderly at the hostel, occasionally used these windows when she was late coming in at night.

Olive reported that every Land Girl had their own wardrobe and drawers. Each of these rooms had a stove and they were allocated one bucket of fuel per day. The Cook travelled from a farm each day, while another Cook lived in. The staff prepared the sandwiches for the girls' lunch boxes. This was unusual, because in most hostels the Land Girls prepared their own sandwiches. The Nurse, Mrs Roberts, had her accommodation in the sick bay block, which was at the other end of the site. There were seven beds in the sick bay, which still stands on the site and has been converted to a large, modern family house.

There was a gigantic recreation hut where regular dances were held.

This led on to a large dining area with a hatch to the kitchen, numerous stores and the sandwich-making room. The food was of an excellent standard. Each item of food used was meticulously weighed to comply with the rationing rules. Should any girl remain hungry there was always the village bakery, but the buns and bread would apparently fall like stones if dropped, so it was not popular!

Pollington Hostel, site of ablution block, still standing today.

Pollington, the remains of the Dormitory Block as it is today.

There were several long dormitories, which still exist, and a washing and ablution block with a tower for storing the water tank, which provided the necessary water pressure. Much of the original hostel can still be seen, but it is in disrepair. Now, the site is divided into two farms, St Lawrence Farm and Animal Farm (named after the George Orwell novel).

The girls used their bikes to travel to farms within a four to five mile radius. Girls working at farms further away were transported by army lorries. There were four of these lorries and six drivers in total. They also serviced and cared for the bikes. If they found a bike around the site they would take it to the bicycle hut. This happened to Olive's bike when she left it outside her quarters. Sometimes a farmer would call for the girls in his own lorry. Four German Prisoners of War worked on the site doing repairs. The site used by the WLA was vast as the dormitories were set apart from other huge buildings. It was quite different from the usual hostel and numerous repairs had to be completed in consequence.

The Warden was thought to be very kind and she was also fair to the staff and girls. They all respected her. The girls were allowed to have a long weekend every fortnight, from Friday night to Sunday evening. Orderlies had a long weekend once a month. The Forewoman was extremely efficient and always put foremost the best interests of the girls. She often did battle with the farmers on behalf of the girls. Some of the farmers tried to be too friendly to the girls and the Forewoman would immediately stop sending girls to their farms.

Olive Elcock joined up to work as an orderly at the hostel when she was still only sixteen. Although she was not a member of the Land Army she still had to wear the uniform, which she travelled to Leeds to collect. She lived happily at the hostel from 1946 to 1949, when she left to get married and then she worked part-time until the hostel closed in 1950.

The Land Girls at Pollington had a wonderful social life. There was a cinema down a long narrow lane which linked the RAF base with the hostel, although only a small number of RAF personnel remained there. The village hall served as a Christian Social Base where the Land Army girls could meet the local lads. The most popular meeting pub was the George and Dragon. There were two other pubs in the village, one used mostly by the Poles. In 1947, for six weeks all the girls from Brooklands Hostel, Selby, were evacuated to Pollington as their hostel had been flooded.

On 18 January 1947 a recording was made at the hostel for the Wilfred Pickles radio show. Hired charabancs and coaches came from as far as Skipton Hostel to bring Land Girls to the performance. Wilfred was dressed in a natty blue suit and striped tie. He coaxed and cajoled the girls before the microphone. Eight happy girls went home with £1 18s 6d each. The Forewoman at Pollington said to Wilfred that she liked watching little piglets growing and her worst experience had been falling backwards into a muck cart. A girl from Pollington had been due to get married soon after the recording. She had her wedding dress and trousseau bought, but after the radio programme discovered that her intended was already married.

In 1947, after a particularly severe cold winter, the whole hostel site was flooded. There were no rivers nearby, so the water table must have risen. All the girls were sent home.

There is still one surprising reminder of the Land Army at the hostel. The author observed some graffiti in the toilets in which a Land Girl had signed her name and the hostel address!

Ripon Hostel, North Yorkshire

This hostel was the first to open in the three Ridings, in 1941 (see Chapter Two for more details of the opening). Land Girl Mary Tetlow, who had previously been at Catterick, moved to Ripon in the winter of 1943. She described the hostel as being set amongst rows of houses at the bottom of the slope, near the cathedral. It had been a YWCA hostel and consisted of two log huts, dormitory and recreation/dining room joined by a passage where the Land Girls stored their coats and boots. The dormitory was divided into cubicles accommodating four persons with bunks, two dressing tables and four folding chairs. Two stove heaters were in the gangway. The baths were beyond.

Outside the Ripon Hostel. (*Eileen Jones Collection*)

Miss McLeod was in charge of this hostel, assisted by Miss Blanche and two girls who did the housework. On the evening of Mary Tetlow's arrival the girls' Halloween decorations were evident in the dining room. There was also a protest meeting about the untidiness of the girls versus the domestic staff. One Land Girl made an offer to the domestic staff, that she would clean the hostel if one of them would muck out her pigs!

Each day, they were divided by the Forewoman into gangs and each assigned to different farms. They were transported there in a van by the Head Land Girl. Mary was at Ripon for three months and it was almost inevitable during that time that she was put on threshing. Apart from the four Land Girls who were working at Markenfield Hall, threshing was the inevitable fate of all of them!

Mary recalled the Christmas dinner at the hostel. There were white cloths on the tables and plates of tarts, which they munched in the kitchen, while singing 'O Come all Ye Faithful'. Mrs McLeod, the Warden, made a short speech wishing them a Happy Christmas and saying she hoped there would be more Land Girls at the hostel next year! They had recently acquired a wireless and it made a pleasant evening sitting by the stove reading.

One year, the girls at Ripon were told that the Harrogate WLA Office had demanded they should be come back on the following Tuesday after Christmas Day in time for work that afternoon. Mary decided her plan was going to be

Girls with troops at a party at Ripon Hostel. (*Eileen Jones Collection*)

either: '1) To forget it, 2) To not know, 3) To not understand.' She had not decided what to do. Despite this and the alarm felt at the WLA Office at the Land Girls' negative attitude, all the girls returned as demanded!

When they arrived back they had a feast with a small cake, parkin and an apple. One girl had come back in new clothes and said she felt really cold. She found her wait in Harrogate for the bus was stressful, as it was so dark she nearly got on the wrong bus to Knaresborough instead of Ripon. The stove was out of use, so it was especially cold and Mary consoled herself with a hot bath.

On Wednesday, 23 February 1944 there was a dance at the base camp. The soldiers had promised to send transport to the hostel but it did not arrive. The girls asked Mrs McLeod to ring up the base, but she refused, so they went in style by taxi! The next day Mary went into the kitchen, Mrs McLeod had her lips drawn down on her cigarette and was looking very unamiable. Miss Clegg said, "There's no sign of your cough now, eh Mary!"

Two new girls arrived and one looked thoroughly miserable. She said she had been separated from her friend, who had been with her at the Westwood Hostel. She wanted to know the times of trains to Harrogate, so she could go home. Mary borrowed some gum boots and went to the camp cinema, although the roads were covered with ice. The picture was *Thunderbirds* about the air training schools in Canada. It was followed by a western, which Mary particularly enjoyed because of the horses. She and her friend also went to the YMCA soon after, where they played cards with two soldiers. The men seemed very impressed when the girls told their fortunes.

202

It was hard work threshing during the day, Mary said. They used old threshing machines driven by tractor engines. Some of the machines dated from the early twentieth century. They took it in turns band cutting on top of the machine, chaff carrying from under it, straw carrying from the back (Mary's record was four bales at one go) with a pitchfork. Their only protection from the dust was a scarf over the mouth. No one complained, although Mary said she was slow. It was much harder work than she had done at Catterick but there was no nonsense with a pernickety sergeant.

She said that a spirit of camaraderie existed amongst the girls and between them and the thresher men. Two of them travelled from farm to farm with their machines, so the girls were always welcomed by the farmers and their staff. By way of a break, they sometimes were sent to 'burn up', clearing the land of shrubs and trees. They shifted a lot each day with saws and hatchets. The woods had already been uprooted and it seemed easy work. Their sandwiches seemed a little better when eaten by a bonfire. One of the older Land Girls, who was aged about forty, entertained the girls by reciting long narrative poems. They all sang popular songs – and only one that was rude!

Back at the hostel, their meals were always well cooked and plentiful. Mary marvelled at the contrast to the rations at home. She wished they could have eaten like that at midday, as the sandwiches seemed inadequate. Most evenings were spent in the hostel as they were too tired to go out, especially when it was dark and cold. Sometimes a few of the girls would go up to town to the cinema or to the various Forces canteens. One evening they went to the fair.

Ripon girls receiving instruction in a technical subject. (*Eileen Jones Collection*)

Mary could never remember anyone visiting from the Harrogate WLA Office. When their wages arrived late the forewoman always said, "Don't blame me. It's them in Harrogate." Sometimes a voluntary worker connected with the Cathedral used to call. She said she had nothing to do with working conditions or the running of the hostel. Her work was with moral welfare and she gave confidential talks to girls who were about to get married.

Eventually, Mary developed a terrible rash like goose flesh all over her chest and a stubborn racking cough. She left the WLA as a result and returned to her former job as a librarian.

Settle, North Yorkshire

Settle Hostel opened in 1942. This was a purpose-built hutment hostel on the site where the Mill Bank housing estate is situated today, according to Malhamdale Local History Society. It was a machinery hostel, accommodating tractor drivers and machinery workers. There was a social life of dances and visits to the local cinema. Land Girls from Cappleside often took a taxi to Settle to join in the social merriment. The RAF built a hut with a dance floor and stage alongside the Falcon Hotel in Settle. Every Saturday dances were held there.

Several girls were transferred to Settle from Skipton but they found the facilities were poor with insufficient food and bedding. They organised a petition requesting a return to Skipton. They said that new recruits were going to Skipton when they should have been placed at Settle. The girls were allowed to go back to Skipton. (Bullock, 2002.)

The hostel became redundant early in 1948, as machinery accommodation was transferred to the Labour Sub Committee. The hostel closed in 1949.

Sherburn, near Malton, North Yorkshire

Situated between Malton and Scarborough, Sherburn Hostel was brick-built. In May 1943 the *Hull Daily Mail* described the hutment as a light airy place, with a comfortable dining room, a recreation room and a capacious kitchen where appetising meals were prepared. The girls slept in bunk beds and there was plenty of room for drying, washing and depositing wet clothes. There was a constant supply of hot water. The three baths were in constant use after the Land Girls returned from a hard day's work in the fields.

Mrs Morrison, the Warden, was considered the ideal person to look after the Land Girls, as she was a mother with a large grown-up family. She ensured the hostel ran smoothly and she acted as a guide and mentor to the girls. She was helped by an assistant warden and willing staff. Soon after the hostel opened, preparations were being made for a special dance for the WLA Benevolent Fund and to buy a piano.

A male Foreman supervised the girls at work. At first, he was sceptical about girls working on the farm but he later told the *Hull Daily Mail* that he had been impressed by their enthusiasm and determination to learn as quickly as possible. The girls interviewed were wearing bib and braces, brightly coloured blouses and wellington boots. The charge woman was described as a 'sparkling brunette'. She had been a machinist in her previous life, while another girl had been a bandage roller and a third a packer. One girl said she had put on 2st in weight since she had joined the WLA nine months previously.

Emily Chant was at Sherburn Hostel. After arriving at the hostel, aged eighteen or nineteen, she felt she had friends for the first time in her life and found a wonderful camaraderie at the hostel. Life at the hostel gave a real sense of freedom to her, because before joining the WLA she had worked 'in service' and had been very badly treated. She and her friends would swap life stories. They had all been in the same boat, Emily said, knowing a miserable existence until the War Effort was needed and they joined the Land Army.

Emily and her friends at the hostel would play games and reminisce and, she said, they always looked out for each other. Sometimes they would sneak out the hostel for a drink and a laugh, whilst the others would cover for them. Sometimes they even went as far as Scarborough. In the evenings they kept busy making things out of old clothing and bric-a-brac. One hot day Emily said she took off her shirt and worked in her underslip and she was so badly sunburned that she got into trouble from the farmer for having a day off work.

After the WLA left the hostel it was occupied by German prisoners of war. Then, the former hostel was subsequently used as timber store, also a piggery and a shed for battery hens. It then fell into disrepair and was demolished seven or eight years ago to make room for a housing estate. Vicarage Farm Close was built on the site of the derelict hostel.

Sherburn-in-Elmet, near Selby, North Yorkshire

Some of the information on this hostel has been taken from Winifred Emmingham's notes (provided by her son, John Sykes). Winifred was a Land Girl at Sherburn-in-Elmet from 1941 to 1945. She had lived in Batley before joining the WLA. The issue of uniforms when they arrived caused some merriment, she remembered, as the smallest girls got the largest outfits and the largest girls were given small uniforms. There was a great deal of swapping until everyone was suitably clad.

Sherburn-in-Elmet hostel, located in Moor Lane, housed forty girls aged from nineteen to twenty-five and they enjoyed life as a big happy family. Miss Beaumont was the Warden and Winifred said she was called 'Our mother, our provider and a wonderful person' by one of the girls. She was a great help to all those girls who felt homesick.

Sherburn-in-Elmet Hostel members, 1944. (*Eden Camp Collection*)

The hostel organised beetle drives and whist drives to raise money. Some of that money was used to purchase a piano so they could organise their own dances and concerts. The girls used to help in the YMCA in the village. Unfortunately, they were denied money-saving goods on offer to the other armed services. Sherburn-in-Elmet was a sleepy village but there were airmen there, as well as at Church Fenton. There were lots of dances at the camps and they were given invites to most of these. There were four or five men to every woman.

When the girls started work they found it hard, as they were unused to farming ways. One girl was sent to sort potatoes and found herself surrounded by mice. She ran screaming out of the field. The farmers were wary of the farming novices and the girls themselves were fearful of the cows and cart horses. Gradually, the farmers and girls grew to respect each other and the girls found the locals were very kind to them.

In 1946, the Forewoman at Sherburn in Elmet spoke at the inaugural ceremony for the special recruiting campaign for the West Riding at Leeds. She said she had been posted two days after the war began to horticultural work. It was hard work but she thoroughly enjoyed it, she said. Another Land Girl, who was also a Forewoman at the hostel, was chosen to be in the guard of honour to the King and Queen at the Harvest Festival at Westminster Abbey on 30 October 1948.

The hostel was situated next to a poultry farm and continued to be used into the late 1940s. It is still used today by a flying club.

Skipton Hostel, North Yorkshire

This hostel was situated in Shortbank Road, Skipton. The *Craven Herald* reported in August 1941, noting that the site had been selected for the construction of a purpose-built hostel for women land workers in Settle and Skipton. This was a machinery hostel. It had been resolved that WLA tractor drivers and personnel should be accommodated together in hostels, apart from general workers, as it was thought that discontent could arise from the two types of workers living together.

Skipton Hostel consisted of two single-storey brick buildings, with a dormitory block to sleep forty. Their work was organised by the War Agricultural Executive Committee (WAEC), also known as 'War Ag', and was, in turn, organised by their HQ at the back of Millbridge House, between the Castle Inn and the then New Ship Inn. The girls worked alongside other WAEC workers travelling from the hostel by bicycle or sometimes by truck or van. Dora Varley (née Watson) who had formerly been a cashier in a Bradford office, lived in the hostel and she remembers that they were well fed, paying 17s 6d a week for board out of a week's wage of £2 or so, although overtime could be earned in busy periods. They were expected to be in by 10.30 pm each night, unless they had requested a special pass. (The war time memories of Dora Varley, Malhamdale History Group.)

The Land Girls were sent to work from depots such as Carleton, West Marton, Gargrave or Bolton Abbey. Dora was taught to drive a tractor by an Irish man, who assured her she would get it 'through the eye of a needle'. As the gates to fields were so narrow, it was essential that the tractor driver was accurate, even if the gate post had to be removed, as there was so little space! Dora was so accomplished that she became a 'Flyer driver', which was the nickname given to a person who drove a double tractor unit. She explained that: 'The spiked wheel tractors used for heavy work could not travel on the roads, so they were transported on a trailer, pulled by a tractor with rubber wheels. This tractor also pulled a fuel trailer, and at harvest time a reaper/binder too, making the whole outfit long and difficult to manoeuvre, especially if it needed to be reversed for any distance.'

Another of her jobs was at the Carelton Fuel Depot, where she reconciled the fuel dispensed with what was left in the tank. Other work involved ploughing, back-breaking potato picking, sugar beet lifting on cold mornings, hay making and harvesting and threshing. Ploughing competitions were organised on a county basis. In January 1944, local heats were at Aireville and finals at Wetherby. Dora won the Land Army Employees class at Aireville and was runner-up at Wetherby.

Dora still lives in Skipton, having met her husband as a result of her work with the WLA. She is now the organiser of the Skipton Land Army Reunion Society. (Malhamdale Local History Society.)

207

In the *Land Girl*, (published May 1943), H Driver wrote of the hostel:

'There were forty of us at Skipton. We are in the mechanical section and we can all drive tractors. We go out each day to our depots and from there we are sent to farms round and about. At present I am ploughing by the side of a deep ravine with a Yorkshire stream bubbling along the bottom. It was great fun watching the expression on the faces of the local farmers when first the Land Girls started to plough. "Nay, Nay, Lassie, "was torn from their usually silent lips and now they even admit that we make" a Middlin fairish job on't". I consider like other hostels that ours is the cosiest, nicest and friendliest of its kind. I enjoy ploughing and my life here very much!'

The hostel was located down Shortbank Road, towards a steep rise to Rombaids Moor, where a dirt road branched off to the right. The members of staff at Skipton with Miss Rolston, the YMCA Warden, included a Cook and a former high school teacher who had worked in China, and now took charge of the linen. The Warden, Mrs Rolston, was a Canadian woman, the wife of a Canadian officer serving in Britain. She was kind, firm, sympathetic and could be unpredictable, but she was always on the girls' side. Whatever trouble the girls were in she would defend them. The girls were fond of her but she would also drive them mad with her way-out schemes (one of Mrs Rolston's cooking disasters is related earlier in the book).

The hostel was not beautiful but it remained homely and comfortable. The dormitory blocks slept forty girls. There were ten double bunks down each side, which were divided into sets of four by rows of single wardrobes. Each faced a corresponding four across the central gangway. This made small families of eight. At the end of the dormitory block were washing facilities which consisted of rows of wash basins, three bathrooms and lavatories.

The bath rota was tightly organised and bathing together was the norm. Beyond the dormitory block were the sick bay and small staff bedrooms furnished with economy. The sick bay overlooked the Rombalds Moor and the wonderful scenery. The sitting room/dining room and kitchen and the Warden's quarters were in the other block. The dining tables were at one end near the serving hatch and two rings of fireside chairs were grouped around coke stoves.

Many of the girls had boyfriends and some had husbands in the Forces. They would spend their time going to the cinema or knitting or sewing around the hostels stoves. Some girls worried about letters that failed to arrive or listened avidly to news bulletins, as they could never forget it was wartime. When a telegraph boy was sighted up the road the suspense gripped everyone. (Driver, 1975.)

As for a social life, there was a picture house and dances were held at Skipton Town Hall. The Warden often arranged the use of a gramophone and sometimes a local band for dances at the hostel. The whole community would be invited. Hostel sales were held to raise money for the Red Cross and Great Ormond Street Hospital. There was also a tap dancing troupe called the 'Landolettes'. They travelled by bike to outlying isolated villages, where they would put on skimpy outfits in village hall kitchens and then dance on tables on the main hall. (Bullock, 2002.)

The Warden would often say a prayer each evening and a short service was held on Sundays. One recruit noted that on most occasions the hymn chosen was 'Dear Lord and Father of Mankind, forgive our foolish ways'. She was unsure whether it was the only hymn the Warden knew or whether it was considered to have particular significance for the Land Girls! (Bullock, 2002.)

In 1948, the hostel became redundant, as machinery accommodation was transferred to the Labour Sub Committee. It remained open, however, as accommodation for men working on drainage and open cast restoration work.

Staveley Hostel, North Yorkshire

This hostel opened in 1943. (Staveley has already been discussed in relation to Miss Jowett's visits to requisitioned houses.) Miss Jacob-Smith made a few visits to the hostel, which are mentioned below.

The hostel was formerly known as the Old Rectory, opposite the village church, and it is now used as a family home and called Staveley Court. The hostel opened on 3 July 1943, with fifteen girls. The Ministry of Works decided to open before they had finished the work necessary for the full number of girls. The house was still full of workmen during the first few weeks, but the basins, two WCs and a bath were working and most of work was finished in the kitchen. Mrs Colman, of the Ministry of Works office in Leeds, came out to see the work and when it was finished she said it would make a nice hostel.

Miss Whittington, the new Warden, who had previously been the Assistant Warden at Blois Hall and Mrs Home had carried on. The dormitories, recreation room and dining room looked very nice, although the linoleum was not laid down. Lady Lawson Tancred and Miss Jacob-Smith came to meet the girls. Only nine girls had appeared by 6.00 pm and Miss Jacob-Smith thought they seemed a sullen lot. With the exception of three from other counties, their forms said they were from the Leeds and Barnsley areas.

Lady Lawson Tancred spoke to the girls, telling them she had opened the first hostel in 1915, before the Women's Land Army had officially been formed (see Chapter One for more information). The girls were not interested in anything like that, though!

The Forewoman, who had been at Knaresborough, did not appear for the tea but came down afterwards in a tweed suit and simply walked in without a word to anyone, handing the girls some forms to fill in. The Warden at Knaresborough, Mrs Budlark said that the Forewoman at Staveley had been the instigator of all the trouble at Knaresborough and they had been glad to be rid of her. Miss Jacob-Smith felt it was unfortunate that she had been sent to Staveley, as this was bound to affect the name of the WLA in that hostel.

Hazel Bennet was a Land Girl at Staveley. She was just eighteen years old and only just tall enough to join the WLA. She used a shovel almost as big as herself. It was hard work, she found, especially digging potatoes. She got jaundice and was sent home on the bus from Staveley, with her skin all yellow, carrying two dead rabbits.

In December 1943 Staveley Hostel wanted a piano and a sewing machine, so the hostel organised a dance at Boroughbridge to raise money. An epidemic of influenza in the district had upset the arrangements made for the room, which had been kindly lent for the dance and another room was obtained at the last minute. Staveley was now able to have both, a piano and sewing machine, as £23 was raised.

28/2/44 Miss Jacob-Smith went to see a girl who was upset because of the removal of her friend. The friend had been an excellent worker but she had created mischief in the hostel and the Forewoman had arranged for her to be removed to Ripon. The Doctor thought the upset girl should have her release from the WLA, as she had not been well and was now suffering with a sore throat.

The lavatories were overflowing at the hostel, the roof was leaking over the stairs and the tap heads needed new washers. One of the girls had been sent to a Salvation Army hostel as she was considered very dirty!

4/3/44 Miss Jacob-Smith was asked to call at the hostel. A party had been arranged the previous night and the troops who usually went could not attend so others came. Approximately nine girls went to a local pub and the troops they met came back to the party at the hostel. Two girls were so drunk when they came back to the hostel that they could not stand up. Two others were not so drunk and three more were also slightly drunk. These girls and the troops brought in bottles of beer. Several of them were sick on the recreation room floor and one chair was broken.

The Warden was away for the weekend and Mrs Hower had been in charge. She had stopped the party at 11.40 pm and told the girls not to go out of the hostel. In spite of this, one of the girls was missing and did not return until 1.00 am. Mrs Hower told the girl she was not fit to live in a hostel, whereupon the girl packed her bag and said she was leaving. The WAEC did not want her back and the Warden was anxious that the other eight girls were also transferred to another hostel. The Forewoman said the girls concerned also behaved very badly when out working and she would like them removed.

17/3/44 Miss Whittington was very anxious to know when the girls who had been drunk at the party would be moving to another hostel. Two of them had returned slightly drunk again that week.

23/3/44 Miss Jacob-Smith took Miss Whittington and two girls to Blois Hall for a whist drive. Twelve dice were needed so the hostel could run a beetle drive. A total of £5 had been paid to the hostel Benevolent Fund. This was the proceeds of the recent dance. The remainder was used to buy a sewing machine. The Staveley Land Girls were moved to Arkendale at the end of 1944.

Stockton House, Stockton on Forest, North Yorkshire

This hostel, located four miles from York, has been discussed in a previous chapter. This requisitioned house is now a private dwelling.

Stokesley Hostel, North Yorkshire

The hostel was of the hutment variety, mostly consisting of wood on a brick foundation. It was sited in North Road in Stokesley, next to a large three-storey Georgian House called North Villa (now demolished). The hostel closed in 1948 and was subsequently used by displaced persons and Poles.

Bessie Bowes (née Eyre) was interviewed in 2004 for the BBC People's War Website (from which Ian Pearce supplied the following information). Bessie had been working at Slazengers in Wakefield before she joined the WLA. She was sent to the YWCA hostel at Stokesley and she lived there from 1943 to 1948, when the hostel closed.

There were forty-two girls at Stokesley, mostly from Bradford and Leeds. Bessie's memories of the hostel were of bunk beds and coke fires all the way down the dormitory. They had a wonderful time, she recalled. The Warden used to give parties for everything – Valentine's day or anything like that. There was also the hostel Concert Party, which was organised by a girl from Huddersfield. The Warden allowed her to make dresses out of blackout curtains and the girls had little white blouses and black skirts. She used to tear up old sheets and make all sorts for concerts. They used to give concerts at local villages for such as 'Salute the Soldier' week.

There were soldiers stationed at the Manor in Stokesley and at the Camp in Station Road. If a party had been organised and a girl had not got a boyfriend, the Warden would count the number of lads short and sent for a supply from the camp. Many met their husbands that way. One good thing about being in the Land Army, Bessie thought, was that they could wear civvies, whereas the forces had to wear uniform. At first, the girls wore their corduroy breeches to go to dances at the Town Hall and to go to Middlesbrough to the pictures. At parties they put their dresses on, though clothing coupons put restrictions on their choice of attire. There were beetle drives and whist drives organised.

At first Bessie, like the others was homesick, and she used to go home at weekends, but later she stayed at Stokesley for the weekends. There were only a few remaining at the hostel eventually and the Warden used to make them a nice tea and let them bring their boyfriends in. The food in the hostel was good and sandwiches, made by the girls each morning, were of ham, spam, dripping, beetroot or cheese.

Two girls at Stokesley Hostel. (*Eden Camp Collection*)

Like most Land Girls, Bessie and her colleagues regarded threshing as one of the worst jobs. With barley threshing, the barley awns went down and scratched their necks. Often the farmers would keep them extra time, which made them late in to the hostel, with no time to wash or bathe before eating. Bessie said this used to 'nark' them. At threshing time, if they were not cutting the bands of corn then they had to carry the chaff, which was collected in a big sheet.

A girl from the hostel once went missing during the threshing. She was supposed to be carrying the chaff, but she had fainted and had fallen underneath

Entertainment at Stokesley. (*Eden Camp Collection*)

the threshing machine, after which the chaff blew all over her. The girls pulled her out and she went home. She never came back to the hostel.

One thing Bessie disliked about her work was the presence of rats and mice. When the girls got to the bottom of the stack they often found rats. It was necessary to have their trousers tied up to stop the rats climbing up their trouser legs! While cutting bands Bessie once saw a hole in her companion's trousers and a mouse looking out. Bessie dared not tell her friend in case she screamed and jumped into the thresher. Threshing machines were potentially quite dangerous, with lots of moving parts.

Wardens did change, but one stayed at Stokesley a long time and she was very good to the girls. Mrs Bottomley visited the Hostel as the representative of the WLA and she was friendly with the Warden. She always arrived on a motorbike with a sidecar. In 1947, Tina Goss (also at Guisborough Hostel) was involved with the tremendous task of snow-cutting. Italian prisoners of war arrived by transport, whilst the girls still went everywhere by bicycle to work in the fields.

In October 1946 a Harvest Ball in aid of the WLA Benevolent fund was organised at Stokesley, when the excellent sum of £178s was raised. Hostel wardens did their best to make the life exciting for their charges. There were soldiers up the Station Road at a camp there. In February 1947 the Stokesley hostel girls went to the York pantomime and this was followed by tea in York. The hostel organised a dance in the Town Hall, Stokesley on 7 March, ending at 1.00 am. The entry fee of 2s 6d included a buffet supper.

The concerts given by the Stokesley girls were well-known for their fun and originality. A young girl who went to one of these concerts about sixty-four years ago can still remember the first verse of one of the songs:

'I'm a little prairie flower,

Getting wilder every day

Nobody cares what happens to me

So I'm as wild as wild can be.

Umpa Umpa Umpa...'

Putting on a show at Stokesley Hostel. (*Eden Camp Collection*)

Eileen Conlin (née Thomas) was at Stokesley from 1946 until 1949 when the hostel disbanded. She worked for the Thomas family on farms at Seamer Moor and Moor Farm and married Clifford Thomas.

In April 1949 Stokesley closed and girls were transferred to Croft.

Strensall, near York, North Yorkshire

This was a hutment hostel, which was probably opened in 1942. The WLA closed the hostel in 1944, when they moved out to Stockton on the Forest, a few miles away. Prisoners of war were then billeted at the Strensall Hostel.

Kay Farrell, who was also at Thirsk and Easingwold, stayed at Strensall as Forewoman for a short time, in order to select suitable girls for tractor driving and machine handling. She took them to Easingwold Hostel, where they learned to plough the grass land and work the flax fields.

Eleven girls at Strensall had 'dirty heads'. Two of the girls were particularly bad. The doctor who gave them all a medical certificate, advised them to go home until they were clean. One of the girls had been warned several times about being dirty and no one would share a bunk with her.

24/1/44 Miss Rudd was very unsettled, as she had not had a day or weekend off since Christmas. Miss Davis had offered to take over one weekend but Miss Rudd had refused! The staff consisted of her Assistant Warden, together with a cook of twenty-one years, a hostel orderly and a daily cleaner.

24/2/44 Miss Rudd appeared to be tired of the hostel and threatened to leave. The Assistant Warden had not yet arrived. The Forewoman said the girls were poor workers and needed constant supervision, but hoped that in time they would improve. Thirty-three girls were working in the hostel garden, which was much improved.

29/2/44 Miss Rudd had sent in her resignation to YWCA and was to leave on 26/3/44. She complained about the lack of staff, as she had only had an Assistant Warden for two weeks in five months. The girls were not working but they were going to creosote the hostel outside in the afternoon. ENSA was giving a film slide show once a week. Mrs Rudd thought this was too often and suggested once a fortnight.

16/3/44 It was proposed closing the hostel in six weeks' time and moving the Land Girls to Stockton House. Strensall Hostel would have prisoners of war instead.

31/3/44 The new Warden Mrs Mcleod had made the hostel look much cleaner and more comfortable, with cushions and flowers in the common room. Miss Jacob-Smith found the girls in the hostel helpful and well behaved. The hostel orderly needed to be told that orderlies do not have every weekend and evening free.

11/4/44 Mrs Mcleod informed Miss Jacob-Smith that she thought Mrs Porter was to be the new Warden and she would be coming on 17/4/44. She still found the Orderly of little use and very slow at work.

24/4/44 The hostel was to close on 5 May. Mrs Mcleod had not been notified of the food allocation and she was to leave in three days. She complained of the lack of cooperation from the WLA.

21/5/44 Miss Hardy to be the new Assistant Warden at Stockton on Forest. The kitchen floor had not been repaired as agreed. Strensall Hostel was to be closed on 29/5/44 and all thirty-five girls moved to Stockton.

Swinton, near Malton, North Yorkshire

The only surviving mention of this hostel located in print was an advertisement for a housekeeper to look after eight girls in a hostel on a farm. A further advertisement appeared in March 1947, when a housekeeper was required to look after three Land Girls in a modern cottage with hot water and electric light. Applications were to be sent to C Bowles, Home Farm, Swinton. Swinton Grange, where the girls from the hostel worked, was renowned for its Pedigree Ayrshire Cattle.

Delia Holding (née Pickard) lived in the cottage with two other WLA girls. Her home was near Helperby. The cottage at Swinton was very small with tiny rooms, and it was nicknamed 'Trigger Castle'. There was a housekeeper who cared for them and she had a small son who lived in with her. The girls tended the poultry and rabbits, which were reared for meat to supply the army convalescence home at Swinton Grange. When the small cottage was closed, Delia took home the cottage cat. Delia and her two friends were moved to Terrington Hostel.

Tadcaster Hostel, North Yorkshire

This hostel was built sometime during the war and intended for wartime use. It was used by the WLA as a hostel and subsequently as part of the nearby hospital. Miss Jacob-Smith visited this hostel and made the following notes.

20/12/49 She called at hostel and found the Ripon staff quite happy. The girls Miss Jacob-Smith questioned seemed concerned about the food and lack of entertainment. She suggested they waited until the Warden, Miss Campenot, had settled in. Miss Campenot thought the girls were tough, especially five of them, but thought she could cope. She needed twenty-four hooks, for working coats, as there were no hooks. The girls had left their dirty coats on the beds, making the dormitory dirty. Miss Jacob-Smith took the hostel batteries for the wireless, twelve quilts and one bag of sago.

4/1/50 The hostel had been improved considerably by Miss Campenot, with pots of bulbs, a bookcase, chair backs etc. The hostel now looked nice and the Warden thought the girls appreciated her efforts. There were over a hundred blankets for twenty girls and one Forewoman. This left no surplus for laundry purposes. It was suggested that they needed six more grey and white blankets.

16/2/50 One of the girls had left the hostel about three weeks before, suffering with suspected TB and had said she was in hospital. Her sister said she had a high temperature and must not be upset, so requested that the WLA should not send her notice to the hospital. She was suffering from Crevica Adenitis (inflammation of the lymph nodes). Could her home be visited, Miss Jacob-Smith asked? The girl had not taken proper care of herself and she still wanted to go to work, although she had a signing-off certificate, and was annoyed when the Forewoman would not let her.

28/1/50 The girls said that the hostel had improved. They felt the pack-up could be improved. The water went cold after four baths. They said they would like sausage rolls sometimes. They had not complained to Miss Campenot, as she was too upset about her father's recent death. Miss Campenot said she was not able to stop cooking until 10.00 am and has no time to cook sausage rolls. Mrs Campenot said the tap washers needed repair. At present the water was being wasted.

The girls had being playing football in the field alongside the hostel and wanted a new football.

16/2/50 Two girls complained to Miss Jacob-Smith about the weekends. According to these two girls, they have a good midday meal on Saturdays and then for tea just bread and jam. When they complained they were told that Miss Campenot had no intention of encouraging them to remain for the weekend, as she thought they should go home to give the staff a rest. Miss Jacob-Smith told her she was quite wrong and they should be fed properly. Miss Campenot she did not like criticism of her methods.

6/3/50 Miss Jacob-Smith asked to see the hostel menu book and Miss Campenot said she had not kept this recently, as no one had asked to see it whilst she was at Ripon and Settle. Miss Jacob-Smith wondered whether she should insist that Miss Campenot kept one now. She usually inspected the books two monthly.

The girls had made the following complaints: they were not allowed to sit in the dormitory, nor to have any chairs there; they were only allowed five minutes to get undressed and Miss Campenot stood and watched them, which they disliked; there were insufficient cups for them each; all the locks in the dressing tables had been forced when the Warden had been looking for cups.

16/3/50 Miss Campenot was very annoyed at the girls' complaints and Miss Jacob-Smith suggested a Hostel Committee should be set up. Miss Jacob-Smith felt the Warden should be more tactful and considerate with the girls, but thought she resented any criticism from Miss Jacob-Smith. Miss Campenot said she did not approve of the girls sitting in the dormitories and said they should sit in the recreation room. The girls said they cannot do this when they have had a bath and are undressed, as other girls had their boyfriends in the recreation room. They had always sat in the dormitory at other hostels they had been in. Miss Camponot said she went to the dormitories to see them undress because otherwise they would spend time gossiping and they had fifteen minutes to change, not five. She said they all had a cup but they had broken some of them and there were no replacements.

Terrington Hostel, near Malton, North Yorkshire

This hostel opened in 1943 and closed in 1946.

Delia Holding (née Pickard) was sent to Terrington when the cottage she was posted to at Swinton closed. It was a long Nissen-type hostel. She said that prisoners of war had lived in the hostel before the Land Army took over. Their social life was restricted, as there was only one bus a week to Malton.

The following information is taken from Miss Jacob-Smith's notes on the hostel:

Dec 1943 The hostel held a children's party, in addition to a hot pot supper.

29/2/44 The Warden complained about the Forewoman, who was late up in the morning and late in at night. She was not helpful in the hostel. The Warden, Miss Lilling, suggested she be transferred to another hostel or removed to a local billet.

6/3/44 The new Forewoman appeared satisfactory.

7/3/44 Miss Lilling complained that the new Forewoman undermined her authority, as she was insolent and would not keep hostel rules. She came in at 11.10 pm instead of 11.00 pm and came in through the window. The Forewoman complained that the Warden also undermined her authority and was rude to her. The Forewoman and the Warden were not speaking to each other and neither would give way.

Miss Jacob-Smith suggested that the Forewoman found a billet. Miss Jacob-Smith met Miss Jife and Mrs Diggle, the Welfare Officer, to discuss the problems at Terrington. Mrs Diggle may have given Eileen the impression that the Forewoman was equal in status to the Warden, and should have special privileges

218

such as a key of her own and not have to keep hostel rules. She may have given her the idea that she was better than the Warden. As a result of this, the Warden felt Mrs Diggle was favouring the Forewoman. As this was a YWCA hostel, the WASE have power over the Warden.

16/3/44 Miss Lilling was not settled and she had told the YWCA that she may leave. The Forewoman said she would make every effort to work with Miss Lilling.

5/4/44 Miss Lilling knew nothing about the new Assistant Warden. If she did come, then the Forewoman will have to move out of the dormitory. There was one small sick bay with double bunk in it and no other furniture.

There was only one bucket of coal left, so Miss Jacob-Smith telephoned to get some coal from the Easingwold Hostel.

The Forewoman and Warden situation had not altered but they had tried their best to agree. When Miss Jacob-Smith mentioned that the Assistant Warden was coming, she did not mention moving the Forewomen out! Miss Lilling did not mention her former accusations.

27/6/44 The Forewoman called Miss Jacob-Smith about the possibility of having a bedroom, as she was sleeping in the dormitory. The rooms at the hostel consisted of the Warden's room, sick bay, cooking room, the Warden's bedroom and the scullery. The Assistant Warden's bedroom was large and empty. The domestic's bedroom was used. The situation over the bedrooms was acute.

28/8/44 The new Forewoman was excellent said Miss Lilling and the Forewoman also said she was most helpful. Miss Lilling had offered her a separate bedroom, as the hostel was so empty. She had the whole bay to herself which she enjoyed!

9/10/44 There had been considerable confusion over travel on a Sunday, since there were no buses running on Sundays.

The Forewoman was worried about the hostel being bottom of the WLA hostels competition. Miss Lilling felt rejected by YWCA and WAEC and said she had not had the support of either.

5/9/44 New chairs were needed but had never arrived, although they had been ordered for sometime.

3/1/45 There were only ten girls in the hostel when Miss Jacob-Smith arrived. The Forewoman was eating dinner in Miss Lilling's room and did not move when Miss Jacob-Smith came in. The Forewoman did not want to move from Terrington. Obviously she had got too fond of Miss Lilling, Miss Jacob-Smith suggested to the WLA Office and said that she should be moved as far as possible from Miss Lilling.

All ten girls at the hostel seemed depressed and emphasized the isolation of the hostel now there were no troops nearby. Entertainment was suggested, but no one could play the piano. Miss Lilling had tried to get ENSA films, but Terrington was too far from their usual route.

21/2/45 Miss Lilling said the Forewoman was permanently miserable.

17/3/45 The hostel bring and buy sale collected £26 for the WLA Benefit Fund. A girl asked for a transfer as she had quarrelled with her boyfriend who lived at the farm she worked on. She was a good worker but inclined to use bad language.

7/6/45 The Forewoman had settled down and was quite friendly with Miss Lilling but not too much so, and she ate her meals with the girls. Three girls wanted to be bridesmaids for a girl at another hostel. One of the girls asked for help to find dresses and said they would like long white dresses, if possible. A girl sent her mother to the hostel to try to get shoes to fit, as since an accident she needed size six and a half on one foot and size five on the other. She had been at home for fourteen weeks.

25/6/45 Miss Jacob-Smith ordered twelve Evan Williams camomile shampoos, twelve henna, three Amani, also two lipsticks and four large Ponds vanishing creams at a total of £5 13s 9d.

26/7/45 A sack full of gum boots was collected.

27/7/45 Miss Jacob-SMith ordered two exotic tattoo lipsticks for the hostel.

13/8/45 Everything was satisfactory except for the bugs! The Ministry of Works were to come as soon as possible and the hostel was to close for three days.

In 1946 the hostel closed.

The Limes, Weeton, West Yorkshire

The Limes opened in 1943, (as reported in the *Land Girl* of November 1943) and closed in 1948.

The following information was taken from a letter by Ernie Wilson, who lived near The Limes when it was occupied by the WLA. The village of Weeton is small and spread out and in the 1940s most of the farms were in the ownership of the Harewood Estate. The Limes was a very large, stone built, three-storey house, set in about fifteen acres, including the Weeton cricket ground.

It was the home of the Dyson family and just before the Land Girls moved in alterations were made to the house, including a large single-storey extension to the side. This was used as the dining area and for social activities, including dances to which the locals were invited. There was also a film show one Friday

The Limes, Weeton. (*Courtesy Brian Lye*)

evening per month, for which locals paid sixpence to attend. There was also a team of domestic staff there; Ernie Wilson's brother married one of the cooks.

The arrival of the Land Girls caused great excitement and gossip in the village, but it was soon proved that they were a very hard-working and skilful group. There were few tractors at the times, so much of the ploughing, hay making and harvesting was done by using horses.

Ernie's everlasting memory is of an incident on a threshing day at a local farm where another brother of his was working with a Land Girl called Alma. She was sitting on top of the machine, feeding the sheaves into fast revolving blades, when she lost her balance and fell on to them. Unfortunately, she lost one of her legs. Alma returned to the village about a year later to thank everyone for their help and generosity.

The WLA left Weeton in 1948 and the property returned to private ownership, with the extension being converted into a two-bedroom bungalow. The whole property was demolished in the 1980s and replaced by two modern houses.

Thirsk Hostel, North Yorkshire

Thirks Hostel opened in October 1942, and was attached to a mid-Victorian villa called Stoneybrough, on the Stockton Road. (This hostel has been discussed at length in the chapter on Thirsk, from the notes of Miss Jacob-Smith.)

Joan Nicholson (née Lund) had been working as a children's nurse but felt that the family she worked for was unfair to her. She went into the WLA recruiting office in York to volunteer. She was nearly seventeen at the time, but when her papers arrived she had some difficulty in telling her father, who thought she was making a mistake. However, she said the Land Army was the happiest time of her life.

She arrived in 1947, after travelling to Thirsk by train from York. She met another girl who was also dressed in the WLA uniform and they battled through an enormous onslaught of hailstones to the hostel in Stockton Road, Thirsk. There they were met by the homely Mrs Keep, accompanied by her bulldog Joe. He had a fierce stance and did not appear too friendly on first acquaintance, as he sniffed and snarled. Subsequently, after her introduction to the dog, she was always welcomed home by him as a true friend. The dog was a true 'softy'. His favourite place in the hostel was in front of the kitchen fire, where he was sprayed with cinders, which appeared to be to his liking.

Joan always regarded the Thirsk Hostel as her home and her female companions as sisters. She had no complaints over the food, and even enjoyed the beetroot sandwiches! She was usually so tired at night that she went to sleep as soon as her head touched the pillow. She thought Mrs Keep was a wonderful role model, confidante and friend. She always found the Forewoman helpful and just.

Joan was sent to work with two other girls to a farm next to the prisoner of war camp. The farmer wanted to use the Germans rather than the Land Girls. However, regulations said that he must have one Land Girl in order to employ the German POWs. He sent the other two girls home, but Joan had been instructed by the Forewoman to stick at the work what ever happened. She was involved with barley threshing and had the worst job following behind the machine. She was covered with dirt, barley and dust all the time. Even the prisoners' supervisor told the farmer that it was no job for a lady and that one of his men should do the work. At lunchtime she had to eat her sandwiches in the wash house, whilst the men were invited indoors.

Joey, Thirsk Hostel's dog.
(*Joan Nicholson Collection*)

By the end of the working day she was feeling very tired, hard done by and fed up. She was given a pure white towel by the farmer's daughter when she tried to clean up. The towel was in a sorry state when she had tried to wash off some of the grime. The girl said her father wanted Joan to accept a ten shilling note for her work – a generous gift at the time! When Joan reached the hostel she was greeted by the Forewoman, who ran the bath water for her and praised her efforts, telling her to keep the ten shillings because the farmer would still have to pay the WAEC for her services.

A WLA girl working with a prisoner of war.
(*Dorothy Buckton Collection*)

Joan Nicolson née Lund on a farm near Thirsk.
(*Joan Nicholson Collection*)

On days when girls was not able to work they spent their times mending punctures and fixing the bikes. Often there were more punctures in the tyres than when they had started!

Other memorable working events Joan recalled were with horses.

On one farm, Captain and Violet always galloped up the field to greet her and on another farm a cow got a potato stuck in its throat. The vet was called and Alf White (James Herriot) arrived and pushed the potato down the cow's throat with a broom handle! Joan continued working in the Thirsk area on a farm, after the hostel closed.

Thorpe Audlin Hostel, near Pontefract, West Yorkshire

Thorpe Audlin, which was nearly five miles from Pontefract, opened in May 1943 and closed in November 1945. It was also known as 'Hill Thorpe'. Thorpe Audlin Hostel was formerly the home of Mrs Cooke and it was converted to a hostel for Land Girls to serve farms in the Pontefract area. There was a real shortage of agricultural labour, so the thirty-two girls in the hostel were most welcome.

In April 1943, a group of girls from the hostel met at the Municipal Office in Pontefract. Among the varied speakers, talking mainly to local sixteen- and seventeen-year-olds was Mrs E Brown, a Forewoman in the WLA. She spoke about hostel life and said the first few weeks could be difficult, especially for girls who had mixed with crowds, but said they soon got used to it. A former journalist, who had become a land army girl talked about horticultural work and said that in the nursery gardening section there was the opportunity to learn a great deal. Another speaker said she had served three years in general farm work and it had been the happiest time of her life. It had been her ambition to be in the WLA and she thought it was not only a wartime job, but after the war it would still be very important. (*Pontefract in Focus*, April 1943.)

There appear to be no further records of this hostel.

Muriel, Dorothy and Iris, WLA veterans, still represent
Yorkshire's Women's Land Army at every national event!

References and Sources of Information

Archives and Records

Imperial War Museum:

Jacob-Smith, W., Interview (9458) (1986).

Shaw, B. (née Bradley), 2013: Papers.

Tetlow, Miss M., Private Papers.

Yorkshire Museum of Farming:

Forth, F., 2012: Manuscript of interview held at Yorkshire Museum of Farming, Murton.

Jones, E. (no date) 'Teenager in War' (self-published memoir, undated).

Miss Jacob-Smith's duplicate books (Graham, E. former Curator of Museum)

Periodicals and newspapers

Down Your Way magazine

Journal of Modern Agriculture

Journal of the Board of Agriculture

The Dalesman

The Landswoman

Yorkshire Post and Leeds Intelligencer